Tried for H.

Emma Dorothy Eliza Nevitte Southworth

Alpha Editions

This edition published in 2024

ISBN : 9789362093691

Design and Setting By
Alpha Editions
www.alphaedis.com
Email - info@alphaedis.com

Contents

CHAPTER I.

SYBIL'S SUBTERRANEAN ADVENTURES.

Dark den is this,

Witch-haunted, devil-built, and filled

With horrid shapes, but not of men or beasts,

Or aught with which the affrighted sense

Hath ever made acquaintance.

When Sybil recovered from her death-like swoon, she felt herself being borne slowly on through what seemed a narrow, tortuous underground passage; but the utter darkness, relieved only by a little gleaming red taper that moved like a star before her, prevented her from seeing more.

A presentiment of impending destruction possessed her, and overwhelming horror filled her soul and held her faculties. Though her life had depended upon her speech, she could not have uttered a syllable. And no word was breathed by the mysterious beings who bore her on. Dumb as mutes at a funeral, they marched. Silent, breathless as one on the brink of death, Sybil held her senses fast and prayed. And the little red spark moved through the darkness before her, like a malignant star leading her to doom. And how long drawn out the dreadful way! minutes seemed months, and hours ages. The awful forms that held her in their hands; their monotonous tread as they bore her on; their utter silence; the deep darkness; the damp, earthy, stifling atmosphere; the agony of suspense; the horror of anticipation!—all these must have sent her into another swoon, but that her vigilant mind still held her senses alert, and she prayed.

Who were these beings? Why had they abducted her? What would they do with her? She asked herself these questions, but shrank appalled from any possible answer. Death? dishonor worse than death? Oh that some miracle might save her in this tremendous peril! She prayed. And what a tedious anguish of anxiety! When would the end come?

At length a breath of fresh air as from the upper world was wafted past her face. Welcome as a drop of cold water to a parched palate, was this breath of fresh air to her fevered lungs. But it passed, and all was close and suffocating again.

Next a faint gleam of pale light glanced through the darkness far ahead, but it vanished, and all was blackness again, but for the little red spark moving before her. All silent, suffocating, dark.

But presently there came another breath of air, together with a faint, fair, blue light as of day, in the far distance. And soon the breath of air became a breeze, and Sybil drew in refreshing draughts that, in renewing her vitality almost restored her courage.

And now they moved on faster, for the path was freer. And now also the dawning light enabled Sybil to see her captors; and if any circumstance could have increased her horror, the looks of these men must have done so. They were of almost gigantic height, and shrouded from head to foot in long black gowns, with hoods that were drawn over their heads, while their faces were entirely concealed by black masks. A shudder ran through her frame, as she looked upon them.

But soon the changing aspect of the subterranean passage forced itself upon her attention. It now seemed not so much a narrow passage as a succession of small caverns, one opening into another, and every advanced one rather larger, lighter, and more beautiful than the preceding; the walls, floor, and ceiling being of bright red sandstone, and lighted here and there with sparkling stalactites. At last, through a narrower and more tortuous winding than any they had yet passed, they suddenly entered a spacious cavern of such exceeding beauty and splendor, that for an instant Sybil lost sight of her terrors in her astonishment and admiration.

The walls and roofs of this dazzling place were completely covered with the purest pearl-like spar, and lighted with pendant crystals and stalactites, that, as they caught the stray sunbeams, glowed, burned, blazed, and sparkled like a million of pendant diamonds, rubies, emeralds, and sapphires. The floor was thickly carpeted with living moss of the most brilliant hues of vivid green, soft grey, delicate rose, and cerulean blue. Into this enchanting palace of nature, the light entered from many almost imperceptible crevices.

All this Sybil saw at a glance, and then her eyes settled upon a figure who seemed the sole occupant of the place.

This was a young girl, who, with her red cloak thrown mat-like on the moss, was seated upon it cross-legged in the Turkish fashion. Her elfin face, her malign eyes, her wild black hair and picturesque costume, were all so in keeping with the aspect of the place, that one might have deemed her the spirit of the cavern.

Sybil had scarcely time to observe all this before her bearers stood her immediately in front of the seated girl, and saying:

"There she is, Princess! So work your will upon her," they withdrew.

Now the worst of Sybil's terrors were over. Those dreadful men were gone. Before her was only a woman, a girl, whom she certainly had no reason to fear.

They looked at each other in silence for perhaps half a minute; and then Sybil spoke:

"What place is this? Who are you? Why am I brought hither?"

"One question at a time," answered the girl. "'What place this is' concerns you little; 'who I am' concerns you less; 'why you are brought here,' ah! that concerns you very much! It concerns your liberty, and perhaps your life."

"I do not believe it! You have had me torn away from my husband! Where is he now?" haughtily demanded Mrs. Berners.

"He is likely in the hands of the constables, who are by this time in possession of the Haunted Chapel. But fear nothing! Him they will release again, for they have no right to detain him; but you they would have kept if they had caught you. Come, lady, do not resent the rough manner in which you were saved."

"I do not understand all this."

"It is scarcely necessary that you should."

"And my husband! When shall I see him?"

"When you can do so with safety to yourself, and to us."

"When will that be?"

"How can I tell?"

"Oh, heaven! he will be half crazed with anxiety!"

"Better that he should be half crazed with anxiety, than wholly crazed by despair. Lady, had we not removed you when we did, you would certainly be in the hands of the constables before this day is over, probably before this hour."

"How do you know this?"

"From information brought in by our spies."

"We came upon the Haunted Chapel by chance, in the dead of night. No one could have known so soon that we were there."

"No one did know it. The constables were coming there for *us*, but they would have found *you*, had we not brought you away with us. That was my doing. I made your removal the condition of my silence."

"Girl, who are you? I ask again; and why do you take this interest in me?"

"Lady, I am an outlaw like yourself, hunted like yourself, in peril like yourself, guiltless like yourself; the daughter, sister, companion of thieves. Yet, never will I become a thief, or the wife or the mother of one!"

"This is terrible!" said Sybil with a shudder. "But why should this be so?"

"It is my fate."

"And why do you care for me?"

"I thought I had answered that question in telling you all that I have told about myself, for 'a fellow feeling makes us wondrous kind;' but if you want another reason I can give it to you. I care for you because I know that you are guiltless of the crime for which you are hunted through the world. And I am resolved, come what may, that you shall not suffer for it."

"In the name of heaven, what do you say?" exclaimed Sybil, in strong excitement. "If you *know* me to be guiltless, you *must* know who is guilty! Nay, you *do* know it! You can not only save my life, but clear my fame."

"Hush! I know nothing, but that you are guiltless. I can *do* nothing but save your life."

"You took me away in the absence of my husband. Why could you not have waited a little while until his return, and—"

"Ha! ha! ha!" laughed the girl, breaking in upon Sybil's speech; "waited until his return, and take two strangers, himself and his servant, into our confidence! Moloch would have brained me, or Belial would have poisoned me if I had done such a thing. We are knaves, but not fools, Mrs. Berners."

"But when will you communicate with him, to relieve his dreadful suspense?"

"As soon as it shall be safe to do so. Our first care must be our own safety, but our second, will be yours."

Sybil said no more at the moment; but sat looking at the speaker, and thinking of all that had befallen her in the Haunted Chapel. Could this bright, warm, spirited creature possibly be the "damp girl" whose two nightly visitations had appalled her so much? She put the question:

"Tell me; are you the one who came twice to my bed-side and lay down beside me, or is there another?"

Her strange hostess laughed aloud, and clapped her hands.

And there immediately appeared before them, as if it had dropped from the sky, or risen out of the earth, a figure that caused Sybil to start and utter a half-suppressed scream.

It was that of a small, thin girl, so bloodless that her complexion was bluish white; her hair and eyes were also very light, and her dress was a faded out blue calico, that clung close to her form; her whole aspect was cold, damp, clammy, corpse-like, as she stood mutely with hanging hands before her summoner.

"For Heaven's sake, who is she?" inquired Sybil, under her breath.

"We call her Proserpine, because she was reft from the upper world and brought down here. She is my maid, my shadow, my wraith, my anything you like, that never leaves me. She it was who visited you in idleness or curiosity, I suppose. She bore the taper before you, when you came through the underground passage. More than this I cannot tell you of her, since more I do not know myself. You may go now, Proserpine. And tell old Hecate to hurry up the breakfast, as we have company this morning. And do you come and let me know when it is ready."

Sybil kept her eyes on the pallid girl to see where she would go, and she saw her slip through an almost invisible opening in the side of the rock. Then Sybil turned again to her strange entertainer, and said:

"There is something more I wish to know, if you do not mind telling me. Why were we drugged with opium that night?"

"Ha! ha! ha! We had some goods to remove from the vault. You were all in our way. We were obliged either to kill you or to drug you. So we drugged you," laughed the girl.

"And nearly killed us, as well."

"Yes; we had to make sure of your taking enough to put you to sleep, so I poured the laudanum into your coffee-pot pretty freely, I tell you."

At this moment the bloodless phantom appeared again, and in the same thin, reed-like voice that sounded so far away, she announced that breakfast was ready.

"Come, then; I know you must need nourishment," said Sybil's wild hostess, rising to lead the way.

And now Sybil saw how it was that the pale girl had slipped through the almost invisible aperture, like a spirit vanishing through a solid wall; for the rocky partitions of this natural underground palace overlapped each other, leaving a passage of about one foot in width and three feet in length between the walls.

Through this they passed into a smaller cavern, which, like the larger one, had its roof and walls incrusted with pearly spars and hung with sparkling stalactites, and its floor covered with living moss.

This cavern was not only beautiful, but comfortable. A large charcoal furnace that stood in the middle of the floor agreeably warmed the place, while the appetizing odor of hot coffee, broiled birds, and buckwheat cakes filled the air.

But the furniture of the place was the most incongruous and amazing that could be imagined. A wooden table of the rudest workmanship stood near the furnace, but it was covered with a white damask table-cloth of the finest description, and adorned with a service of the purest silver plate. With this elegant and costly array was intermingled crockery-ware of the coarsest pattern. Around the table were placed two three-legged stools of the roughest manufacture, and one piano chair of the most finished workmanship, of carved rosewood and cut velvet.

Waiting on this table stood the "damp girl" mentioned before, and also a very small, dark, withered old woman, in a black gown, with a red handkerchief tied over her head and under her chin.

"Come, Mrs. Berners, you are my guest, and I will give you the seat of honor," said Sybil's nameless hostess, as she led her to the little piano chair and put her on it.

Then for herself she took one of the three-legged stools, saying to her handmaid:

"You may take the other two seats away. Moloch and Belial will not be at breakfast with us this morning. They have gone back to the vault to lay the train."

"Dangerous," muttered the old woman between her shut lips.

"Never you mind, Mother Hecate! Moloch's courage and Belial's craft will enable them to take care of themselves," said the girl, as she set a cup of hot coffee before her guest, and placed a broiled partridge and a buckwheat cake upon her plate.

Sybil's long ride of the night before, followed as it had been by a refreshing sleep, had so restored her strength and appetite that, despite her late fright and her present anxieties, she made a very good breakfast.

"And now," said the young hostess, as they arose from the table, "what will you do? Will you lie down on my bed in the next cavern and sleep; or will you sit here where it is warm, and talk: or will you let me show you through this net-work of caverns, that underlies all this mountain?"

"You are very kind, at all events, and I thank you much, and I think I would like to look at this great natural curiosity, whose very existence so near my home I never even suspected," said Sybil; for she really wished to explore the wonderful labyrinth, not only from motives of curiosity, but also of policy; for she thought it would be well to know the ins and outs of this underground habitation, in case she should find it necessary to make her escape.

So her hostess took her back into the splendid outer cavern, saying:

"You do not wish to go back through any of those caverns you passed in coming here, so we will go this way."

And she passed behind another of those over-lapping partitions of rock, and led Sybil into another small division, fitted up as a rude but clean bed-chamber. In one corner was a pile of dried moss and leaves, covered with fine white linen sheets and soft, warm, woolen blankets. On a ledge of rock stood a tin wash-basin, in which stood a pure silver ewer. In a word, the appointments of this apartment were as incongruous as those of the other had been found.

"This is my bed, and if you should be tired when we get back from our tour through the caverns, or at any time, you can lie down here and sleep in perfect safety," said the girl.

"I thank you," answered Sybil, as they passed out of that division into another.

It was as the girl had told her, a net-work or cell-work of caverns, occupying, as far as it had been explored, several acres under the mountain. All these caverns bore a natural resemblance to each other. All had their roofs and walls incrusted with pearly spars and hung with glittering stalactites, and their floors covered with living moss; and all were connected by narrow passages, with the walls lapping past each other.

But some of these caverns were large, and lighted by crevices in the roof, and others were small and dark. Some of the passages between them were also wide and free, and some narrow and impassable. And in some black inaccessible holes was heard the fearful sound of subterranean waters. In one of the larger divisions of the cavern there were boxes and bales of merchandise, and silver plate and jewels; in another there was the complicated machinery of an underground distillery; and in still another was a collection of burglars' tools, counterfeiters' instruments, and firearms.

"I show you all! I do not fear to do so! You will never betray us, even if you have a chance; but you will never have a chance," said the guide.

"What! You would not keep me here for ever?"

"No; for *we* shall not stay for ever. Be comforted, lady! No harm is intended you," said the girl, as, having shown her guest all that was to be seen of the caverns, she conducted her back to the bedroom.

"I am very much surprised at all that I have seen," said Sybil. "I had no idea that there was a cave of such extent and beauty so near our home."

"I believe," answered the girl, "that there are many caves in the mountains, as there are many isles in the ocean, that have never been discovered."

Sybil looked up in surprise. "You call yourself the companion of thieves, yet you talk like a person of intelligence and refinement," she said.

The girl laughed sardonically. "Of course people 'of intelligence and refinement' are all and always honest and true. You should know Belial! He taught me to read. I taught myself everything else. I have read Homer, Danté, Milton, and Shakespeare. But now you are tired; you look so. Lie down on my bed of moss and rest, and I will cover you up warm."

"Thank you, I will do so," answered Sybil, gladly stretching her wearied limbs upon the soft couch.

Her wild hostess covered her carefully, and then left her, saying:

"Sleep in peace, lady, for here you are perfectly safe."

CHAPTER II.

WHAT WAS SOUGHT, AND WHAT WAS FOUND.

They sought her that night, and they sought her next day,

They sought her in vain till a week passed away.

The highest, the lowest, the loneliest spot,

Her husband sought wildly, but found her not.—THE MISTLETOE BOUGH.

When Lyon Berners and his faithful servant returned to the Haunted Chapel, after having comfortably disposed of their horses for the rest of the night, the interior was still so dark that they did not at first discover the absence of Sybil, especially as the covering lay heaped upon the mattress so like a sleeping form, that even in a less murky darkness it might have been mistaken for her.

As it was now very cold, Mr. Berners, who had found a tinder-box and a coil of wax tapers among his other effects in the wagon, struck a light, with the intention of kindling a fire.

Joe brought some broken sticks and dry brushwood from the far corner where Lyon Berners had piled it up just before the flight from the chapel, and between the master and man they soon kindled a cheerful blaze that lighted up every nook and crevice of the old interior.

Then Mr. Berners turned toward the mattress to see how his wife might be sleeping.

"Why, she is not here! She has waked up and walked out," he exclaimed, in some surprise and annoyance, but not in the least alarm, for he naturally supposed that she had only left the chapel for a few minutes, and would soon return.

"Hi! whar de debbil she took herself off to, all alone, dis onlawful time o' de night?" cried Joe, in dismay.

"Oh, not far! She will soon be back again," answered Mr. Berners cheerfully. And then he took one of the blankets from the mattress and folded it up for a seat, and sat down upon it near the fire, and stretched his benumbed hands over the blaze. Joe followed his example, stretching out his hands also, and staring across the fire at his master—staring at such a rate that Mr. Berners, feeling somewhat inconvenienced, sharply demanded:

"What the deuce do you mean by that, Joe?"

"I want to go and sarch for my mistess. I don't feel satisfied into my own mind about her."

"Why, what are you afraid of, man?"

"*Ghostesses.*"

"Absurd!"

"Well, now, no it an't, marster. I've knowed Miss Sybil longer'n you have. I've knowed her ever since she was born, and I don't believe as she'd go out all alone by herself in the dead of night to the lonesome church-yard—that I don't. And I's afeard as the ghostesses have spirited her away."

"Preposterous, Joe! Have you lived in an intelligent family, and in a Christian community all your life, to believe in 'ghostesses,' as you call them? Are you such a big fool as all that, at your time of life?"

"Yes, marster, I's jest sich a big fool as all that, at my time of life. And I want to go out and sarch for my young mistress," said Joe, in the spirit of "dogged persistence," as he began to gather himself up.

"Stop, stay where you are. If one of us must go, it must be myself," said Mr. Berners.

"Which would be a heap the most properest proceedings, any ways," muttered Joe, sulkily settling himself in his seat again, in a manner that seemed to say, "And I wonder why you didn't do it before."

"She really ought to be back by this time, even if she went out but the moment before we returned; and she may have gone out before that," murmured Mr. Berners, with some little vague uneasiness, as he arose and buttoned his overcoat, and went into the church-yard.

The day was dawning, and the old tombstones gleamed faintly from their bushes, in the pale gray light of early morning.

"She cannot have gone far; she would not venture; she must be very near," he said to himself, and he murmured softly:

"*Sybil! Sybil!* where are you, love?"

There was no answer, and he raised his voice a little.

"Sybil, Sybil, my darling!"

Still there was no response. His vague uneasiness became anxiety, and he called aloud:

"SYBIL! SYBIL!"

But nothing came of it, and his anxiety grew to terror, and he ran wildly about shouting her name till all the mountain rocks and glens echoed and reëchoed:

"SYBIL! SYBIL!"

And now he was joined by Joe, whose faithful and affectionate heart was wrung with anxiety and distress for his beloved and missing young mistress.

"You can't find her? Oh, Marster, where is she gone? What have become of her? Oh, what shall we do?" he cried, wringing his hands in great trouble.

"We must search for her, Joe. This is very strange, and very alarming," said Mr. Berners, striking off into the path that led to the fountain, and shouting her name at every step.

But only the mountain echoes answered. In an agony of anxiety they beat about the woods and thickets, and climbed the rocks and went down into the glens, still shouting—always shouting her name.

Day broadened, the sun arose, and its first rays struck them as they stood upon the heights behind the chapel, looking all over the wilderness.

"In the name of Heaven, now what are we to do?" exclaimed Lyon Berners, speaking more to himself than to another.

Joe was standing, leaning upon his stick in an attitude of the deepest despair. But suddenly he raised his head, and a gleam of light shot over his dark face, as he said:

"I tell you what we can do, Marster: where she's took to, we can find out at all ewents. I say where she's took to, for she never went of her own accords."

"Heaven help my poor darling! no; she never did. But how do you think you can trace her, Joe?"

"This a-way! I'll take the freshest of them horses, and ride home as fast as I can for life and death; and I'll snatch up her little dog as has been pining away ever since she left, and I'll bring it here and make it smell to the bedclothes where she lay, and then put it on the scent, to lead us the way she went."

"Eureka, Joe! The instinct of faithful affection, in man or brute, sometimes puts pure reason to the blush by its superior acumen," exclaimed Mr. Berners.

"I don't know no more 'n the dead what you're a-talking about, Marster; but that's the way to find out where Miss Sybil was took," answered practical Joe.

"Come, then, we will go at once and look at the horses. I think, Joe, that one of your cart horses would be better to take, as they have not been so hard worked as ours," said Mr. Berners, as they ran down the steep to the thicket in the rear of the chapel, where they had left their horses.

In a very few minutes Joe had selected and saddled his horse, and stood ready to start.

"I needn't tell you to be prudent, Joe, and to drop no hint of your errand," said Mr. Berners.

"Well, no, you needn't take that there trouble, Marse Lyon, 'cause you'd be a-cautioning of Joe, as is cautious enough a'ready. Good-morning, Marse Lyon. I'll be at Black Hall afore the fam'ly is well out of bed, and I'll be back here with the little dog afore you have time to get unpatient," said Joe, climbing into his saddle and riding away.

Mr. Berners returned to the chapel, where he found the fire smouldering out, but everything else in the same condition in which he had left it when he went in pursuit of Sybil.

Far too restless to keep still, he walked up and down the length of the chapel, until he was fairly tired out. Then he went to the front door and sat down, keeping his eyes upon the entrance of the little thicket path, by which he knew that Joe must return. And although he knew it was much too early to expect his messenger back, yet he still impatiently watched that path.

Presently the sound of approaching horsemen struck upon his listening ear. They were coming up the path through the thicket, and presently they emerged from it—not two or three, but couple after couple, until the old churchyard was filled with sheriff's officers and militia-men. Sheriff Benthwick himself was at their head.

In great surprise, as if they had come in quest of him, Mr. Berners went forward to receive the party.

Lyon Berners was known to have been the companion of his fugitive wife, and therefore a sort of an outlaw; yet the sheriff took off his hat, and accosted him respectfully.

"Mr. Berners, I am greatly surprised to see you here," he said.

"Not less than myself at seeing you," answered Lyon.

"We are here to seek out a set of burglars whom we have reason to believe have their lair in this chapel," said Mr. Benthwick.

"Then your errand is not to me," observed Lyon.

"Certainly not! Though, should I find Mrs. Berners here, as well as yourself, as I think now highly probable, I shall have a most painful duty to perform."

"Ah, sir! within the last terrible month, I have become all too much accustomed to the sight of friends with 'painful duties to perform,' as they delicately put it. But you will be spared the pain. Mrs. Berners is not here with me."

"Not here with you? Then where is she?"

"Excuse me, Mr. Benthwick," said Mr. Berners, gravely; "you certainly forget yourself; you cannot possibly expect me to tell you—even if I knew myself," he added, in an undertone.

"No, I cannot, indeed," admitted the sheriff. "Nor did I come here to look for Mrs. Berners, having had neither information nor suspicion that she was here; nevertheless, if I find her I shall be constrained to arrest her. Were it not for my duty, I could almost pray that I might not find her."

"I do not think you will," said Mr. Berners, grimly.

And meanwhile the officers and the militia-men, at a sign from the sheriff, had surrounded the chapel so that it would be impossible for any one who might be within its walls to escape from it.

"Now, Mr. Berners, as you assure me that your wife is not within this building, perhaps you may have no objection to enter it with me," said the sheriff.

"Not the least in the world," answered Lyon Berners, leading the way into the chapel, as the sheriff dismounted from his horse, threw the bridle to an attendant, and followed.

The interior was soon thoroughly searched, having nothing but its bare walls and vacant windows, with the exception of Sybil's forsaken bed near the altar, the smouldering fire in what had once been the middle aisle, and the little pile of brushwood in the corner.

"There is certainly no one here but yourself, Mr. Berners; yet here are signs of human habitation," said the sheriff significantly.

Lyon Berners laughed painfully. And then he thought it would be safest to inform the sheriff of some part of the truth, rather than to leave him to his own conjectures, which might cover the whole case. So he answered:

"I do not mind telling you, Mr. Benthwick, that myself and my injured wife took refuge in this place immediately after the terrible tragedy that so unjustly compromised her safety. We remained here several days, and then departed. These things that you notice had been brought for our accommodation, and were left here when we went away."

"So you were not at Pendleton's?"

"Not for an hour."

"That is strange. But how comes it that you are here now without your wife, Mr. Berners?"

"Sir, I have told you all that I mean to tell, and now my lips are sealed on the subject of my wife," said Lyon Berners, firmly.

"I cannot and do not blame you in the least," said the sheriff, kindly.

"All that we have to do now, is to pursue our search for the burglars, and if in the course of it we should come upon Mrs. Berners, we must do our duty," he concluded.

"To that proposition Mr. Berners assented with a silent bow and bitterly compressed lips. The sheriff then went to the door of the vault, and stooping down with his hands upon his knees, peered through the iron grating, more in curiosity than in any hope of finding a clue to the robbers. And in fact he discovered nothing but the head of that narrow staircase whose foot disappeared in the darkness below.

"Phew! what a damp, deadly air comes up from that foul pit! it hasn't been opened in half a century, I suppose," exclaimed Mr. Benthwick, taking hold of the rusty bars and trying to shake the grating; but finding it immovable, he ceased his efforts and turned away.

Then he went to the chapel door, and called his men around him, saying:

"There is no sign of the miscreants inside the ruin; we must search for them outside."

And he divided his party into four detachments; and one he sent up the narrow path leading to the fountain, another he sent up on the heights, and another down in the glen; while he himself led the fourth back upon the path leading through the thicket. And they beat the woods in all directions without coming upon the "trail" of the burglars. But Sheriff Benthwick, in going through the thicket with his little party, met a harmless negro on a tired horse with a little dog before him. The sheriff knew the negro, and accosted him by name.

"Joe, what are you doing here, so far from your home?"

Joe was ready with his answer:

"If you please, marster, I am coming to fetch away some truck left here by a picnic party from our house."

"Ah! a picnic party! I know all about that picnic party! I have been up to the old ruin and had a talk with your master, and he has told me of it," said the sheriff cunningly, hoping to betray the negro into some admissions that might be of service to him in tracing Sybil.

But his cunning was no match for Joe's.

"Well, marster," he said, "if Marse Lyon telled you all about that, you must be satisfied into your honorable mind, as I am a telling of the truth, and does come after the truck left in the chapel, which you may see my wagon a-standin' out there on the road beyant for yourself."

"Then if you have a wagon, why do you come on horseback?"

"Lor's marster, I couldn't no ways get a wagon through this here thicket."

The sheriff felt that that was true, and that he had been making a fool of himself. He made a great many more inquiries, but received no satisfaction from astute Joe. He asked no question about the little dog, considering her of no importance. And at length, having no pretext to stop the negro, he let him pass and go on.

Joe, glad to be relieved, touched up his horse and trotted briskly through the thicket, and through the graveyard, to the ruined door of the old chapel. Here he dismounted, tied his horse to a tree, and put down the little Skye terrier, who no sooner found herself at liberty, than she bounded into the church and ran with joyous leaps and barks, and jumped upon her master, licking, or kissing, as she understood kissing, his hands and face all over with her little tongue, and assuring him how glad she was to see him.

"Nelly, Nelly, good Nelly, pretty Nelly," said Mr. Berners, caressing her soft, curly brown hair.

But Nelly grew fidgety; something was wanting—the best thing of all was wanting—her mistress! So she jumped from her master's lap, not forgetting to kiss him good-by, by a direct lick upon his lips, and then she ran snuffing and whining about the floor of the chapel until she came to the mattress and blankets, where she began wildly to root and paw about, whining piteously all the while.

"Nelly, good dog," said Mr. Berners, taking the blanket and holding it to her nose. "Sybil, Sybil! seek her, seek her!"

The little Skye terrier looked up with a world of intelligence and devotion in her brown eyes, and re-commenced her rooting and pawing and snuffing around the bedding, and for some little time was at fault; but at length, with a quick bark of delight, she struck a line of scent, and with her nose close to the floor, cautiously followed it to the door of the vault, at which she stopped and began to scratch and bark wildly, hysterically—running back to her master and whining, and then running forward to the door, and barking and scratching with all her might and main.

"There she is, Marster. Mistess is down in that vault, so sure's I'm a livin' nigger," exclaimed Joe, who now came up to the door.

"Good Heaven! she could not live there an hour; the very air is death! But if there, with a breath of life remaining, she must hear and answer us," exclaimed Lyon Berners, in breathless haste, as he went to the door of the vault; and putting his lips close to the bars, called loudly:

"Sybil, Sybil! my darling, are you there?"

But though he bent his ear and listened in the dead silence and dread suspense, no breath of answer came. And little Nelly, who had ceased her noise, began to whine again.

Lyon Berners soothed her into quietness, and began to call again and again; but still no breath of response from the dark and silent depths below.

"If she is there, she is dead!" groaned Lyon Berners, in a voice of agony, as he thought of all Sybil had told him of the open vault and the mysterious figures that had passed to and from it in the night, and which he had set down as so many dreams and nightmares, reverted to his memory. Oh, if this chapel were indeed the den of thieves; if they had some secret means of opening that vault; if they had come upon his sleeping wife while she was left alone in the chapel, and robbed her of the money and jewels she had about her person, and then murdered her, and taken her body down into the vault for concealment; or if, as was most likely, for there was no mark of violence or stain of blood about the place—they had taken her to the vault first, and robbed and murdered her there.

Oh, if these horrible fears should be realized!

With the very thought Lyon Berners went pale and cold as marble in an anguish such as he had never felt in the severest crisis of their sorely troubled lives.

"Joe!" he cried, "go search the wagon for that crowbar belonging to Captain Pendleton. It must be there somewhere. And I must break this vault door open, or break my heart-strings in the trial."

"The crowbar is all right, Marster. And I'll go and fetch it as fast as I can. But we'll nebber see Mistess alive again! Nebber, Marster, in this world!" sobbed Joe, as he arose from his knees near the door and went upon his errand.

Little Nelly renewed her passionate demonstrations of distress and anxiety; now furiously barking and scratching at the door; now jumping upon her master's breast, and looking up into his face and whining, as if telling him that her mistress was down there, imploring his human aid to free her, and wondering why it was not given.

"I know it, my poor little dog! I know it all!" said Lyon, soothingly.

But little Nelly was incredulous and inconsolable, and continued her hysterical deportment through the half hour which intervened between the departure and the return of Joe.

"Ah, give me the tool!" eagerly exclaimed Mr. Berners, snatching the crowbar from the negro, as soon as he saw him.

And he went and applied it with all his force to the door, straining his strong muscles until they knotted like cords, while Joe looked on in anxiety and suspense, and little Nelly stood approvingly wagging her tail, as if to say:

"Now, at last, you are doing the right thing."

But with all Lyon's straining and wrenching, he failed to move the impassable door one hair's breadth.

Joe also took a turn at the crowbar; but with no more success.

They rested a while, and then united their efforts, and with all their strength essayed to force the door; but without the slightest effect upon its immovable bars.

"I might have known we could not do it this way, for neither Pendleton nor myself could succeed in doing so. Joe, we must take down the altar and take up the flagstones; but that will be a work of time and difficulty, and you will have to go back home and bring the proper tools."

"But the day is most gone, Marster, and it will take me most all night to go to Black Hall and get the tools and come back here. And is my poor mistress to stay down there into that dismal place all that time?" sobbed the negro.

"Joe! if she is there, as the little dog insists that she is, you know that she must be dead. And it is her body that we are seeking," groaned Lyon Berners, in despair.

"I knows it, Marster—I knows it too well; but I can't feel as it is true, all de same. And oh! even to leave her dear body there so long!" said Joe, bursting into a storm of tears and sobs.

"That cannot be helped, my poor fellow. Besides, I shall sit at this door and watch till your return, and we can work down into the vault. She shall not be quite alone, Joe."

So persuaded, Joe, unmindful of fatigue, once more set out for Black Hall. But on this occasion he took another horse, which was fresher. The sun had now set, and the short winter twilight was darkening into night.

CHAPTER III.

THE EXPLOSION.

There came a burst of thunder sound!—HEMANS.

Lyon Berners, chilled to the heart with the coldness of the night, half famished for want of food, and wearied with his late violent exertions, and wishing to recruit his strength for the next day's hard work, kindled a fire, and made some coffee, and forced himself to eat and drink a little, before he drew his mattress to the door of the vault, and stretched himself down as near as he could possibly get to the place where he believed the dead body of his beloved wife lay.

Poor little Nelly, abandoning her efforts either from exhaustion or in despair, crept up and tried to squeeze herself between her master and the door of the vault that she too thought held her mistress. Lyon made room for her to curl herself up by his side, and he caressed her soft fur, while he waked and watched.

It was now utterly dark in the chapel but for the dull red glow of the fire, which was dying out. An hour passed by, and the last spark expired, and the chapel was left in total darkness.

The agonies of that night who shall tell? They were extreme—they seemed interminable.

At length the slow morning dawned. Lyon arose with the sun, and walked about the chapel in the restlessness of mental anguish. The little dog followed at his heels, whining. Presently Lyon took up the crowbar and tried again to force the iron door. He might as well have tried to move a mountain. He threw away the crowbar in desperation, and then he stooped and peered through the iron bars: all dark! all still in those dismal depths! He turned away and rekindled the fire, and prepared a little breakfast for himself and his dumb companion. He must cherish his strength for the work that was before him.

After having eaten a morsel, and given his dog food, he signalled to her to lie down at the door of the vault and watch, while he went out towards the thicket to look for Joe, who might now soon be expected.

He went through the church-yard, and on to the entrance of the thicket path; he even pursued that path until it led him out upon the river road. He looked down the road for miles, but saw no sign of Joe!

Then, not wishing longer to leave the spot where the body of his murdered wife was supposed to lie unburied, he went back through thicket and graveyard to the chapel, where at the door of the vault the faithful little Skye terrier still watched.

He entered and threw himself down beside her, there to wait for the return of his messenger.

But ah! this was destined to be a day of weary, weary waiting! The morning advanced towards noon, and still Joe did not appear. Lyon arose and walked restlessly about the chapel, stopping sometimes to peer down into the vault, where nothing could be seen, or to call down where nothing could be heard, or he took up the crowbar again, and renewed his frantic efforts to force the iron door that nothing could move.

Noon passed; afternoon advanced.

"Something has happened to Joe," said the desperate man to himself, as once more he started out in the forlorn hope of meeting his messenger.

Again the weary way was traversed; again he went through the church-yard and thicket, and came out upon the long river road, and strained his gaze far along its length, but without seeing signs of the negro's approach.

"Yes; some accident has befallen Joe. All goes wrong, all is fatal, all is doomed!" He groaned in despair as he turned and retraced his steps towards the old "Haunted Chapel." As he drew near the building, he was startled by the furious barking of his little deg.

"Poor little Nelly has worked herself up into hysterics again at the door of that vault," he said to himself, as he quickened his pace and entered the building.

He found it in the possession of the constables, with the sheriff at their head. Mr. Benthwick, with an expression on his face oddly made up of triumph and compassion, advanced to meet him, saying:

"We are not at fault now, Mr. Berners. We returned to-day to resume our search through these mountains, and late this afternoon, as we were returning from our unsuccessful pursuit of the burglars, we were met here in the churchyard by these men."

And here the sheriff pointed to Purley and Munson, who were standing at a short distance.

"They told us," proceeded Mr. Benthwick, "that Mrs. Berners, with your assistance, had escaped from their custody."

"Right over my dead body, which I should say, my sleeping body," put in Purley.

"And that she was certainly concealed in this chapel, as they had received unquestionable information to that effect," added Mr. Benthwick.

"Well, sir, if you find her here, you will succeed in the search far better than I have done," replied Lyon Berners, grimly. "We have found *you* here, and under very suspicious circumstances; so we will take leave to make a more thorough search than we did yesterday," replied the sheriff.

"Have you tried the vault?" inquired Purley.

"No; but we will try it now. She may be concealed within it, after all," said Mr. Benthwick. And seeing the crowbar, he took it up and went to work upon that immovable door; but finding it so fast, he threw down the tool, saying:

"It is of no use to work at that door in that way, and it is of no use either to look through the bars, for you can see nothing but black darkness. But, Purley, I will tell you what to do. Do you go and cut the most resinous knot that you can find on the nearest pine tree, and bring it to me."

Purley started off in a hurry, and soon returned with a pine knot fairly soaked with turpentine.

"Now, then," said Mr. Benthwick, as he took the torch from the hand of his messenger. "I think this will throw some light into the darkness below!"

And he applied it first to the fire in the aisle, and then he carried, it, flaming high, to the door of the vault, and putting it through the iron bars, let it drop into the vault.

It was lighted up in an instant, and the sheriff and Purley bent down to look through the grating to see what the interior illumination might show them.

And Lyon Berners, whose anxiety was of course more intense than that of any one present, elbowed his way through the crowd to get nearer the door of the vault.

But before he could effect his purpose, a sound of thunder burst upon the air; the solid floor upheaved; the walls of the old Haunted Chapel fell in a heap of smoking ruins; and all the valley and the mountain tops were lighted up with the flames of destruction.

CHAPTER IV.

AFTER THE EXPLOSION.

Horror wide extends

Her desolate domain!—THOMPSON.

The thunder of the explosion, when the old Haunted Chapel was blown up, was heard for many miles around.

It burst upon the unsheltered wayfarers like the crack of doom!

It stunned the plantation negroes gathered around their cabin fires!

It startled the planters' families at their elegant tea-tables!

Travellers paused panic-stricken on the road!

Home-dwellers, high and low, rushed with one accord to doors and windows to see what the dreadful matter might be!

Was it an earthquake?

Had some unsuspected volcano suddenly burst forth in the mountain? Indeed it seemed so!

Volumes of black smoke ascended from a certain point of rocks, filling all the evening air with the suffocating smell of sulphur.

There was a pause of astonishment among the people for about one minute only; and then commenced a general stampede of all the able-bodied men and boys from a circle of several miles in circumference to the centre of attraction; while the women and girls waited at home in dread suspense!

But the very first on the scene of the catastrophe was a lamed negro.

Poor Joe! Just as his master had surmised, he had met with an accident. He had, indeed, reached Black Hall in safety, near the dawn of that day; but being quite exhausted with twenty-four hours of watching, working, and fasting, he succumbed to drowsiness, fatigue, and famine. In short, he ate and drank and slept.

He did not mean, poor faithful creature, to do more than just recruit sufficient strength to take him back, with the tools, to his master.

But when one, under such circumstances, surrenders to sleep, he loses all control over himself for an indefinite period of time. Joe slept fast and long, and never waked until he was rudely kicked up by a fellow-servant, who demanded to know how he came to be sleeping on the hay in the barn, and if he meant to sleep forever.

Joe started up, at first confused and delirious, but afterwards, when he came to his senses and found that it was past noon, he was utterly wretched and inconsolable. He did not even resent the rudeness of his comrade, in kicking him up; but, on the contrary, meekly thanked him for his kindness in arousing him.

And then he went and gathered his tools together, and saddled his horse, and without waiting for bite or sup, he told his mate that he had work to do at a distance, and mounted and rode off towards the ferry, which he had to cross to reach the river road on the other side, because, with, the weight of iron tools he carried, he could not possibly get over the ford.

All this contributed so to delay Joe's journey, that the sun set while he was still upon the river road, and "the shades of night were falling fast" when he reached the entrance of the thicket path leading to the Haunted Chapel.

He had not ridden more than a hundred yards up this path, before the thunder of the explosion burst upon his appalled ears. And at the same instant his affrighted horse, with a violent bound, threw him to the earth, jumped forward and fled away.

Amazed, stunned, bewildered as he was, Joe did not entirely lose his senses. When recovered a little from the shock, he felt himself all over to see what bones were broken; and found to his great relief that all were sound.

Then he got upon his feet, and looked about him; but a dense, heavy, black vapor was settling down upon the thicket, hiding all things from his view, while the stifling fumes of brimstone took his breath away.

"I'm——!"—Joe in his consternation swore a very profane oath, which it is not necessary here to repeat—"ef I don't b'leibe as de Debbil has blowed de old Haunted Chapel! And oh! my Hebbenly Marster! *ef so*, what have become o' Miss Sybil and Marse Lyon, and Nelly?" he cried in a sudden pang of terror and sorrow, as he tried to hurry towards the scene of the tragedy. He set off in a run, but was brought up short by a sharp severe pain in his right ancle.

"It's sprained! Bress de Lord, ef it an't sprained!" he cried, drawing up and caressing his injured limb.

"It an't no use! I can't put it to the ground no more!" he groaned.

Then standing upon his left foot and holding the other in his hand, he looked around and saw the pick lying among the scattered tools, that had fallen from his hold when the horse threw him. He cautiously bent down and took up the pick, and reversed it, and using it as a crutch, he hobbled on through the thicket towards the ruins of the old chapel. But his progress was so slow and painful that it took him nearly an hour to reach the place.

When at length he emerged from the thicket and entered the old churchyard, a scene of devastation met his view that appalled his soul.

"Oh, my Lord!" he said, stopping and leaning upon his pick-crutch, as he gazed around, "what an awful sight! Joe, you are like—somebody among the ruins of something," he added, as a vague classic similitude about Scipio and Carthage flitted through his half-dazed brain.

It was indeed a scene of horror deep enough to dismay the stoutest heart! Nor was that horror less overwhelming for the obscurity that enveloped it. The Haunted Chapel was gone; and in its place was a heap of blackened, burning, and smoking ruins, with here and there the arm or leg of some crushed and mutilated victim protruding from the mass. And in strange contrast to this appalling scene, was a poor little Skye terrier, preserved from destruction, Heaven only knows how, that ran snuffing and whining piteously around and around the wreck.

"Come, Nelly! pretty Nelly! good Nelly!" called Joe.

The Skye terrier left off circling around the smouldering ruins, and bounded towards her dusky friend, and leaped upon him with a yelp of welcome and a whine of sorrow.

"Oh, Nelly! Nelly! what has happened?" cried Joe.

The little dog howled dismally in answer.

"Yes, I know what you would say. I understand. The devil has blown up the Haunted Chapel," said Joe.

She lifted up her nose and her voice in a woe-begone howl of assent.

"Just so; but oh! Nelly! Nelly Brown! where is the master and the mistress?"

She answered by a cry of agony, and ran back to the ruins, and re-commenced her pawing and whining.

"Ah, yes! just so; buried under all that there," groaned Joe.

But Nelly ran back to him, barking emphatically, and then forward to the ruins, and then, seeing that he still stood there, back to him again, with the most eloquent barks, that seemed to assure him that her master and mistress were under the mass, and at length to ask him what was the use of his being a man, if he could not dig them out.

Never did man and dog understand each other better. Joe replied to Nelly as if she had spoken in the best approved English.

"I know it, honey! I know they are; they are there!" he sobbed, "but you see I'm crippled, and can't do nothing."

But the little Skye terrier could not comprehend such incompetency in a human creature, and so she very irrationally and irritatingly continued her appeals and her reproaches, until Joe hobbled up to the heap of smoking ruins to take a nearer view.

The first thing that met his sight was the sole of a man's boot, belonging to a leg protruding from the mass.

"If it should be hizzen! Oh, good gracious! if it should be marster's! But no," he continued, on a closer examination of the limb. "No! there is a spur on the heel. It isn't hizzen. No! thank goodness, it is Master Sheriff Benthwick's, and sarve him right too."

While Joe was exulting, either wickedly over the destruction of the sheriff, or piously over the possible preservation of his master, there was a sound of crackling footsteps through the thicket, and the forerunners of the approaching crowd appeared upon the scene.

Among them was Captain Pendleton, who, recognizing the figure of Joe even in the obscure light, strode towards him, eagerly demanding:

"What is all this? How did it happen? Do you know?"

"Oh, marse Capping Pendulum, sir, I's so glad you'se come!" cried Joe, on the verge of tears.

"But how did this happen?" impatiently repeated the captain.

"Oh, sir, don't you see as the debbil has blowed up the Haunted Chapel and my young mistess and marster into it all this time," sobbed the man.

"Good Heaven! You don't mean that, Joe!" exclaimed Captain Pendleton.

"Yes, I do, sir; worse luck! which you can see for yourself, as even poor little ignorant Nelly knows it," wept Joe.

And the little Skye terrier, as if to confirm the negro's words, ran and leaped upon the captain, whining pathetically, and then ran backward and forward between him and the heap of ruins, as if to impress upon his mind that her dear master and mistress were really buried there, and to implore him to come to their assistance.

But other people were now pouring rapidly in upon the scene of the catastrophe.

Exclamations of horror and dismay were uttered; then pine knots were sought and lighted, and everybody crowded around the ruins.

"There are human <u>beings</u> buried beneath this pile; for Heaven's sake, friends, lose no time; but disperse and find tools to dig this away!" exclaimed Captain Pendleton, energetically.

Several of the by-standers started at once for the nearest farm-houses to procure the needful tools.

Captain Pendleton turned to Joe.

"Tell me now," he said; "how came Mr. and Mrs. Berners in this place?"

Joe related all that he knew of their escape from the sheriff's officers, their accidental meeting with him, their arrival at the Haunted Chapel, the mysterious disappearance of Sybil, the visit of the constables and militia-men in search of the burglars; the means that his master and himself took to discover traces of Sybil through the instinct of her little dog; the reasons they had, through the behavior of the little Skye terrier, to believe that the lady had been taken down into the vault and robbed and murdered; his own departure in search of tools to take up the flagstones over the vault, and finally his return to the scene of action to find the Haunted Chapel one mass of ruins.

"When I left marster he was sitting at the door of the vault, where we thought the dead body of my poor murdered young mistess was hid; and when I comed back I found this here!" sobbed Joe, pointing to the wreck.

"Good heaven! my man, this is a frightful story that you tell me! Sit yourself down on the ground, and give me that pick which you are using for a crutch! I must go to work here," exclaimed Captain Pendleton, taking the pick from the negro and beginning to dig vigorously at the mass of fallen stone and mortar.

The men and boys who had gone after implements now came hurrying back, with picks, spades, hoes, rakes, etc., over their shoulders.

They immediately fell to work with a zeal and energy inspired by curiosity and terror; and while the boys held the lighted pine knots high above their heads, the men dug away at the mass with all their might and main.

It was a wild scene, that deep glen; the heap of smoking ruins in the midst, the affrighted crowd of workers around it, the flaming torches held on high, the spectral gravestones gleaming here and there; the whole encircled by dark, towering mountains, and canopied by a murky, midnight sky!

In almost dead silence the fearful work went on.

The first body exhumed was that of the unfortunate Sheriff Benthwick, quite dead. It was borne tenderly off to some distance, and laid down on a bed of dried leaves beneath the shelter of an oak-tree.

Then four other bodies were dug out from the mass, among them that of the bailiff Purley. And these were carried and laid beside that of the sheriff.

And now, though the workmen dug away at the ruins as vigorously as ever, they found nothing but broken timbers, stone, and mortar. No sign of Lyon or Sybil Berners was to be seen. A wild hope sprang up in the heart of Joe— a hope that in some miraculous manner his young master and mistress had escaped this terrible destruction—a hope that the little Skye terrier would by no means encourage, for she continued to run around the ruins, and in and out among the legs of the workmen, to the serious danger of her own life and limbs, and to bark and whine and paw, and assert in every emphatic manner a little brute could use, that her master and mistress were really under there and nowhere else.

"You'll drive me to despair, you little devil of a dog! You'd make 'em there, whether they're there or not, and I tell you they an't there!" cried Joe in desperation.

But Nelly held to her own opinion, and clamorously maintained it.

She was soon justified. The workmen, in course of their digging, removed quite a hill of plaster, stone, and broken timbers, and came upon a leaning fragment of the back wall, inclined at an angle of about forty-five degrees, and supported in its place by a portion of the altar and the iron door of the vault, which had stood the shock of the explosion.

Under this leaning wall, and completely protected by it, lay two men, scorched, bruised, stunned, insensible, but still living.

They were Lyon Berners and Robert Munson. Amid the surprise and satisfaction of the crowd, they were carefully lifted out and laid upon the ground, while every simple means at hand were used for their restoration, while the little Skye terrier ran round and round with yelps of joy and triumph, which seemed to say:

"I told you so! and next time you'll believe me!"

"Friends," said Captain Pendleton, addressing some of the men who were still working away at the ruins, "there is no use in your digging longer! You may see from the very position of that wall and the aspect of everything else here, that there can be no more bodies among the ruins. You can do nothing to bring the dead to life; but you can do much to save the living from death. Hurry some of you to the nearest house and bring a couple of shutters, and narrow mattresses also, if possible! These men must be taken to my house, which is nearest, to receive medical attention."

As the captain spoke, a dozen workmen threw down their tools and started on the errand.

Old Joe hobbled up to the spot, where Captain Pendleton sat supporting the head of Mr. Berners on his knee, while little Nelly jumped around, now in a hysterical state between joy and fear; for she saw at last, that though her master was rescued, he was not yet safe. On seeing Joe come up, she jumped upon him with an eager bark which seemed to say:

"You see I was right! Here he is, sure enough!"

"Yes, Nelly, that's all very well as far as it goes. But where's the young mistress, Nelly; where's Miss Sybil?" sorrowfully inquired Joe.

The little dog looked up in his face with a bark of intelligence and distress, and then broke away and ran in among the ruins.

"There still is she!" exclaimed Joe, and he hobbled after the little Skye terrier to the place where the leaning fragment of the wall was supported by the iron door of the vault.

"They must dig into that vault. I'll never be contented until they dig into that vault; and I'll speak to Capping Pendulum about it," said Joe, and he hobbled back to the spot where that gentleman still sat supporting the head of his wounded friend.

"Sir, Marse Capping," said Joe, respectfully taking off his hat, "you heerd what I tell you 'bout marster and me having of good reasons to s'pose as my young mistress was robbed and murdered and hid into that vault?"

"Yes," gravely assented the captain.

"Well, sir, Marse Capping, Nelly do stick to it as she *is* down there. And, sir, I shall neber feel satisfied into my own mind, till the men dig away all the rubbish and lay open 'the secrets of that there prisin house.'"

"Joe, it shall be done, if only for the satisfaction of your faithful heart," said the captain.

"And for Nelly's too, sir. See how she stands and looks up into your face, waiting for you to 'cide, just as if she understood all that I was a axing of you, which of course she do."

"Not a doubt of it," assented the captain.

At that moment the messengers who had been dispatched for shutters and mattresses, returned with the articles, and set them down before Captain Pendleton.

"Now, my men," said the captain, "arrange one of the mattresses upon the shutter, and assist me to lay my wounded friend upon it."

Ready hands obeyed this direction, and the faintly breathing body of Lyon Berners was laid down in comparative ease.

The same service was performed for poor young Munson, who was badly injured, and also quite unconscious.

"Now, my men, this poor negro has reason to believe that the body of his mistress may be found in the bottom of that vault; I want you therefore to go to work as fast as you can, and remove all the rubbish that has fallen into it, even down to the floor," was the next order given by the captain.

And the men seized their picks and resumed their digging with renewed energy.

"Joe, stay here by your master and this poor fellow; and occasionally wet their lips with this brandy and water, while I go and see to the clearing out of the vault," said Captain Pendleton; and leaving Joe in charge of the wounded men, he followed the workmen to the ruins to urge them to the greatest expedition, adding as a reason for haste:

"It is time that Mr. Berners and Munson should be taken to my house, and placed in bed, to receive proper medical attention. But I cannot consent to leave this spot even to attend to them, until I find out whether the body of Mrs. Berners is really under the ruins."

Thus exhorted, the men worked with tremendous energy, and soon dug away all the pile of rubbish, and laid the depths of the vault open to the torch light. But there was nothing to be seen but the damp and slimy walls and floor, and the little heaps of broken stones and fallen plaster in the corners.

"Not there! Well, then, I didn't know whether I was a-hoping or a fearing to find her there, or whether I'm glad or sorry now at not finding her there," said Joe, who in his excessive anxiety had at length deserted his post beside the wounded men, and hobbled up to the opened vault.

"You should be glad, for now you have no evidence of her death; but, on the other hand, good reason to hope that she is somewhere alive and well," said Captain Pendleton.

"That's so too, Marster Capping. But only see what a little story-teller Nelly is!"

"It was her master she scented, and she found him."

"Yes, but she tried to make me believe as her mistess was down there also. And look how she sticks to the story! There she is down there still running round and round like she was crazy, and a snuffing at all the corners!"

"Never mind Nelly, Joe. Come along now. We must take your master and the other poor fellow on to my house. It should have been done before this. I am sorry for this delay, which has been so fruitless," said Captain Pendleton, as he led the way back to the spot where he had left the injured victims of the explosion.

"Marster Capping," said Joe, as he hobbled after Pendleton, "I have got two horses tied up there into the woods, ef they haven't been frighted at the blowing up, and done broke loose; and I have got a wagon down by the roadside, if so be as you would like to convey my wounded marster and the t'other gemplan that a way."

"No, Joe; the jolting of a wagon might be fatal to them in their present condition. They must be carried carefully on shutters. But the wagon will be just the thing to convey the dead bodies to Blackville, where an inquest must be held upon them," answered the captain.

And he requested some of the men present to go in search of the horses, and to harness them to the wagon for the required services to the dead, while others he detained to help in care of the wounded.

When the shutters upon which Lyon Berners and Robert Munson lay were each carefully lifted by the hands of four men, and the little procession was about to start, Captain Pendleton called to Joe, saying:

"You must go with me to have your limb looked to, and also to be with your master, who will need familiar faces near him when he comes to himself."

"Yes, sir; Marse Capping Pendulum, I will go. But oh, my Hebbenly Lord, what will I have to tell my poor marster, when he opens his eyes and looks at me?" cried Joe, bursting into tears.

"Come, come, be a man! Stop howling, and do your duty—which is now to follow your master," expostulated the captain.

"Yes, sir, I'll do it; but I must get Nelly fust. I couldn't leave her, poor little dog, here to pine away and die in the vault," sighed Joe, who then lifting his voice, cried, "Nelly! Nelly!"

But no dog answered. So Joe hobbled his way back to the opening of the vault, and looking down into it, exclaimed:

"Bless my two eyes! ef there she an't a-whinin and a-pawin' and a-sarchin' as persemoniously as ever!—Nelly! Nelly!"

At the sound of his voice the little terrier ran up from the vault, and leaped upon him.

Joe stooped and picked her up in his arms, and hugged her affectionately to his bosom, as he said:

"You see it's no use stayin' here, my poor little dog. Our mistess an't nowheres about here."

Nelly was however of a different opinion, and she whined and struggled to be released; and when Joe held her faster, she growled and threatened him with her teeth.

"Can't help it, my little darling. Our mistess an't nowhere round, and it an't no use your staying here to grieve yourself to death among the ruins. You've got to go along with me—OWTCH! you little devil, you!" exclaimed Joe, suddenly breaking off in his discourse, and dropping the dog; who, having found that all her efforts to release herself had been in vain, had made her little teeth meet in the fleshy part of the negro's hand.

"Was there ever sich a vicious little beast?" cried Joe, as he hobbled away, sucking the blood from his wounded member. "Now she may stay there for me. I don't care ef she do pine herself to death, agrawatin' little brute!"

And so, grumbling and growling, he hobbled after the little procession that was now well on its way through the thicket.

Meanwhile little Nelly ran back into the vault, and re-commenced her irrational investigations.

The hours of the night wore on. The men who had been sent in search of the horses, with great difficulty found and caught them, and brought them back to the scene of the explosion. The dead bodies were bound upon their backs, and they were led through the thicket to the road, where the empty wagon was waiting. As there were five bodies and but two horses, and as only one body could be bound upon one horse at a time, it was necessary to make three trips through the thicket, before they could all be got upon the wagon. So it was a work of time and trouble to remove all the dead from the scene of the catastrophe. At length, however, the last body was bound upon the last horse and led away by the last man that left the spot.

And of all the living crowd that had filled the churchyard and surrounded the ruin, none was left but the little Skye terrier Nelly, who was still at work in the vault.

What was she doing?

She had concentrated her attention and her energies upon one spot—a moderate sized heap of densely packed rubbish in one corner. She was scratching away at this heap; she had already burrowed a hole of some depth; and still she scratched away, with all her might and main, until her strength failed; and then she sat down on her hind quarters and panted until she recovered her breath; and then she re-commenced and scratched away for dear life until something fell on the other side, and with a bark and bound of joy, she leaped through the aperture and ran snuffing along the damp ground.

EUREKA!! the little Skye terrier had discovered what human intelligence had failed to do! She had found the secret subterranean passage, and now be sure she will find her mistress.

CHAPTER V.

THE ROBBERS' CAVE.

There's ae thing yet; there's twa things yet,

To brag on that ye know;

They never, never failed a friend,

And never feared a foe.—NICOLL.

We left Sybil sleeping on her sylvan couch, in the cavern chamber of her nameless hostess. She slept on as they sleep who, being completely conquered by mental and bodily fatigue, surrender unconditionally to Nature's great restorer.

Late in the afternoon she awoke, much refreshed in mind and body, though at first somewhat confused as to her "local habitation." But the voice of her strange hostess at once restored her memory and self-possession.

"You have slept long and well," said the girl. "I have been in here half a dozen times at least to look at you, and always found you fast asleep. You never even changed your position. I think you must feel much better."

"I feel very well, thank you, if only I could hear from my husband," replied Sybil.

"Always the same subject! that is stupid and tiresome. But I can tell you about your husband. He is just now at the Haunted Chapel, waiting for the constables to go away, so that he may resume his search for you."

"Poor Lyon! But how do you know this?"

"Moloch, who has just come in, told me."

"'Moloch!' You have mentioned that name several times. Who is Moloch?"

"The lieutenant of the band. Belial is the adjutant. Satan is the captain, but we seldom see him. He is a very fine gentleman, of the very first society. I have no doubt that you have met him often in the drawing-rooms, of wealth and fashion."

"Good Heaven! girl, what story is this that you are telling me?"

"The very truth. Satan is a gentleman. Belial also is no stranger to good company. Hem! they were both at your masquerade."

"Both at—!" gasped Sybil, losing her breath in astonishment.

"Your masquerade! Yes, for I tell you that they are both men of fashion and pleasure. As for poor old Moloch, he is just what he seems—a rude, rugged robber! And then there is Vulcan."

"But who are these men?" inquired Sybil, recovering her lost breath.

"I told you. Gentlemen in the drawing-room! Robbers on the highway."

"But why do you give them such diabolical names?"

"Because they are devils, each in his way! Moloch is a brutal and ferocious devil; Belial is a smooth, deceitful devil; and Satan is an intellectual and commanding devil."

"What are their right names?"

"It would be hard to tell! Each one having a score of aliases at his disposal."

"I hope I shall not be obliged to see any of these wretches!" imprudently exclaimed Sybil.

"They are devils, not wretches, if I know them and know the meaning of words! But reflect, madam, that to these wretches, as you call them, you owe your liberty and perhaps your life," said the elfin-like hostess, resentfully.

"My liberty! And here I am a captive among you."

"Only for a time; only until we can place you in perfect safety on a foreign shore. And that we are sworn to do. And is not this comparatively honorable captivity; better than the degrading one of the county jail?"

Sybil paled and shuddered through all her frame as she answered:

"I should be grateful for all this—but—but—my husband!"

"Oh, bother, there it is again! Always the same *mew*! If there's anything in the world makes me feel ill, it is a love-sick woman!" exclaimed the strange girl. But her short-lived anger quickly disappeared, and holding out her tiny brown hand to her guest, she said:

"Come, get up and wash! There is some fresh water and clean towels. And there is a change of clothing, if you wish to have it. And here am I, to serve as your lady's maid. And when you are dressed, there will be a dinner ready for you, of which I may say that the Govenor of the State will not sit down to a better one to-day."

Sybil gave her hand in token of reconciliation, and then arose from her couch of leaves. Very glad was she of the opportunity of washing and changing her dress; for of all the petty privations that were mixed up with her great troubles, she felt most the want of fresh water and clean clothes.

The girl waited on her kindly and skilfully. And Sybil would have been well pleased had she not, in taking up one of the fresh damask towels, saw on it the initials of her friend Beatrix Pendleton. She held it up to the view of her hostess, and looked inquiringly.

"Yes, to be sure! we wanted face towels, and they brought away a dozen or so of them from a house they recently visited. But you cannot help it. I advise you to make the best of everything," said the girl, answering the look.

Sybil said not a word in reply; but she thought within herself, "I am forced to consort with thieves, and to use their stolen goods; but I will profit by nothing which I shall not make good to the owner; and so as soon as I shall be freed, I will privately send Miss Pendleton a fourfold compensation."

And thus, having satisfied her conscience, Sybil took her hostess' advice, and made "the best of everything."

When she was thoroughly renovated by a complete change of clothing, every article of which she recognized as the property of Miss Pendleton, her strange hostess conducted her into the spacious and beautiful cavern that has been already described.

There was a large round table set in the middle of the floor, covered with a fine white damask cloth, and furnished with a heterogeneous service of the richest silver plate, the most delicate Sevres china and the coarsest earthen ware and rudest cutlery. There were plates laid for about a dozen persons. Around the table were seats as miscellaneous in quality as was the service; there were three-legged stools, stumpy logs of wood set on end, one very large stone, and one elegant piano chair.

"We always eat our great meal of the day in this place. You would call it dinner; we call it supper, but it is all the same," said the girl.

"Oh!" exclaimed Sybil, looking in dismay at the many plates—"Oh! have I got to meet all these horrid men?"

"Yes, my lady! You must meet these horrid men who have saved you! They do not often have the honor of a lady's company to supper, and they will not dispense with yours now," replied the elfin hostess, sarcastically.

A shudder ran through Sybil's frame; but she rallied all her strength to resist the creeping terror.

"These thieves are men, after all," she said to herself. "They are not beasts nor devils, as their companion calls them; they are human beings, why should I fear them?" And she spoke very cheerfully to her hostess, inquiring:

"When do you expect your companions in?"

"They drop in at any time in the evening. Some of them will be here soon, and then we will have supper."

The darkening of the cave now indicated that the sun was setting. And soon the wild hostess clapped her hands and called in her pale attendant to light up the cavern. And the phantom vanished for a few moments, and then returned with two tall silver candlesticks, supporting two such large wax candles that Sybil saw at a glance that they must have been stolen from the altar of a Catholic chapel. And she shivered again at perceiving that she was the guest of the worst of outlaws—sacrilegious church-robbers! But soon her attention was attracted by the splendor of the scene around, when the stalactite walls of the cavern, lighted up by the great candles, emitted millions of prismatic rays of every brilliant hue, as if they were encrusted with diamonds, rubies, emeralds, sapphires, amethysts, topazes, and carbuncles, all of the purest fire.

"Splendid, is it not? What palace chamber can compare to ours?" inquired the girl, on observing the evident admiration with which her guest gazed upon the scene.

Before Sybil had time to reply there was the heavy trampling of feet near at hand, and the next moment four rough looking men entered the cave.

Involuntarily Sybil shrank closer to her hostess, as they passed near her. But not one of them either did or said anything to alarm or offend her. Each one, in his turn, gruffly greeted her by nodding, as he pulled off his hat and threw it into a corner, and then seated himself at the table.

The elfin girl clapped her hands, and when her attendant appeared, she ordered that supper should be immediately brought in.

Meantime Sybil furtively observed the four robbers, but one of them especially fascinated her gaze, with something of the terrible fascination that the boa-constrictor is said to exercise upon the beautiful birds of the Brazilian forest.

He was a great red-haired and red-bearded giant, whose large limbs and coarse features had well earned for him the nick-name of "Moloch;" and Moloch, Sybil instinctively knew this man to be. The other three were ordinary, hirsute, dirty ruffians, upon whom she scarcely bestowed a glance. Her eyes continually reverted to Moloch, from whom she could not long keep them. He was huge, ugly, brutal, ferocious; but he commanded attention, if only from the power that was within him.

But what terrified Sybil the most was this—that her own fascinated eyes at length attracted his, and he looked at her with a devouring gaze that made her eyelids fall and her very heart sink within her.

The two women—the dark and shrivelled old Hecate, and the pale, cold Proserpine—now brought in the supper. And as the elfin hostess had declared, a more luxurious meal did not grace the table of the State's Governor that day. There were green-turtle soup, rock fish, ham, wild turkey, and partridges, with every variety of vegetables and of condiments. And there were pies, puddings, custards, and pastries of every description. And jellies, jams, and fresh and preserved fruits, of every sort. And there were priceless wines, and fragrant coffee and tea. All these luxuries were placed at once upon the supper table, or a side table in full view of the company.

"We have no printed bill of fare," laughed Sybil's strange hostess; "but the fare itself is before you!"

"Let the lady be seated in the place of honor," growled Moloch, glowering at Sybil with his dreadful eyes.

"Which means the piano stool, I suppose," said the strange hostess, taking Sybil by the hand, and leading her to the seat in question.

She suffered herself to be put into it; but the next instant she was horrified by the insolence of Moloch, who deliberately arose from his seat and came around and placed himself beside her, and laid his great hand upon her shoulder.

"You are handsome," he said "Do you know it? But of course you do. The swells have told you so a many times."

"Don't touch me!" said Sybil, shrinking from him.

"Now don't put on airs. You're one of us, you know, and so we'll 'fend you to the last drop of blood in our weins. Only don't put on airs; but be kind to them as are kind to you," growled the brute.

"But take your hand away—please do. I cannot bear it!" cried Sybil, shrinking farther off still.

"Why, now, if you only knowed what this here hand have done in your sarvice, you'd fondle on to it, instead o' flinging it off like it was a wasp," coaxed the ruffian, stealing his arm around her neck.

But Sybil, with a sudden and violent gesture, cast it off, and started to her feet, seizing the knife beside her as a weapon of defence.

"Lord bless your pretty little soul, what's the good of that? Why, when I was a lad, I always liked to tease the kittens best that spit and scratched and fit the most! That only makes me like you better. Come now, sit down alongside o' me, and let's be good friends," said the ruffian, throwing his arms around Sybil, and forcing her into her seat.

"Stop that, you devilish beast! Let the lady alone!" cried Sybil's nameless hostess, in a voice of authority.

"Don't be jealous, my darling," replied Moloch, tightening his clasp around Sybil's waist.

"Men! why don't you interfere? He is rude to the lady!" cried the girl, appealing to the others.

"We never meddle between other men and their sweethearts. Do we, mates?" called out one.

"No, no, no!" answered the others.

"Oh, if Satan were here!" cried the girl in despair.

"SATAN IS HERE!" responded a voice close by.

And the robber captain stood among them as if he had risen from the earth!

Moloch dropped Sybil, and cowered in the most abject manner.

Sybil looked up, and turned cold from head to foot; for in the handsome, stately, graceful form of the brigand chief, she recognized the finished gentleman who, in the character of "Death," had danced with her at her own Mask ball, and—the probable murderer of Rosa Blondelle!

CHAPTER VI.

THE ROBBER CHIEFTAIN.

He was the mildest mannered man

That ever scuttled ship, or cut a throat;

With such true breeding of a gentleman,

You never could divine his real thought;

Pity he loved adventurous life's variety,

He was so great a loss to good society.—BYRON.

While the walls of the cavern seemed wheeling around Sybil, the robber captain calmly came up to her, lifted his hat, and said:

"Spirit of Fire, I am happy to welcome you to your own appropriate dwelling place. Behold!"

And he waved his hat around towards the stalactite walls and ceiling of the cavern, now burning, sparkling, blazing, in the reflected light of the candles.

"DEATH!" uttered Sybil, under her suspended breath.

"Yes, Death! I told you, Spirit, that Death and Fire were often allies! But now, as we are no longer masquerading, permit me, Mrs. Berners, to present myself to you as Captain Inconnu," he said, with another and a deeper bow.

"That name tells me nothing," replied Sybil.

"What name does more?" inquired the stranger; and then, without expecting an answer, he turned to Moloch, and said in his smoothest tones:

"Be so good as to give me this seat, sir."

But Sybil saw that the giant turned pale and trembled like the fabled mountain in labor, as he left the seat by her side, and slunk into another at some distance; and she felt far more fear of the graceful "Captain Inconnu," who now placed himself beside her, and behaved with so much deference, than she had felt of the brutal "Moloch," who had treated her with the rudest familiarity. And this fear was not at all modified by a whisper that reached her acute ears, from the man at whose side the giant had now seated himself.

"I could a' told you what you'd get, if you meddled wi' the Captain's gal! Now look out."

But the "Captain" conducted himself with the greatest courtesy towards his guest.

"Come here, Princess!" he said, addressing the girl, "come here and place yourself on the other side of this lady. If you are Princess, she is Queen."

The girl immediately came around and seated herself. And the master of the house helped his guest to the most delicate morsels of the viands before him.

Sybil, though in deadly fear of her gentlemanly attendant, accepted every one of his attentions with a smile. She knew poor child, to whom she was now obliged to pay court. Her one idea was her husband; her one want, to be reunited to him, at all risks or costs to liberty or life; and she knew that this man, the autocrat, as well as the Captain of his band, had the power to restore her to her husband, and so she exerted all her powers of pleasing to win his favor.

Poor Sybil! if she was rather ignorant of books, (for a gentleman's daughter,) she was still more ignorant of mankind. She might have learned something from the case of Rosa Blondelle, but she did not. And now no guardian spirit whispered to her:

"You saw how the blandishments of a beauty affected even your own true-hearted husband; and yet, with the best intentions, you are using the same sort of blandishments upon a brigand. What can you expect but evil?"

No; the voice of her guardian angel was silent; and the beautiful, honorable lady continued to smile on the robber captain, until his head was turned.

Near the conclusion of the feast, he filled a goblet to the brim with wine, and rising in his place, said:

"Fill high your glasses, men! Let us drink to the health of our new sovereign. Dethroned and outcast by the law, we will enthrone her and crown her the Queen of Outlaws! Fill to the brim with this best of wine. And mind, this cup is a pledge of amnesty to all offenders, of union among ourselves, and of devotion to our Queen!"

The toast was honored by full glasses and loud cheers. And none filled higher or cheered louder than the giant Moloch, who now felt himself secure from the captain's vengeance, by virtue of the general proclamation of amnesty.

The long-protracted feast came to an end at last.

The robber captain was not an impetuous brute like the giant Moloch. He was a refined and cultivated being, who could bide his time, and enjoy his happiness by anticipation.

So at the end of the supper, seeing that his guest was very weary, he signed to the girl to rise. And then he took the lady's hand, pressed it most respectfully to his lips, and placed it in that of the girl, saying:

"See your queen to her apartments, and serve her royally."

Poor Sybil! In her infatuation she smiled upon the brigand, with a look that deprived him of the last remnant of reason, and then she followed her conductor from the room.

The girl led the lady to the same cavern chamber where she had before slept, and then said:

"Listen to me. Satan is not himself to-night. Satan is in love. That is a more fatal intoxication than any produced by wine; and when the devil is drunk with love or wine, he is very dangerous. You must stay with me to-night."

"Your eyes are wide open, and as bright as stars! You are not sleepy at all," said the girl gazing upon Sybil's excited face.

"How can I be, when I slept so long to-day, and when I have so much to occupy my thoughts besides?" sighed Sybil.

"Do you wish to sleep?"

"Indeed I do; to sleep and forget."

"Here then," said the girl taking a full bag from a corner and drawing over it a clean pillow-case. "Here is a sack of dried hop-leaves. It is as soft as down, and soporific as opium. Put this under your head and you will find it to be a magic cushion that will convey you at once to the land of Nod."

Sybil took her advice and soon grew calm, and soon after lost all consciousness of her troubles in a deep repose, which lasted until morning.

The glinting of the sun's rays through the crevices in the cave, and the sparkling of the stalactites on the walls, first awakened Sybil. She saw that her hostess was already up and dressed; but had not left the cave. She was in truth setting the place in order after her own toilet, and, laying out fresh towels for that of her guest.

Sybil watched her in silence some time, and then spoke:

"I have been with you twenty-four hours, and yet do not know your name. Will you never tell it to me?"

"Yes, my name is Gentiliska; but you may call me Iska."

"Iska? Gentiliska? Where have I heard that singular name before?" inquired Sybil of herself; for in fact so many startling incidents had happened to her lately, that her mind was rather confused. She reflected a moment before she could recall the idea of the Gipsy girl, in the legend of the "Haunted Chapel." She turned and gazed at her hostess with renewed interest. A superstitious thrill ran through her frame. Yes; here were all the points of resemblance between this strange being and the spectral girl of the story! Here were the Gipsy features, the long black elf-locks, the jet black eyes, and arch eye-brows depressed towards the nose and lifted towards the temple, the elfish expression, the manner, the dress, the very name itself!

"Why do you look at me so strangely?" inquired the girl.

"Gentiliska!" repeated Sybil, as in a dream.

"Yes, that's it! Most of the girls of my race have borne it; but my great-grandmother was the last before me."

"Your great-grandmother?" echoed Sybil still as in a dream.

"Yes; she had no daughter or granddaughter, else they also would have been Gentiliska's. She had only a son and a grandson, and her grandson had only me," calmly replied the girl.

Sybil gasped for breath; and when she recovered her voice she exclaimed:

"But you have another name—a family name!"

"Oh, to be sure; most people have."

"Would you—would you tell it me?" inquired Sybil, hesitatingly.

The girl looked at her quizzingly.

"Believe me, I do not ask from idle curiosity," added Sybil.

"Oh, no; to be sure not. We are not a bit curious—we!"

"You needn't tell me," said Sybil.

"Oh, but I will. My family name? It is not a very noble one. It is indeed a very humble one—Dewberry."

"DUBARRY!" exclaimed Sybil, catching her breath.

"Oh bother, no. I wish it was. That was the name of the great family who once owned all this great manor, which went to wreck and ruin for want of an heir!—oh, no; my name is Dewberry—the little fruit vine, you know, that runs along the ground, and takes its name from its cool berries being always found deep in the dew. Besides, I am English, and descended through my great-grandmother Gentiliska from the English gipsies. *She* was a gipsy queen."

"Gentiliska," said Sybil, "Tell me something about your great-grandmother. I feel interested in all that concerns gipsies."

"Well, but get up and dress for breakfast. I can talk while you are making your toilet."

"Certainly," said Sybil, immediately following the advice of her hostess, who with nimble hands began to help her to dress.

"My ancestress Gentiliska was the daughter of a long line of gipsy kings. On the death of her father, she became queen of the tribe."

"Her father had no sons?"

"Oh, yes, he had. But his daughter was made queen, I don't know why. She was very beautiful, and she sang and danced as charmingly as that beautiful Jewish princess, who danced off the head of holy 'John the Baptist.' She was an astute reader of human nature, and therefore a successful fortune teller. She always promised love to youth, money to the mature, and long life to the aged. One day at the races she told the fortune of a rich young man, in return for which he made hers."

"How?"

"He married her."

"He *did* really marry her? You are sure?"

The girl flared up. "He took her abroad with him; and *of course* he married her."

"Of course he should have done so," sighed Sybil, as the fairy castle she had built for the girl fell like a house of cards.

"I tell you he not only *should* have done so, but he *did* so. My ancestress was no fool. She was married by special license. I have the license in a silver casket. It was the only heirloom she left her descendants, and they have kept it in the family ever since. They had a notion, I think, that there was wealth or honor hung on to it," laughed the girl.

"Honor certainly, wealth possibly."

"Ha! ha! ha! I don't see how. Little good for one or the other, it ever did us. My father was a tramp; my grandfather a tinker."

"But how was that? Your ancestress married a gentleman?"

"Yes, she married a gentleman, and her tribe discarded her when she deserted them. They would have discarded her all the same, if she had married a king who was not of her race. She went abroad with her husband, and visited, I have heard, the four quarters of the globe. She returned after two years, bringing with her a dark infant boy. She was about to go with her husband on another long, long voyage. He refused to allow her to take her child, but said, for the little lad's own sake, he must be left at nurse in England. The only point she could get him to yield was this, that the child should be left with her tribe until it should be five years old, when they would reclaim it."

"That was a very strange disposition for a gentleman to make of his son."

"It would have been, if he had cared a snap for his son, which he didn't, as after events proved. The gipsy wife sought out her own old grandmother, who was a famous doctress of the tribe. In the beldame's care she left the babe. Then with her husband she slipped away to sea, and neither the one nor the other was ever seen or heard of afterwards. The boy, deserted by his father and his mother, grew up a poor degraded little half-breed among the gipsies, scarcely tolerated by them, but loved and petted by his foster-mother, whose great power in her tribe only sufficed for his protection. When at length the old crone lay upon her death-bed, she called the youth to her side, and placed in his hand the silver casket, saying:

"Take it, my lad. It was put in my hands by your mother, when she left you with me. Take it, then; guard it as the most sacred treasure of your life; for it may bring you to wealth and honor yet.'

"And then she died, and the lad, with the casket for his only fortune, left the tribe, and took to the road alone, mending pots and kettles for a living, often suffering hunger and cold, but never, under any stress of poverty, parting with the silver casket." The girl paused for a moment and then resumed:

"But poverty never yet prevented a gipsy from taking a mate. He found one in the daughter of another travelling tinker, poorer, if possible, than himself. She lived only long enough to bring him one child, and then died, it is said, from the hardships of her life."

"That was miserable," sighed Sybil.

"It was so miserable that her widowed husband never tried marriage any more; but he brought up his son to his own trade—that of a travelling tinker. And when the time came for him to give up the ghost, he placed the casket in the hand of the boy, saying:

"Your mother died of want, rather than let it be sold for a sum that might have saved her life and made her comfortable; because she said that in it was her child's destiny. Keep it and guard it as you would guard your heart's blood.

"And so the old tinker died, and the young tramp, with the heirloom in his possession, set out to seek his fortunes.

"But he did not go upon the quest alone. Like most improvident young tramps, he took a mate. His wife was my mother. I remember both my parents while they were yet young and handsome, and very happy despite their poverty. My father—But let me stop! Before I go any further, I wish to ask you a question."

"Ask it."

"Do you believe that any one may become so maddened with causeless jealousy as to commit a crime?"

"I not only believe it, but know it."

"Then I will go on. My father doted on my mother—just doted on her! But my poor mother had a friend and benefactor, of whom my father grew insanely, furiously, but causelessly jealous.

"One day he did a cruel murder, and found out when it was too late that he had slain the father of his wife, who, in coming after her at all was only looking to the interests of his poor, unowned daughter. Ah! a volume might be written on that tragedy; but let it pass! My mother died of grief. But long ere that my father had fled the country an outlaw and the companion of outlaws.

"Once his still absorbing love for his wife drew him back to England, at the imminent risk of his life. His wife was dead, and his daughter was a little wretched child, knocked about among beggars and tramps, and in extreme danger of that last evil—that last, and worst evil that could have befallen her—being taken care of by the parish!"

"That is a severe sarcasm," said Sybil, rebukingly.

"Is it? If ever you are free again, lady, visit the most destitute homes in the world, and then the best alms-houses in your reach, and find out for yourself whether it is not better to die a free beggar than to live an imprisoned pauper. The manner in which Workhouse Charity 'whips the devil round the stump' by satisfying its conscience without benefiting its object, is one of the funniest jokes, as well as one of the most curious subjects of study, that can be found in social life."

"I am sorry to hear you say so; but go on with your story."

"My father, bowed down with remorse for his crime, and grief for the loss of his wife, found yet something to live for in me, his only child. He brought me away to the coast of France, where he and his pals were carrying on a very successful business in the smuggling line.

"They run goods to and fro between the French and English shores of the Channel. One day he was fatally wounded in an encounter with the Excise officers, near St. Margaret's. He was taken prisoner, but all the other members of his band escaped. When he knew he was dying, he sent for me, and the officers were kind enough to have me looked up.

"I was then wandering about the village in a state of destitution, in which I must have perished but for the kindness of the poorest among the poor, who shared their crusts and their pallets with me.

"I was taken to my father, who was dying in the Dover jail. He gave me the silver casket, telling me what a sacred heirloom it was, and how he had kept it through every temptation to part with it, and that I must guard it as the most precious jewel of my life; for that one day it might be the means of making me a lady."

"I didn't say 'Bosh' to my dying father; but I have said 'Bosh' ever since, every time I have thought of that bauble! It never did any good to my father, or my grandfather, and it is not likely to relent in my favor. Beyond the fact that it proves my great-grandmother, the Gipsy Queen, to have been an honest woman, I don't see any use it is to her descendants."

"I have it still, as I told you before; because from the hour of my poor father's death, I have never known a want, or felt a temptation to part with it. I was adopted by his band, who have always treated me like a princess."

"But I have a sort of spite against it, for all that, for it never yet did what was expected of it; and so, the first time I find myself hungry without the means of procuring food, I will sell the silver casket to the first purchaser I can find; and the first time I want to light a candle and can't find any other piece of paper, I will burn the marriage license."

"Don't you do it!" exclaimed Sybil, eagerly, earnestly; "burn, sell anything you possess sooner! I believe that that casket has been preserved through three generations for your sake, *yours*! And if, as your poor father hinted, it does not make you a lady,—for nothing but nature and education can make one a lady, you know—it will be sure to make you a woman of wealth and position!"

"Bosh! I *will* say 'bosh' to you; for you are not my father," sneered the girl.

"Suppose I were able to furnish you with the key to the lock of this sealed family history of yours? Suppose I could point out to you the place where Philip Dewberry, as you called him, carried his gipsy wife Gentiliska; where she died without other children; and where he also subsequently died without other heirs?" inquired Sybil.

"If you could do that, you could do wonders!" laughed the girl incredulously.

"I believe I can do all this! I believe I can give you the sequel and complement of the family history you have told me!" said Sybil seriously.

"How is it possible? You can know nothing of it. I am English, you are American. The ocean divides our countries, and the century divides that past history from the present."

"Divides and *unites*!" said Sybil.

"But how is that?"

"Gentiliska, did you never think of connecting the two circumstances; your race of Dewberrys searching for the estate to which they had a claim, but no clue; and this manor of the Dubarrys, waiting in abeyance for the heir who never comes to claim it?"

"*No!*" exclaimed the girl in some excitement, "I never did! But the coincidence is striking too. Only—one name is Dubarry and the other is Dewberry. Bosh, I say again! One name is even French, and the other is English! They are not even of the same nation; how can they have any connection with each other?"

"My dear; don't you know how easy it is to corrupt a name? Don't you see how inevitably the aristocratic French name Dubarry would be corrupted by ignorant people into the humble English name Dewberry?"

"Yes; but I never thought of that before."

"Now, will you let me look at that license?"

"I don't care. Only whenever I put my hands upon it, I am tempted to tear it up."

"Do nothing of the sort; guard it as you would guard your precious eyes. And now let me see it."

CHAPTER VII.

GENTILISKA DUBARRY.

"And Iska,

And Iska,

And Iska's a lady."

The girl went to a little trunk, unlocked it, and brought out the small silver casket. She touched a spring and the top flew open revealing a packet of papers, from which she selected one brown with age, and worn almost into squares by folding. She laid it before Sybil, who carefully unfolded it, and scrutinized it.

"There, you see!" said the lady at length, speaking in triumph. "There is the name of Philip Dubarry, as plain as a proctor's clerk could write it. Not Dewberry, mind you, but Dubarry. See for yourself."

"So it is!" exclaimed the girl in amazement. "Now do you know I never examined it so closely as to see the difference in the spelling of the name before? We were always called Dewberry; and Dewberry I thought we were."

"No; you were and are Dubarry, and in all human probability the sole heiress of this great manor."

"Stop a bit; oh, my eye! I mean, oh, my nose!"

"What's the matter?"

"I smell a mice!"

"What do you mean?"

"Satan knows I am a princess in disguise, and that's the very reason why he wants to marry me."

"Please be clear, if you can't be brilliant."

"Why, I'm as clear as mud. Satan has found out that I am the rightful heiress of the Dubarry manor, and he wishes to make me his wife in order to become master of the estate," the girl explained.

Sybil raised her eyes in surprise, then dropped them again upon the license, and repeated:

"So Satan wishes to wed you."

"You bet. And I never could imagine why a gentleman of his cultivated tastes should want me for a wife."

"Did he ever happen to see that marriage license?"

"Oh, yes, he has seen it and studied it. He told me it was an important document, and advised me to take good care of it."

"Then that is probably the way in which he discovered your right to the Dubarry estate."

"To be sure it was; for from the time he first saw that paper, he began to treat me with more respect and attention. And I do believe that was also the reason why he came down to this place."

While the girl spoke, Sybil was thinking hard and fast. Was the gentleman brigand the husband of Rosa Blondelle? Had he deliberately murdered his wife that he might marry this young gipsy heiress of the great Dubarry manor? But the girl would not let the lady reflect in peace for many minutes. She suddenly broke out with—

"I can't credit it. Not even in the face of the facts. What, a poor little beggarly wretch of a half-breed gipsy like me, the sole heiress of an old aristocratic manor? Stuff and nonsense! Even if I have a right to it, I shall never get it."

"Oh, yes, you will," said Sybil, confidently. "I never heard of a clearer case than yours, as you have stated it. You have only to prove three marriages, three births, and one identity. And as marriages and births are always registered in your country, there will be no difficulty in that."

"*Our* marriages and births were always registered for the same reason that this license was kept, that some of us might come into the family fortune sometime and be made a lady or a gentleman of. And it begins to look like I was going to be the lady."

"Well, but don't spoil your fortune by marrying Satan," said Sybil.

"Marry Satan? I'd see him in Pandemonium first!" exclaimed the little student of Milton.

"I'm glad to hear you say so! Keep to that, and get out of this den of thieves as soon as ever you can," added Sybil.

"Now, may Satan fly away with me if ever I desert my friends. They risked their necks to rescue me from want in Dover, and have provided for me like a princess. If *that's* the way you good people requite kindness, I think I'll stick to my poor scamps. At least, I will never leave them, until I can give them each and all money enough to retire upon honestly."

"But you will have to leave them, before you can do that. You will have to live among law-abiding people, before you can get a lawyer to take up such a case as yours. I think, if ever I am free again, I would like to have you home with me; and I am sure my dear husband would take up your cause, as he has taken up that of many a poor client, without money, and without price."

Here the girl burst into such peals of laughter, that Sybil could but gaze on her in astonishment.

"Oh, you know, that is too good!" exclaimed Iska, as soon as she recovered from her mirthful paroxysm.

"What is too good?" inquired Sybil, slightly displeased.

"Oh, that you should invite me to your house, and recommend me to your husband's good offices! One would think that you had had enough of taking up stray women and flinging them at your husband's head!" exclaimed the girl, with another paroxysm of laughter.

Sybil turned pale, and remained silent for a few moments; then she said very gravely:

"Your gay rebuke may be a just one. I will think twice before I repeat the folly."

"And now I have lost a friend by my jest. I am always losing friends by jests," said Gentiliska, sadly.

"No, indeed you have not, poor child," exclaimed our magnanimous Sybil. "I might think once, or twice, but I should never think long without offering you a home in my heart and in my house. You are no saint, poor girl; but that you are an honest woman, with your antecedents and your surroundings, is as much to your credit, I think, as sanctity is to the most holy."

And the lady arose and kissed the little gipsy.

"That was good," sighed Gentiliska; "that is the first time I have ever been kissed since my poor mother died."

They were interrupted by the apparition of Proserpine, who glided into the inner cavern.

"What do you want?" demanded Gentiliska.

"Nothing. Breakfast has been ready this half-hour. We thought you were asleep, so we waited. But just now I heard you laughing. So I came in to tell you everything would be spoiled, if you didn't made haste and get ready."

"All right; we are ready. Put breakfast on the table directly," said Gentiliska.

The girl disappeared, and the two temporary companions, Sybil and Gentiliska, soon followed.

They found a comfortable breakfast laid out in the kitchen, and, as on the preceding morning, Sybil did justice to the delicacies set before her.

"Where are your companions?" she inquired of Gentiliska, not seeing any sign of the robbers' presence.

"I don't know. Where are the men, Hecate?" inquired the hostess, turning to the crone.

"Bless you, Missis, as soon as they got through with their supper, which they kept up until midnight, they one and all put on their gowns and masks, and started out on business."

"Business! Yes, that means stopping a stage-coach, or breaking into a house!" sneered the girl. "And they have not got back yet?" she inquired.

"Bless you, Missis, no! I sorter, kinder, think as they've gone a good distance this time."

Sybil said nothing; but she felt relieved, and grateful to be rid of those terrible men, even for a few hours.

When breakfast was over, Gentiliska said to Sybil:

"You must not suppose that I live entirely under ground, like a mole! No, indeed; every day when it is fine, I go to the surface. I get out on the roof. I walk on the mountain heights, 'where never foot fell,' except my own! I went out yesterday, and would have taken you; but that you were so dead asleep. Will you climb with me to-day?"

"With great pleasure," said Sybil.

"And while we go, we will take little baskets and some luncheon, and we will gather some nuts—there are so many on the mountain—walnuts, chestnuts, hickory-nuts, hazle-nuts, and chinkapins," added the young hostess, as they walked back to the sleeping cavern, where they began to prepare for their ramble.

"There, take that, and wrap yourself up warm. I wish it was nicer, but I haven't a choice of garments here, you know."

Sybil picked up the articles thrown her by her hostess, and saw, to her astonishment, that it was a priceless India shawl, belonging to her friend Miss Pendleton.

"This! this!" she exclaimed, indignantly; "do you know what this is?"

"It is an old shawl," replied the girl, contemptuously.

"Yes, it is an 'old shawl,' a rare old camel's hair shawl, worth thousands upon thousands of dollars, an heir loom of the Pendleton family, that has

- 51 -

descended from generation to generation, until now it is the property of Miss Beatrix Pendleton. Oh, I am so sorry she has lost it."

"What, that old thing? I'm blessed if I didn't think it was a most uncommon coarse, thick, heavy old broche."

"It is a priceless India camel's hair shawl! Such a one as could not be bought in this century at any price. Oh. I wish she had it back!"

"Lor' bless you! she may have it back if she wants it! Why do you think they took it? For its value? They knew no more of its value than I did! No! they took it for its uses! They took it to tie up some of the silver plate in, because they hadn't sacks enough. You take it, and keep it! And when you have a chance, give it back to your friend. But for to-day, you had better give it an airing on your shoulders."

So exhorted, Sybil wrapped herself in the costly shawl, and followed her hostess through many labyrinths of the caverns, until they came out on a lonely height apparently yet untrodden by the foot of man.

It was a clear, bright December day. The morning, if sharp and cold, was fresh and invigorating.

They spent the middle of the day in rambling through the loneliest parts of the mountain fastnesses, and gathering treasure of many sorts of the sweetest nuts. The sun was sinking in the west when they turned their steps towards the caverns.

"The men will be sure to be home to supper. They never fail supper! And now we will be able to give them walnuts with their wine!" said Gentiliska, as they reëntered the labyrinth that led them from the mountain top to the caverns underneath.

Sybil's heart shrunk within her. To the delicate and conscientious, there is always an exquisite torture in the immediate contact of the coarse and reckless.

They reached the large cavern to find its walls brilliantly lighted up, and the supper table laid and well laden, as on the preceding evening.

"We will go to the sleeping cavern, and lay off our bonnets and shawls. Then we will be ready for supper. Fortunately we don't have to dress for the evening at our house!" laughed the girl, leading the way to the little cave.

When they had thrown off their wraps, they returned to the larger cavern to find it half full of the men. Supper was already on the table; and Satan, who was now in full evening dress, came forward and bowed to Sybil, and with much empressment led her to the place of honor at the board, and seated himself beside her.

Moloch took a stool immediately opposite the pair, where he could gaze at will upon the new beauty.

When all were seated the feast began. Satan gave his whole attention to Sybil, whom he treated with tender deference.

As the supper progressed and the wine passed around, the men, under the exhilarating influence, grew merry and talkative.

"Hope the beaks'll have a good time up at the old Haunted Chapel to-day! This is the second day they've been there looking for us! And oh! didn't they think they'd struck a rich lead when they found that swell Berners up there! They thought they had got his wife too, for certain! That's what's brought them back to-day! they know they can't find us there; but they hope to find her," said one of the robbers.

But his speech was not received with general favor. And when he stupidly pursued the theme, not understanding the menacing look of Satan, one of his companions dug an elbow in his side, and called out:

"Stow all that, you stupid donkey! Don't you see the lady you are talking about is at the table?"

The rebuke was almost as bad as the offense had been; but it had its effect in silencing the talkative offender.

But good-humor was soon restored. The walnuts were placed upon the table with the dessert, and many compliments were passed upon the pretty hands that had gathered them for the feast.

But just in the midst of their merry-making the whole party were startled by a tremendous explosion, that seemed to shake the mountain side.

All sprung to their feet, and stood gazing in amazement at each other until the echoes of the thunder died away. There was silence for a moment after, and then Moloch suddenly burst into a peal of laughter, in which he was soon joined by all his companions, with the exception of Satan, who sat frowning upon them.

"What is the meaning of this rudeness?" he sternly demanded.

"Oh, boss! don't you know? We are laughing at the beaks! They have blown themselves up in the old Haunted Chapel!" answered one of the party.

"Good Heaven! A wholesale murder! I was not prepared for that!" exclaimed the captain.

"A wholesale murder, or a wholesale accident, if you please, boss! but no murder. Nobody told them to take lights down into that vault, where there was gunpowder lying around loose! And if the trap was set for one meddler and caught a dozen, why, so much the better, I say! And I don't think it could a caught much less than a dozen, seeing as there were about fifteen or twenty men in the chapel when I spied it this afternoon from my cover in the woods on the mountain behind it, and I reckon there must a' been more than half of them killed."

"Hush!" said Satan; "don't you see that this lady is nearly fainting with terror?"

Sybil was indeed as white as a ghost, and on the very verge of swooning. But she managed to command nerve enough to ask:

"Was—can you tell me—was my husband in the chapel this afternoon?"

"Oh, no, ma'am!" answered the robber, who had immediately taken his cue from the glance of his captain's eye. "Oh, no, ma'am, I met him on his road to Blackville early this afternoon."

This was partly true, for the man *had* really seen Lyon Berners when he was walking along the river road to meet Joe. Sybil believed it to be wholly true, and uttered an exclamation of thankfulness.

The wine passed more freely, and the men grew merrier, wilder, and more uproarious. Sybil became very much alarmed; and not so much by the noisy orgies of these rude revellers, as by the dreadful gaze of Moloch fixed upon her from the opposite end of the table where he sat, and the offensive language of Satan's eyes whenever they turned towards her.

At length, unable to bear the trial longer, she arose from her seat, and courtesying to these brigands as she would have done to any set of gentlemen of whom she was taking leave, Sybil left the cavern, followed by Gentiliska.

"I must take you to another grotto. You cannot occupy mine to-night," said the girl, with evident reluctance.

"But, oh! why, why may I not stay with you? I am afraid to sleep alone in this terrible place!" pleaded Sybil.

"I have a reason, but I cannot tell it to you now. Yes, I will, too! I will tell you at all risks! Then it is this: My chamber is no longer safe for you! I myself am not strong enough to protect you! You might be carried off forcibly from my side! I must hide you where no devil may find you to-night!" whispered the girl.

"My blood curdles! Oh, help me if you can!" cried Sybil.

"I cannot help you! I can only hide you! I could perhaps save you from insult by sober men; but who shall save you from maniacs, mad with drink?"

"Yet you have always saved yourself! How have you managed to do so?"

"I have grown up among them, their child! That makes all the difference!"

"Oh, Heaven help me! Would I were dead!" cried Sybil, in an agony of terror.

"Oh, bosh! that's the cry of weakness! I've seen some hard times, but I never wished myself dead yet!" said the girl, as she led her guest through a labyrinth of small caverns until she reached one smaller and more remote than the others.

"Oh, do not leave me here alone!" pleaded Sybil. "If I must stay, stay with me! I do not fear death; but oh! I fear these men! Do not leave me!"

"I must, for your own safety. They must not miss me, or their suspicions will be aroused."

Then pointing to a bed of moss, and recommending her guest to lie down and seek repose, Gentiliska glided away through the labyrinth of caves and was lost to sight and hearing.

Sybil's first impulse was to start up and run after her hostess, but she restrained herself, and sank half fainting upon the heap of moss.

There was but a faint sparkling of light in the cave, coming from a crevice in the roof through which the moonlight entered, and glancing down, struck here and there upon the stalactites on the walls.

"Seek repose," had been the advice of Gentiliska.

Sybil dared not seek it if she could, and could not have found it if she had. She lay there with her eyes wide open, staring towards the entrance of the cavern, as if she feared the sudden apparition of some horrid shape. She lay there with every nerve strung up to the severest tension, and every faculty of mind and body on the alert. She scarcely breathed, but lay motionless, and watched and listened intently. Hour after hour passed in this stern tension of her frame, this trance-like stillness and silence, when at length she fancied she heard a creeping, stealthy step approaching. Nearly frozen with terror, she listened and watched more intently than ever. Alone, helpless, in darkness and solitude, what horrid fate must she meet! The creeping, cautious footstep drew nearer, nearer!

Oh, Heaven! it was no fancy! The entrance of the cavern was more deeply darkened for one moment, and then the huge form of Moloch stood within the cavern and nearly filled it up.

Paralyzed with horror, Sybil could neither move nor cry out—not even when the monster approached the bed and put his profane hand upon her face.

CHAPTER VIII.

NELLY TO THE RESCUE.

She never, never failed a friend,

And never feared a foe.—NICHOLL.

Help was at hand. There came a sound as of the rushing of tiny feet, and suddenly the little Skye terrier rushed into the cavern, and with joyous barks darted upon her mistress's bed; but instantly these barks of joy were changed into a howl of rage and pain, as she sprang at the throat of the robber, and closing her teeth upon his windpipe, hung there like "grim death."

With a yell of agony, the giant threw up his hands and seized the dog, to tear her off; but Nelly held fast. He might have torn her in two, but he could not have made her let go her hold upon his throat. He raised his huge fist to brain her.

"DON'T hurt the dog," cried Sybil, starting up and seizing his arm; her palsy of terror dispelled by her love for her faithful little four-footed friend.

"DOWN, traitor and coward!" shouted another voice.

And all started and looked around to recognize the robber captain standing before them, with a pistol levelled straight at the head of his lieutenant.

"Call this brute off, then. She's cutting my throat with her cursed teeth. Call her off, I say, or I'll wring her in two, like a worm," gurgled the half-strangled monster, as he shook off the clasp of Sybil, and seized the little dog.

"DROP YOUR HAND, you villain, or I'll shoot you where you stand!" thundered the captain, cocking his pistol.

The bully instantly obeyed.

"Come, Nelly! dear Nelly!" called Sybil, sinking to a sitting posture on the side of her bed.

The obedient little terrier immediately let go her hold, and leaped down into her mistress' lap, and with barks of delight began to lick her hands and face.

Sybil, utterly overcome by the rapid events and conflicting emotions of the last few minutes, burst into a passion of tears, as she clasped the little creature to her bosom.

"Madam," said the robber captain—suddenly changing his whole manner as he turned towards the lady, took off his hat, and subdued his voice to its softest and smoothest tones—"Madam, I will relieve you of the presence of this ruffian; and to-morrow I will make such amends to you, for this insult, as may lie in my power."

Sybil did not and could not answer him. She only clasped her little dog closer to her heart and wept.

"And now, sir," said the captain, sternly, wheeling around upon his huge lieutenant, and pointing to the outlet of the grotto, "go before me out of this! This crime must be accounted for at another time and place."

The crestfallen monster slouched out of the cavern, followed by his captain, who turned once more, at leaving, to say:

"Rest in peace now, lady. You shall no more be disturbed. And I will send Gentiliska to stay with you."

"Oh thanks! thanks! do so! pray do so!" said Sybil, eagerly.

When she was left alone with her little dog, she fell to caressing and fondling her, as with all her heart and soul.

"Oh, Nelly! darling Nelly! what a little heroine you are! But how did you come here, Nelly?" she inquired, holding the little creature's curly head between her hands, and gazing down into its soft brown eyes. "How did you find me, Nelly?"

Nelly lapped her lady's cheek, and then jumped down and ran to the outlet of the cavern, and then ran back and jumped again into her lady's lap.

"Oh, yes, Nelly dear, I understand. You came that way and found me here. But that tells me nothing. How did you know I was here, little doggy?"

Poor little Skye terrier! She knew that a question was asked her, and she tried her best in her eloquent dumb way to answer it. And while she was jumping off and on her mistress' lap, and whining and caressing, the cavern door was darkened once more, and Gentiliska entered.

"Oh, I am so glad you have come! Be quiet, Nelly, darling; that's a girl, you know," exclaimed Sybil, speaking first to her visitor, and then to her little dog, who seemed inclined to make some hostile demonstrations against the supposed enemy.

"Why, what dog is that?" inquired Gentiliska, her mouth and eyes wide open with amazement.

"She is *my* dog, my dear, darling, devoted, brave little Nelly," replied Sybil, piling on the complimentary adjectives. And I leave it to any reader of mine if Nelly did not deserve them all.

"But—how on the face of the earth did she come here?" gasped Gentiliska.

"She didn't come on the face of the earth, but through the bowels of the earth. So she says, and I never knew her to tell a falsehood."

"But—how came she to trace you here?"

"Ah! that's just what I have been inquiring of her, and she has been trying to explain to me. You know these four-footed friends of ours have a good deal of difficulty in communicating with us—through *our* stupidity, bless you, not theirs. *They* can understand *us* a great deal better than *we* can comprehend *them*. Nelly knows very well what I ask her, and she answers my question; but I don't in the least understand what she says."

"But—when did she come? You know that."

"She came in the nick of time to fly at Moloch's throat and hold him till Satan came to deliver me."

Here the girl burst into a peal of laughter that almost offended Sybil, who gravely inquired:

"What is the matter?"

"I am laughing at your hallucination that Satan came to deliver you."

"What do you mean?" inquired Sybil, surprised and displeased at the girl's untimely mirth.

"Why, you goose," laughed Gentiliska, "don't you know, can't you see, that Satan is a hundred times worse and a thousand times more dangerous than Moloch? I tell you that Captain 'Inconnu' came to your cave on the same errand that brought his lieutenant here. Only, as he happened to be the last comer, and as he found the other here, he chose to take credit as your deliverer! Bosh! your little dog saved you. No other under Heaven did!"

"How do you know these facts?"

"By watching. You know when I left you?"

"Yes; go on."

"As I was returning to my own den, I saw a shadow pass before me, and then I knew that we had been tracked to this place, but whether by Satan or Moloch, or any other one of the band, I could not tell. By the time I had crept back to the entrance of the large cavern, the spy must have regained his place, for they were all at the table as I had left them."

"Why then did you not return to me, since you knew that my place of concealment was discovered?" inquired Sybil, reproachfully.

"Because I could do you better service by staying outside and watching, which I did. About an hour ago, as I sat watching and listening in my own den, I heard a stealthy step, and peeping out, I saw the huge form of Moloch stealing towards your retreat. I stepped out silently, and stole softly after him, with the full intention of running back, giving the alarm, and raising the whole band, in case my suspicions should be true, that he intended to harm you. Of course I could not have helped you at all, if I had been in here with you. He wouldn't have let me pass out to have roused the men. He would have brained me on the spot, and had you at his mercy, do you see?"

"Yes, yes, I see. Oh, Heaven! deliver me from this dreadful place!" sighed Sybil.

"All in good time. I followed Moloch, until I saw him take the little turn that led to your den. Then I turned and fled, or was about to fly to rouse the men to your rescue, when I saw the graceful figure of Satan gliding towards me. As in that half-darkness I had recognized Moloch only by his huge form, so now I knew Satan only by his graceful, gliding motions. I drew back into a crevice of the rock, and waited until he had passed me and taken the same turn towards your den. And then I knew that you were quite safe. Either of these men alone would have been fatal to you; but together they were perfectly harmless. But just then I heard a dog bark, where never a dog had barked before. I stole after Satan towards the entrance of this place, and hid myself to listen to the fun. I heard the row. Oh, wasn't Captain 'Inconnu's' righteous indignation fine? At length I heard Satan order Moloch to leave the place, and then I heard him tell you that he would send me to stay with you. Then I thought it was about time for me to leave, and I stole away and fled as fast as I could towards my own den. And when I got there I covered myself up in my bed and feigned sleep, when the gallant captain came to call me. So here I am."

"Oh that Heaven would deliver me from this dreadful place!" repeated Sybil.

"All in good time, as I said before. And now I think you had better try to sleep. The little dog will watch us and give the alarm, in case any other daring marauder should venture to intrude on us," counselled the girl.

"Sleep! I have scarcely slept a whole night since I was forced to leave my home. Sleep! the best sleep I have had has been more like swooning, and has befallen me in the day-time. I cannot sleep."

"Well, then, please to be quiet while I sleep. I'm fagged out with all this," said Gentiliska, throwing herself down on the mossy floor of the cave, and settling herself comfortably to rest.

Meanwhile Sybil sat with her tired little dog lying on her lap. She was too wretched to think of resting, too anxious to think of anything but escape. Nothing that could happen to her in the outer world seemed so appalling as the dangers that surrounded her here. And while her companion slept soundly, Sybil racked her brain for means of escape.

People before now, chained in dungeons and weakened by imprisonment, have nevertheless contrived to burst their fetters and break through bolts and bars, and press through guards, and effect their freedom. And here was she, a captive certainly, but neither fettered nor locked up, nor guarded except by one sleeping girl. Why could she not make good her escape? What should hinder her, if only she knew how to find her way out of this labyrinth?

In her restlessness and distress, she groaned and lifted her hands to her head.

Her little dog immediately woke up, and in quick sympathy climbed up to her bosom, and whining, licked her face.

A sudden inspiration filled the soul of Sybil, and directed her course.

"If this poor little four-footed friend of mine, with nothing but her instinct and her affection to guide and sustain her, if *she* contrived to find me, hid away as I was from all human help, surely *I*, with my higher intelligence and greater powers, should be able to find my way out of this labyrinth with her help."

Saying this to herself, Sybil tenderly caressed her little dog, then lifted it to her bosom, wrapped Beatrix Pendleton's camel's hair shawl closely around her, and went to the entrance of the cavern through which little Nelly had entered.

Here she paused for a moment to listen. All was silent except for the deep breathing of Gentiliska, that only proved how profound was the sleep of the girl.

Then she caressed her little dog again, saying in a low voice:

"*Lyon*, Nelly! Where is *Lyon*?"

The little Skye terrier pricked up her ears and whimpered.

Then Sybil was sure that Nelly understood her words.

"Let us go find *Lyon*, Nelly; *Lyon! Lyon! Lyon!*" said Sybil, setting the little dog down and harking her on by the way she had come.

Nelly remembered where she had left "Lyon," and so with a glad bark she leapt forward and ran on as fast as the tortuous nature of the dark subterranean passage would permit her to do; pausing now and then to rest herself, and to allow her mistress time to overtake her.

"Poor, dear little faithful Nelly! don't run so fast. You were tired almost to death when you came in from your first journey, and now you set out immediately on this the moment I ask you to do it; but abate your zeal, dear little friend, or you will not be able to hold out to the end," said Sybil, sitting down and caressing her little dog while they both rested.

When they re-commenced their journey, they found the passage growing narrower, darker, and more tortuous than before. They were compelled to move slowly and cautiously.

Sybil had already recognized the natural underground road by which she had been brought to the robber's cave; but she did not know this portion of it. So she supposed that she must have been brought through it while in that state of unconsciousness into which she had fallen from terror on first being seized by the masked and shrouded forms of the men who had carried her off. She therefore hoped that she was near the outlet of the subterranean passage.

But where that outlet might be, she could not guess. The last she remembered before falling into that swoon of horror, was the vault of the Haunted Chapel. The first she saw, on recovering herself, was the middle of the subterranean passage. But whether that passage had started from the vault, or whether the men had carried her any distance over the upper earth, before descending into it, she had no means of knowing or surmising. She must wait for the revelation at the end of this underground road.

The end was fast approaching. Far ahead, a little, dim dot of gray light kept dodging right and left before her eyes, following as it were the abrupt turning of the passage. It drew nearer, nearer, and now at last it was before her.

The little dog that had been trotting beside her mistress, now sprang past her and began to dig away at the hole with her paws.

Sybil stooped down, and peered through it. By the early light, of the now dawning day, she discerned a section of a foundation wall, that she felt sure must be a part of the old vault under the Haunted Chapel.

The little dog now jumped through the hole, and turned around and pawed and whimpered, as if inviting and expecting Sybil to follow her.

She understood the situation well enough now. She knew that this small hole was the entrance from the underground passage into the vault, and that it must have become partly filled up by the falling in of the bricks and mortar at the blowing up of the church. She went to work to try to remove the obstructions. It was a work of more time and toil than of real difficulty. With her delicate hands she began to take away the broken stones, timbers, and plaster, until she pulled out a short, narrow piece of plank, which she immediately began to use as a tool to dig away the refuse. A half an hour's hard work cleared her way into the vault. She passed in, and once more saw the dome of heaven above her head.

Little Nelly jumped around her with delighted barks, and then ran up the broken walls of the vault, and turned around and looked at her and barked, as if to say:

"This way! this way!"

But the irregularities in the dilapidated wall, that furnished a sure foothold for Nelly's little feet, would not serve her mistress's turn. So Sybil looked about the place, and cast around in her mind to consider how she should contrive to reach the upper ground. She soon saw the way, but she had to rest before she could commence a new work. So she sat down and called the dog to her, and both remained quiet for about ten minutes. And then Sybil arose and went to work, and piled up the bricks and stones, until she had raised for herself a rude stairway half up to the top. By these, at some little risk of life and limb, she climbed out of the vault, and found herself standing on the edge of a heap of rubbish, which was all that remained of the old Haunted Chapel.

Here again she sat down to look around her. The sun was just rising from behind the mountain, and tinging all the wintry scene with the golden hues of autumn. Though it was a clear, cold, frosty morning, Sybil was perspiring from her late hard work, so she drew her heavy shawl around her shoulders to protect her from a chill while she rested. The little terrier, who had leaped up after her mistress, would not rest, but continued to jump about and bark, as if to testify her joy and triumph in a work accomplished. Every leap and bark said as plainly as tongue could have spoken the words:

"I have found her, and brought her back! I knew I could! I knew I could! I have done it at last! I have done it at last!"

"I know you have, Nelly dear, and I love you better than anybody in the world except Lyon! But now I want you to help me to find Lyon, Nelly! *Lyon! Lyon!*" said Sybil, holding the little terrier's face between her hands and gazing into its loving brown eyes.

Nelly jumped away at her bidding and ran all over the place snuffing zealously for some moments, and then finding herself clearly at fault, ran back and whimpered her disappointment on her mistress' lap.

"You have lost trace and scent of Lyon! Oh, Nelly! Nelly! what shall we do? Venture back boldly to Black Hall? Run right in the teeth of the law officers, and be snapped up by them?" sighed Sybil.

Nelly understood "a horror in the words, if not the words," and howled dismally.

Just at that moment a halting step was heard approaching, and a sad voice sighing:

"I sorter can't give her up! No, I can't! Ef she did bite me, it wa'n't outen malice to me, but outen dewotion to the mistess—on'y to make me drap her down, so she could go back to dis vault and wait for her mistess, which I do expect she have starved to death by dis time! But I'll see. Nelly. Nelly!"

Sybil's heart leaped with joy at recognizing the voice of her faithful servant Joe. And Nelly jumped forward with a cry of delight to meet him.

"So you is here yet in dis supernumerary speer. Thank my Marster in Heaven for dat!" exclaimed Joe, stooping painfully, while he leaned upon his crutch, to lift the little dog to his bosom. "But who dat young o'man, Nelly?" continued Joe, whose eyesight was none of the best, pausing abruptly and staring at Sybil, who was completely disguised by the large India shawl and the red merino gown, both of which were entirely opposite to her usual style of dress.

Joe hobbled towards the supposed stranger cautiously.

"Don't you know me, dear old Joe?" inquired Sybil, dropping the shawl from her head and rising to her feet.

"*Ah-h-h-ah!*" yelled Joe in a prolonged howl of horror at what he took to be a ghost!

And then, as he could not run away, he dropped dog and crutch, fell flat upon his face and roared for mercy.

Sybil and her little dog both tried to soothe and reassure him—Sybil by repeating to him over and over again that she was alive and well, and that there was nothing whatever to fear at that moment; and little Nelly, by running around him and trying to poke her nose under his face to find a place to kiss or to lick.

But Joe for a time was perfectly inaccessible to reason; and Sybil, in discouragement, left him to recover himself alone, while she went and sat down at some distance to wait the issue of the event.

After a little while Joe slowly lifted up his head, and cautiously glanced around, whispering:

"Is she gone?"

"No," answered Sybil, sharply; "I am not gone! I am sitting here waiting for you to come to your senses!"

Joe, who after the first glimpse had not dared to look upon the ghost, now ventured from this safe distance to steal a glance. The glance grew into a gaze, and then he spoke:

"Miss Sybil—"

"Well, Joe?"

"Is it you?"

"Yes, it is I."

"But is you alibe?"

"Yes, I'm alive."

"Is you sure?"

"I am hungry and mad! That should make me sure."

"—Mad 'long o' me, Miss Sybil?"

"Yes; mad with you for being such a fool!"

"But I thought you was a ghostess!"

"Bosh! you haven't as much sense as little Nelly!" exclaimed Sybil, affecting more anger than she really felt.

"But an't you dead?" mysteriously inquired Joe, gazing at the pale face of his mistress, now very pale indeed through all that she had suffered. "An't you really dead, Miss Sybil?"

"Not much, Joe."

"But wan't you robbed and murdered by them riporate willains?"

"Neither the one nor the other, Joe! I am safe and sound, and have my money and jewels still about me."

"But—wan't you reduced?"

"I was *ab*ducted, Joe; but not harmed! It is a long story, Joe. I cannot tell it now, because I want to know about my husband. Is he safe?"

"Yes, Miss Sybil, he's all right now! only grieving arter you! 'cause everybody beliebes as you perished in the blowing up of the old chapel. Lord! where was you all the time? Did Nelly find you?"

"Yes, Nelly found me; but—"

"Lord! the sense of that little thing!"

"—But tell me about my husband! Where is he!"

"He is at Capping Pendulum's, a doing very well now."

"Doing very well *now!* That means he has been doing badly lately! Has he been ill?" exclaimed Sybil, in breathless anxiety.

"No, Miss Sybil; but he was in the old Haunted Chapel when de debbil blowed it up."

"Oh, good heavens!" cried Sybil, clasping her hands, and unable to speak another word.

"Don't be scared! he wasn't hurt not to speak of; only stunned and bruised a bit. And he's all right now. On'y grievin' of hisse'f to death, which is perfec'ly nateral, you see. Goodness knows as I myse'f hasn't eat a meal's wittels, nor likewise sleeped a wink o' sleep, since gone you's been! And oh! how I thank my Heavenly Marster as has 'stored you to us once more alive and well!" cried Joe, hobbling towards Sybil, sinking at her feet, and giving way to his feelings in a burst of sobs and tears.

Sybil raised him up, and then noticed for the first time how lame he was.

"It's nothin' to speak on, Miss Sybil. On'y a sprained ankle. I can get on well enough with a crutch. And here I am as willin' and *able* to sarve you as ever," said the poor fellow, earnestly.

"Thanks, dear Joe! I want you, if you can, to go with me to my husband immediately."

"But, Miss Sybil, honey, you look so pale and weak and wore out. Better stay here while I go and get a conweyance."

"No, no, no, Joe! It would take you too long, and I cannot wait. I can walk," said Sybil, impatiently rising and drawing the shawl up over her head, for she had no hat or bonnet.

"Name o' de Lord, then come on, honey," replied Joe, who knew it would be useless to oppose his mistress when she was fully bent on any purpose.

They set out together, picking their way slowly over the heaps of rubbish that filled the churchyard and lay between them and the narrow path leading through the thicket to the river road.

Little Nelly followed faithfully at their heels.

CHAPTER IX.

THE SECOND FLIGHT.

A beam of comfort, like the moon through clouds,

Gilds the black horror and directs their way.—DRYDEN.

It was yet early morning, and Lyon Berners still lay on his comfortable bed in the spacious front chamber, at Pendleton Hall. The window shutters were open, admitting a fine view of the wooded mountains, not yet wholly divested of their gay autumn hues. A fine wood fire blazed in the broad fireplace. A nice breakfast stood on a little stand by the bed-side. A good-humored, motherly looking negro woman presided over the little meal, while Captain Pendleton stood by the invalid, trying to persuade him to take nourishment.

"But I have no inclination, dear friend," pleaded Mr. Berners, as he reached out his pale hand, took a morsel of bread from the plate, and put it to his lips.

"You must eat without inclination, then, Berners. It is your duty to live," remarked Captain Pendleton.

"But, in the name of Heaven, what have I left to live for?" groaned the bereaved husband.

"For a future of usefulness, if not of happiness; for a future of duty, if not of domestic joys," replied the captain, earnestly.

Footsteps were heard upon the stairs without, but no one heeded them.

"'Duty,' 'usefulness!'" bitterly echoed Lyon Berners. "I might indeed have lived and labored for them, and for my country and my kind, if—if—*Oh, Sybil! Sybil! Oh, Sybil! Sybil! My young, sweet wife!*" He broke off, and groaned with the insufferable, tearless agony of a strong man's grief.

"HERE SHE IS, MARSTER! Bress de Lord, here she is, and Nelly too! Nelly found her!" frantically exclaimed Joe, bursting open the chamber door, while Sybil flew past him and threw herself with a sob of delight into the arms of her husband. His brain reeled with the sudden, overwhelming joy, as he clasped his wife to his heart.

"Good Heaven, man! why did you not prepare your master for this?" was the first question Captain Pendleton thought of asking the negro.

Joe stared, and found nothing to answer. He did not understand preparation.

Nelly jumped upon the bed, and insisted upon being recognized; but nobody noticed her. Noble humanity is singularly ungrateful to their four-footed friends.

Lyon Berners, forgetful of everybody and everything else in the world, was gazing fondly, wonderingly into his wife's beautiful pale face. *His* face was like marble.

"My own, my own," he murmured. "By what miracle have you been preserved?"

Sybil could not answer; she could only sob for joy at this reunion, forgetful, poor child, of the awful danger in which she still stood.

Captain Pendleton remembered it. He first looked around to take note of who was in the room. There were Mr. and Mrs. Berners, himself, Joe, and the colored woman Margy—only *one* new witness, if there were no others outside who might have seen the entrance of Sybil.

He went and locked the door, that no one else should enter the chamber. And then he called Joe apart to the distant window.

"You very reckless fellow! tell me who besides ourselves have seen Mrs. Berners enter this house."

"Not a singly soul, marster, outen dis room. We walk all de way from de Haunted Chapel, and didn't meet nobody we knowed. Miss Sybil she keep de shawl over her head. Dem as did meet us couldn't a told who she was or even if she was white or brack. When we got home here, I jes opens de door like I always do, and Miss Sybil she follow me in, likewise Nelly. Nobody seed us, likewise we seed nobody, 'cept it was Jerome, as was jest a passin' outen de back door wid a breakfast tray in his hands; but he didn't see us, acause his back was to us, which that fellow is always too lazy to look over his own shoulder, no matter what may be behind him," said Joe, contemptuously.

"That is true; but lucky on this occasion. Then you are certain that no one out of this room knows of Mrs. Berner's presence in the house?"

"Sartain sure, marster!" answered Joe, in the most emphatic manner.

"Then I must warn you not to hint—mind, Joe—not so much as to *hint* the fact to any living soul," said the captain, solemnly.

"Hi, Marse Capping! who you think is a 'fernal fool? Not dis Joe," answered the negro, indignantly.

"Mind, then, that's all," repeated the captain, who then dismissed Joe, and beckoned the motherly looking colored woman to come to him.

"Margy," he whispered, "do you understand the horrible danger in which Mrs. Berners stands?"

"Oh, my good Lord, Marse Clement, don't I understand it? My blood runs cold and hot by turns every time I look at her and think of it," muttered the woman, with a dismayed look.

"I am glad you feel and appreciate this peril. It is said that no secret is safe that is known to three persons. This secret is known to five: Mr. and Mrs. Berners, Joe, you, and myself! I think I can rely on the secresy of all," said Captain Pendleton, with a meaning look.

"You can rely on *mine*, Marse Clement! I'd suffer my tongue to be tored out by the roots afore ever I'd breathe a word about her being here," said the woman.

"Quite right! Now we must see about concealing her for a few days, until we can ship her off to some foreign country."

"To be sure, marster; but are you certain that no one down stairs saw her when she came in?"

"Quite certain," answered the captain.

Meanwhile Sybil sat down on the chair at the side of Lyon's bed, and with her hand clasped in his, began to tell the story of her abduction and captivity among the robbers.

Lyon Berners, seeing his host now at leisure, beckoned him to approach and hear the strange story.

Sybil told it briefly to her wondering audience.

"And if they had not carried me off, I should not now be at liberty," she concluded.

That this was true, they all agreed.

Now Sybil had to hear the particulars of the explosion, and the names of its victims. She shuddered as Captain Pendleton went over the list.

"One feels the less compassion, however, when one considers that this was a case of the 'engineer hoist with his own petard.'"

"Don't you think, Marse Clement, as Mrs. Berners would be the better for a bit of breakfast?" inquired Aunt Margy.

"Certainly. And here is Berners, touched nothing yet. And everything allowed to grow cold in our excitement and forgetfulness," said Captain Pendleton, anxiously examining into the condition of the tray.

"Oh, never you mind, Marse Clem, I can go down and fetch up some hot breakfast, and another cup and sasser, and then may be the master and missis will take a bit of breakfast here together," put in Margy, as she lifted the tray to take it from the room.

"Be careful to let no word drop concerning our new visitor," said Captain Pendleton, as he cautiously locked the door after the woman.

While she was gone on this errand, Sybil told her friends further details of her life among the mountain robbers; among other matters, she related the story of Gentiliska Dubarry, at which her hearers were much surprised.

"I think it is easy to see through this matter," said Lyon Berners, after a pause; "this robber chief—this Captain Inconnu—this Satan of the band must be, or rather must have been the husband of Rosa Blondelle, and most probably her assassin. The motive for all his crimes seems clear enough. He could never have been a gentleman. He must always have been an adventurer—a criminal adventurer. He married the beautiful young Scotch widow for her money, and having spent it all, and discovered another heiress in this poor vagrant girl, he put Rosa out of the way, that he might be free to marry another fortune.

"No devil is so bad, however, but that there is a speck of good about him somewhere; and this adventurer, gambler, smuggler, robber, murderer was unwilling that an innocent woman should suffer for his crime; therefore he had you abducted to prevent you from falling into the hands of the law."

"I do not know," said Sybil; "but I think that in having me carried off, he yielded to the threats or persuasions of Gentiliska, who certainly seemed to know enough of the matter to give her great power over him. Indeed she hinted as much to me. And she certainly knew of his presence at my mask ball."

"The daring impudence, the reckless effrontery of that man!" exclaimed Captain Pendleton, in astonishment and disgust.

"You said, dear Sybil, that he came in the character of Death?" inquired Mr. Berners.

"Yes," replied his wife, with a shudder.

"Ah, then I do not wonder at that poor woman's great—instinctive horror—of that mask! I remember now that, every time he approached her, she shivered as with an ague fit. And yet she could not have suspected his identity," said Mr. Berners.

Next Sybil spoke of the discovery of the Pendleton plate and jewels in the possession of the robbers.

"I am glad of that, at all events, Clement, since it gives you a sure clue to the recovery of your stolen goods," suggested Mr. Berners.

"A clue that I shall not now follow, as to do so might seriously compromise the safety of Mrs. Berners. Our first care must be for her," answered Captain Pendleton.

"Always thoughtful, always magnanimous, dear friend," warmly exclaimed Lyon Berners, while Sybil eloquently looked her gratitude.

At that moment there was heard a low tap at the door, and a low voice saying:

"It's only me, Marse Clem, with the breakfast things."

The captain stepped to the door, unlocked it, and admitted Margy with the breakfast tray, and then carefully locked it again.

As the woman drew nearer to Sybil, she began to stare in astonishment at the India shawl that lady wore around her shoulders.

"You know it, do you, Margy? Well, yes, you are right. It is the celebrated Pendleton shawl that the captain's great-grandfather brought away from the palace of the Rajah, at the siege of some unpronounceable place in Hindostan," smiled Sybil.

"That's it," laughed her host. "My great-grandfather, a captain in the British army, *stole* it from the Rajah, and Mr. Inconnu, a captain of banditti, took it from us!"

But Margy was much too dignified to relish such jokes at the expense of her master's family, even from her master's lips. She put the tray upon the stand and arranged the breakfast, all in stately silence.

Captain Pendleton, with old-fashioned hospitality, pressed his guests to their repast; and so Lyon Berners being propped up with pillows, and Sybil sitting in the easy-chair, with the stand placed between them, ate their breakfast together; not forgetting to feed little Nelly, who was certainly the most famished of the party.

When the breakfast was over, Margy went out with the tray, followed by Joe.

Mr. and Mrs. Berners being left alone with their host, the captain began to devise means first for her temporary concealment in the house, and afterwards for her successful removal to a seaport.

"I confess, Mrs. Berners," began the captain, "that when I saw you enter this room I was as much alarmed for your safety as astonished at your appearance. But since your servant has told me, and you have confirmed his story, that no one recognized you, either on the road or in the house, until you reached this room, my anxieties are allayed. The prevalent belief that you perished in the explosion at the Haunted Chapel has caused all pursuit of you to be abandoned for the present. And so long as we can keep you out of the sight of others than the few who have already seen you, you will be perfectly secure."

"Yes; but we must not trust to this security," interrupted Mr. Berners; "we must rather avail ourselves of this lull in the excitement, this cessation of all pursuit, to get as fast and far away from this place as possible.

"Oh, yes! yes! dear Lyon!" eagerly exclaimed Sybil, "let us get as fast and as far away from this place as we can. Let us get to Europe, or anywhere where we can have rest and peace. Oh! Heaven only knows how I long for rest and peace!"

"You are both right. I shall not oppose your going; but shall rather speed your departure, just as soon as Berners shall be able to travel. But in the meantime we must contrive some place of safe concealment for you in the house," said the captain, as he arose and opened an inner door leading to a small adjoining chamber. "Could you live in there for a few days, Mrs. Berners?" he inquired, in some uneasiness.

"Live in there! Why, that is a palace chamber compared to what I have been lately accustomed to!" exclaimed Sybil, gratefully.

"Well, then it is all right. That room is unoccupied and has no outlet except through this. That shall be your private withdrawing room when the doctor, or any one else who is not in our secret, happens to come into this room. At all other times you may safely take the freedom of both chambers," said the captain cheerfully.

"A thousand thanks in *words*; for, ah! in all *else* I am bankrupt, and can never repay your goodness, unless Heaven should show me some singular favor to enable me to do it," said Sybil, fervently.

And Lyon Berners joined warmly in her expressions of gratitude.

"If you, either of you, knew how much gratification it gives me to serve you, you would not think it necessary to say a single word more on the subject!" exclaimed Clement Pendleton, flushing.

"And now tell me about my dear, bonny Beatrix. Surely *she* may see me! I hope she is quite well," said Sybil.

"Trix is always well. She is now at Staunton. She is one of your most devoted friends, Mrs. Berners, and she will regret not to have been home to receive you. But as for myself, great as my faith is in my sister, I hardly know whether I am glad or sorry for her absence on this occasion. Certainly the fewer witnesses there are to your presence here, the better. Beatrix would die before she would knowingly betray you; but she might do it unconsciously, in which case she would never forgive herself," gravely replied Captain Pendleton.

"Well, I am sorry not to see her. But at any rate, after I have gone I wish you to send her this shawl, with my love, by some safe messenger," Sybil requested, smiling sadly.

"I will be sure to do so. She will be glad to get the old heirloom, which she has been bewailing ever since it was lost; and she will also be well pleased to owe its restitution to you," replied the Captain; and then, surmising that his guests might like to be left alone for an hour or two, he arose and retired from the room, cautioning Sybil to turn the key to prevent the intrusion of any one who was not to be let into the dangerous secret of her presence in the house.

Three precious hours of each other's exclusive company the young people enjoyed, and then Captain Pendleton tapped at the door to announce the approach of the village doctor. Sybil unlocked the door, and hastily retreated into her withdrawing room, where she remained during the doctor's visit.

As soon as the physician departed, Aunt Margy came in with fresh water, clean towels, and everything else that was necessary to make the inner chamber comfortable and pleasant for the occupation of Mrs. Berners.

When the early dinner was ready, Sybil took hers with her husband at his bed-side.

And from that time, as long as they remained at Captain Pendleton's house, they ate their meals together.

Twelve tranquil days they passed at Pendleton Park. Their secret was well kept, at least during their stay at the house.

On the thirteenth day, Mr. Berners being sufficiently recovered to bear the journey, the fugitive pair prepared for their new flight.

Upon this occasion their disguise was admirably well arranged. They were got up as mulattoes. Their faces, necks, and hands were carefully colored with fine brown umber; Sybil's black tresses were cut short and crimped; Lyon's auburn hair and beard were also crimped, and dyed black; Sybil was dressed in a suit of Margy's Sunday clothes, and Lyon in a holiday suit of Joe's.

Serious as the circumstances were, the lady and gentleman could not forbear laughing as they looked into each other's faces.

"When we introduced mask balls into this quiet country place, we had no idea how long the masquerading would last, so far as we were concerned, had we, dear?" inquired Lyon Berners.

Sybil smiled and shook her head.

They were armed with a pass such as colored people were required to have from their masters to show to the authorities before they could be permitted to travel.

Our fugitives were not now going to Norfolk, where their story and their persons were too well known; but to Baltimore, where they were perfect strangers. So their pass was to this effect:

PENDLETON PARK, }
Near Blackville, Dec. 15th, 18—.}

"To all whom it may concern: This is to certify that my man Cæsar, with his wife Dinah, are permitted to go from this place to Baltimore to return between this date and the first of next March.

"CLEMENT PENDLETON."

This was designed to protect the supposed darkies until they should reach the Monumental City, where they were to take the first opportunity of throwing off their disguises and embarking under another name in the first outward bound ship for a foreign port.

Provided with this protection, and with a well-filled old knapsack that "Cæsar" slung over his shoulders, and with a well-stuffed old carpet bag that "Dinah" carried in her hand, the fugitive couple took a long last leave of their friend, and entered the farm wagon, by which Joe was to drive them to the hamlet of Upton, to meet the night coach for Baltimore.

The night was very dark; they could scarcely see each other's faces, much less the road before them.

"Marster," said Joe, in his extreme anxiety, "I hopes you'll pardon the liberty, sir; but has you thought to take money enough for you and the missis?"

"Plenty, Joe! Pendleton, Heaven bless him, has seen to all that," smiled Mr. Berners.

"And, Marster, sir, I hopes as you've made some 'rangements as how we may hear from you when you gets over yonder."

"Certainly, Joe. A correspondence that will be both sure and secret has been contrived between the captain and myself."

"And, Missis," said Joe, turning weepingly towards his lady, "when you're over yonder, don't forget poor Joe; but send for him as soon as ever you can."

"Indeed I will, Joe," promised Sybil.

"And, missis! please don't let little Nelly forget me, neither. I love that little thing like a child!"

"Nelly will not forget you, Joe."

And the little dog, that Sybil had insisted on taking with her, even at the risk of its being recognized as hers, now jumped up from her place at her mistress' feet, and ran and licked Joe's face, as if to assure him of her continued love.

At which, for the first time, Joe burst out crying, and sobbed hard.

"Come, my man, prove your devotion to your mistress by deeds, not tears! Drive fast, or we will miss the coach," Lyon Berners advised.

Joe wiped his eyes with the cuff of his coat, and whipped up his horses, and they rattled over the rocky road for an hour or more before they reached the little hamlet, where they were to wait for the coach. It was very late, and all Upton was asleep, with the exception of the hostlers at the stable, where the coach stopped to change horses. Here Joe drew up his wagon, but his passengers retained their seats while waiting for the coming of the stage-coach. They had not waited more than five minutes, when they heard the guard's warning horn blow, and the huge vehicle rumble down the street, and pull up before the stable door.

Very quickly the tired horses, were taken out and led away to rest, and the fresh ones brought forth.

Meanwhile Lyon Berners alighted, and spoke to the agent, to take places for himself and his wife.

"Show your pass, my man! show your pass! We can't take you without a pass. How do we know but you are running away?" objected the agent.

Lyon Berners smiled bitterly to think how near the man had inadvertently approached the truth. He handed up the pass, which the agent carefully examined before he returned it, saying:

"Yes, that's all right; but you and the girl will have to get up on top, there. We can't have any darkies inside, you know. And in fact, if we could, there's no room, you see; the inside is full."

"Cæsar" helped "Dinah" up on the top of the coach, and then climbed after her. Joe handed up the little dog; and was about to take a dangerously affecting leave of his beloved master and mistress, when luckily the coachman cracked his whip and the horses started.

Joe watched it out of sight, and then got into his seat on the wagon, and drove back to Pendleton Park, the most disconsolate darkey under the sun.

Meanwhile the flying pair pursued their journey, almost happy, because at length they were together.

Soon after sunrise the next morning the stage reached the station at which it was to breakfast. Not wishing to subject their disguise to the too prying eyes of strangers in broad daylight, they took the provisions that they had brought along, and went apart in the woods to eat them, after which they resumed their places on the top of the coach, in time for its starting.

At noon, when the coach stopped to dine, they went apart again to satisfy their hunger.

It was not until night, when they reached an obscure road-side inn, that they dared to enter a house or ask for a cup of tea. Being "darkies," they were sent to the kitchen, where they were regaled with a very hot pot of the beverage that "cheers but not inebriates."

Here also, as they had to change coaches, they were required to show their pass before they could be permitted to take their uncomfortable seats on the top of the vehicle to continue their journey.

They travelled both by day and night, never giving themselves any rest. The policy of the first day was continued to the end of their journey. They always took their meals apart from other people during the broad daylight, denying themselves the comfort of a cup of tea or coffee until night, when, in some dimly lighted country kitchen, they could safely indulge in that refreshment.

At the end of the third day they arrived at Baltimore.

It was just nightfall when they reached the inn where the stage stopped. They alighted, with knapsack, carpet bag, and dog, and found themselves on the sidewalk of a crowded street.

"This way," whispered Lyon Berners to his wife, as he turned into a by-street. "Sybil," he continued, when they felt themselves comparatively alone in the less thronged thoroughfare—"Sybil, if we are to drop our disguises here, we must do so before we enter any inn, because we should have no opportunity afterwards, without detection."

And relieving her of the carpet bag and carrying that as well as the knapsack, he led her by a long walk to the woods on the outskirts of the city, where, by the side of a clear stream, they washed the dye from their faces and hands, and then changed their upper garments. Their knapsack contained every requisite for a decent toilet; and so, in something less than half an hour, they had transformed themselves back again from plain, respectable darkies, to plain, respectable whites; and "Cæsar" and "Dinah" became in their next phase, the Reverend Mr. and Mrs. Martin. The only thing that could not be changed was the color of Lyon's hair, which, having been dyed black, must remain black until time and growth should restore its natural color.

As the Reverend Mr. and Mrs. Martin, they walked back to the city. At the first hack stand "Mr. Martin" called a carriage, placed "Mrs. Martin," with her pet dog, knapsack, and carpet bag in it, entered and took a seat by her side, and told the hackman to drive to the best hotel.

"For it is our policy now to go boldly to the best," he said, as he took Sybil's hands, cold from her outdoor toilet, into his and tried to warm them.

They were driven to the "Calvert House," where Mr. Berners registered their names as the Reverend Isaiah Martin and wife; and where they were received with the respect due to the cloth, and shown to a handsome room on the first floor, which was cheerfully lighted by a chandelier, and warmed by a bright coal fire in the grate.

Here poor Sybil enjoyed the first real repose she had seen since the commencement of her flight. Here Lyon ordered a comfortable and even luxurious supper; and the fugitive pair supped together in peace and safety.

Although it was late when the table was cleared, Lyon felt that no time was to be lost before he should make inquiries about the outward bound ships. So having ordered the morning and evening papers to be brought to their room, he first examined the shipping advertisements, and finding that the "Energy," Captain Strong, was to sail for Havre on the next day but one, taking passengers as well as freight, he put on his hat, and leaving Sybil to amuse herself with the newspapers during his absence, he left the hotel to see the shipping agent.

A strange sense of peace and safety had fallen upon Sybil, and she sat there before her cheerful fire reading the news of the day, and occasionally contrasting her situation now, in the finest room of a large and crowded hotel, with her position but a few days before in the Robbers' Cave. The time passed pleasantly enough until the return of Mr. Berners.

He entered very cheerfully, telling her that he had engaged a cabin passage in the "Energy," which would sail on the day after to-morrow, and that they must be on board the next afternoon.

Sybil was delighted to hear this. Visions of perfect freedom, and of foreign travel with her beloved Lyon, flitted before her imagination.

They talked over their plans for the next day, and then retired to bed, and slept well until the next morning.

They arose and breakfasted early. The morning was fine and clear, and they wrapped themselves in their outer garments, and started with the intention of going out to purchase a couple of trunks and other necessaries for their long voyage.

Lyon was cheerful; Sybil was even gay; both were full of bright anticipations for the future. For were they not flying toward freedom?

They had reached the great lower halls of the hotel, when they were stopped by a sound of altercation in the office, which was on their right hand as they went out.

"I tell you," said the clerk of the house, in an angry voice, "that there is no one of that name here!"

"And I tell you there *is*! And there she is now! I'd know her among ten thousand!" exclaimed a harsh, rude-looking man, who the next instant came out of the office and confronted Sybil, saying roughly:

"I know you, madam! You're my prisoner, Madam Berners! And you'll not do *me*, I reckon, as you did Purley! I'm Jones! And 'tan't one murder you've got to answer for now, but half a dozen!"

And without a word of warning, he snapped a pair of handcuffs upon the lady's delicate wrists.

"VILLAIN!" thundered Sybil's husband, as with a sweep of his strong arm he felled the ruffian to the floor.

It was but a word and a blow, "and the blow came first."

He caught his half-fainting wife to his bosom, and strove to free her from those insulting bracelets; but he could not wrench them off without wounding and bruising her tender flesh.

Meanwhile the fallen officer sprung to his feet, and called upon all good citizens to help him execute his warrant.

A crowd collected then. A riot ensued. Lyon Berners, holding his poor young wife to his bosom, vainly, madly, desperately defended her against all comers, dealing frantic blows with his single right arm on all sides. Of course, for the time being, he was insane.

"Knock him down! Brain him! but don't hurt the woman," shouted some one in the crowd. And some other one, armed with a heavy iron poker, dealt him a crashing blow upon the bare head. And Sybil's brave defender relaxed his protecting hold upon her form, fell broken, bleeding, perhaps dying at her feet.

A piercing scream broke from her lips. She stooped to raise her husband, but was at that instant seized by the officer, and forced from the spot.

"Shame! shame!" cried a bystander. "Take the handcuffs off the poor woman, and let her look at her husband."

"Poor woman indeed!" exclaimed Jones, the officer, "she's the biggest devil alive! Do you know what she's done? Not only murdered a beautiful lady; but blown up a church and killed half a dozen men!"

A shudder shook the crowd. Could this be true? A score of questions was put to Bailiff Jones. But he would not stop to answer any one of them. Calling his coadjutor Smith to help him, they each took an arm of Sybil and forced her from the scene.

Faint, speechless, powerless under this sudden and awful accumulation of misery, the wretched young wife was torn from her dying husband and thrust into a stage-coach, guarded by three other bailiffs, and immediately started on her return journey.

Resistance was useless, lamentations were in vain. She sat dumb with a despair never before exceeded, scarcely ever before equalled in the case of any sufferer under the sun.

There were no other passengers but the sheriff's officers and their one prisoner.

Of the first part of this terrible homeward journey there is but little to tell. They stopped at the appointed hours and stations to breakfast, dine, and sup, and to water and change the horses, but never to sleep. They travelled day and night; and as no other passenger joined them, it was probable that the sheriff's officers had engaged all the seats for themselves and their important charge.

During that whole horrible journey the hapless young wife neither ate, drank, slumbered, nor spoke; all the faculties of mind and body, all the functions of nature, seemed to be suspended.

It was on the night of the third day, and they were in the last stage of the journey.

They were going slowly down that terrible mountain pass, leading to the village of Blackville. The road was even unusually difficult and dangerous, and the night was very dark, so that the coachman was driving slowly and carefully, when suddenly the bits of the leaders were seized and the coach stopped.

In some alarm the bailiffs thrust their heads out of the side windows to the right and left, to see what the obstacle might be.

To their horror and amazement they found it surrounded by half a score of highwaymen, armed to the teeth.

CHAPTER X.

THE NIGHT ATTACK ON THE COACH.

"The sound of hoof, the flash of steel,

The robbers round her coming."

"The road robbers, by all that's devilish!" gasped Jones, falling back in his seat.

"Good gracious!" cried Smith.

And all the brave "bum-baillies" who had so gallantly bullied and brow-beaten Sybil and her sole defender, dropped panic-stricken, paralyzed by terror.

"Get out of this, you vermin!" ordered a stern voice at one of the windows.

"Ye—ye—yes, gentlemen," faltered Jones.

"Ta—take, all we have, but spa—spa—spare our lives!" pleaded Smith.

"Well, well, get out of this, you miserable cowards! Empty your pockets, and you shall be safe! It would be crueler than infanticide to slay such miserably helpless wretches!" laughed the same voice, which poor Sybil, as in a dream, recognized as belonging to Captain "Inconnu."

The trembling bailiffs descended from the coach and gave up their pocket-books and watches, and then submitted to be tied to trees.

The coachman and the guard yielded to the same necessity.

The horses were taken from the coach and appropriated to the use of the victors.

And lastly, Sybil, who was rendered by despair indifferent to her fate, was lifted from her seat by the strong arms of Moloch, who held her a moment in suspense, while he turned to his chief and inquired:

"Where now, Captain?"

"To the rendezvous! And look that you treat the lady with due deference!"

"Never you fear, Captain! I'm sober to-night!" answered the giant, as he threw the half-fainting form of the lady across his shoulders and strode up a narrow foot-path leading through the mountain pass.

Indifferent to fate, to life, to all things, Sybil felt herself borne along in the firm embrace of her rude abductor. As in a dream she heard his voice speaking to her:

"Now don't you be afeard, darlint! We an't none on us agwine to hurt a hair o' your head, or to let anybody else do it! Bless your purty face, if we didn't carry you off you'd spend this night and many more on 'em in the county jail! and end by losing your liberty and your life for that which you never did! But you's safe now! And don't you go to mistrusting on us 'pon account o' that night! Why, Lord love ye! we was all drunk as dukes that night, else we never would a mislested you! Lord! if you'd seen the lots of liquor we'd took aboard, you wouldn't wonder at nothing! But we's sober now! And so you's safe! Where's your little dog? Lord bless my life and soul how that little creetur did take hold o' my throat, to be sure! Where is she?"

Sybil could not answer. Indeed, though she heard the voice, she scarcely comprehended the question.

"What! you won't speak to me, eh? Well, that's natural too, but precious hard, seeing as I risked my life to save your'n; and mean you so well into the bargain," continued the ruffian, as he strode onward to a place where several horses were tied.

He selected the strongest of the group, mounted and lifted the helpless form of the lady into a seat before him, and set off at full speed, clattering through the rugged mountain pass with a recklessness of life and limb, that at another time would have frightened his companion half out of her senses.

But now, in her despair of life, there was even a hope in this mad career— the hope of a sudden death.

But the gigantic ruffian knew himself, his horse, and his road, and so he carried his victim through that fearful pass in perfect safety.

They reached a deep, narrow, secluded valley, in the midst of which stood an old red sandstone house, closely surrounded by trees, and only dimly to be seen in the clouded night sky.

Here the robber rider slackened his pace.

The deep silence that prevailed, the thick growth of leafless weeds and briars through which their horse had to wade, all showed that this house had been long uninhabited and the grounds long uncultivated.

Yet there was some one on guard; for when Moloch rode up to the door and dismounted, and holding Sybil tightly clasped in his left arm, rapped three times three, with his right hand, the door was cautiously opened by a decrepit old man, who held a lighted taper in his withered fingers.

"Ho, Pluto! who is here?" inquired Moloch, striding into the hall, and bearing Sybil in his arms.

"No one, sir, but the girls and the woman; and they have just come," answered the old man.

"No one but the girls and the woman! and they have just come! And no fire made, and no supper ready? And this h—ll of an old house colder and damper than the cavern! Won't the captain be leaping mad, that's all! Come, bestir yourself, bestir yourself, and make a fire first of all. This lady is as cold as death! Where is Iska?"

"In this room, sir," answered the old man, pushing open an old worm-eaten door that admitted them into a large old-fashioned oak-pannelled parlor, with a wide fireplace and a high corner cupboard, but without other furniture.

On the hearth knelt Gentiliska, trying to coax a little smouldering fire of green wood into a blaze.

"What the d—l is the use of puffing away at that? You'd just as well try to set fire to a wet sponge," impatiently exclaimed Moloch.

And he went to one of the windows, wrenched off a dry mouldering shutter, broke it to pieces with his bare hand, and piled it in among the green logs. Then from his pocket he took a flask of whiskey, poured a portion of it on the weak, red embers, and in an instant had the whole mass of fuel in a roaring blaze.

Meanwhile Sybil, unable to stand, had sunk down upon the floor, where she remained only until Gentiliska saw her by the blaze of the fire.

"You are as cold as ice!" said the kind-hearted girl taking Sybil's hands in her own, and trying to warm them. "Come to the fire," she continued, assisting the lady to rise, and drawing her towards the chimney. "Sit here," she added, arranging her own red cloak as a seat.

"Thanks," murmured Sybil. "Thanks—you are very good to me."

"Moloch, she is nearly dead! Have you got any wine? If you have, give it to me!" was the next request of the girl.

The giant lumbered off to a heap of miscellaneous luggage that lay in one corner, and from it he rooted out a black bottle, which he brought and put in the hands of the girl, saying:

"There! ha, ha, ha! there's some of her own old port! We made a raid upon Black Hall buttery last night, on purpose to provide for her."

"All right. Now a tin saucepan, and some sugar and spice, old Moloch! and also, if possible, a cup or tumbler," said Gentiliska.

The giant went back to the pile in the corner, and after a little search brought forth all the articles required by the girl.

"Now, good Moloch, go and do for old Hecate what you have done for me. Make her a fire, that she may have supper ready for the captain when he comes," coaxed Gentiliska.

"Just so, Princess," agreed the robber, who immediately confiscated another shutter, and carried it off into the adjoining back room to kindle the kitchen fire.

"You were wrong to leave us! You got into trouble immediately! You would have been in worse by this time, if we had not rescued you! Don't you know, when the laws are down on you, your only safety is with the outlaws?" inquired Gentiliska, as soon as she found herself alone with her guest.

"I don't know. I don't care. It is all one to me now. I only wish to die. If it were not a sin, I would die by suicide," answered Sybil with the dreary calmness of despair.

"'Die by suicide!' Die by a fiddlestick's end! You to talk so! And you not twenty years old yet! Bosh! cut the law that persecutes you and come with us merry outlaws who protect you. And whatever you do, don't run away from us again! You got us into awful trouble and danger and loss when you ran away the last time; did you know it?"

"No," sighed Sybil, wearily.

"Well, then, you did; and I'll tell you how it all happened: the secret of your abode at Pendleton Park was known to too many people. It couldn't possibly be kept forever by all. It is a wonder that it was kept so long, by any. They kept it only until they thought you were safe from pursuit and arrest. Then some of Captain Pendleton's people—it is not known whom—let it leak out until it got to the ears of the authorities, who set inquiries on foot; and then the whole thing was discovered, and as usual misinterpreted and misrepresented. You got the credit of voluntarily consorting with us, and of purposely blowing up the old Haunted Chapel. And the new warrants that were issued for your arrest charged you with that crime also."

"Good Heaven!" exclaimed Sybil, forgetting all her indifference; "what will they not heap upon my head next? I will not rest under this imputation! I will not."

"Neither would I, if I were you—that is, if I could help it," said the girl, sarcastically.

But Sybil sat with her thin hands clasped tightly together, her deathly white face rigid as marble, and her large, dilated eyes staring into the fire heedless of the strange girl's irony.

"But now I must tell you how all this hurt us. In the first place, when your flight from the cavern was discovered, we felt sorry only on your account, because you ran into imminent danger of arrest. We had no idea then that your arrest would lead to the discovery of our retreat; but it did. When *our* detectives brought in the news of the warrants that were out against you, they also warned us that the authorities had the clue to our caverns, and that there was no time to be lost in making our escape."

With her hands still closely clasped together, with her pallid features still set as in death, and with her staring eyes still fixed upon the fire, Sybil sat, heedless of all that she heard.

The girl continued her story.

"We let no time be lost. We gathered up the most valuable and portable of our effects, and that same night evacuated our cavern and dispersed our band; taking care to appoint a distant place of rendezvous. Satan watched the road, riding frequently to the way-side inns to try to discover the coach by which you would be brought back. He was at Upton this evening, when the stage stopped to change horses. He recognized you, and immediately mounted, put spurs to his fast horse and rode as for life and death to the rendezvous of his band, and got them into their saddles to intercept the stage-coach. He also gave orders that we should come on to this deserted house, which he had discovered in the course of his rides, and which he supposes will be a safe retreat for the present. That is all I have to tell you, and I reckon you know all the rest," concluded Gentiliska.

But still Sybil sat in the same attitude of deep despair, regardless of all that was said to her.

While Gentiliska's tongue was running, her hands were also busy. She had prepared a cordial of spiced and sweetened port wine, and had set it in a saucepan over the fire to heat. And now she poured it out into a silver mug and handed it to Sybil, saying:

"Come, drink: this will warm and strengthen you. You look like death, but you must not die yet. You must drink, and live."

"Yes, I must live!" said Sybil. "I must live to throw off this horrible imputation from the fame of my father's daughter."

And she took the goblet and drank the cordial.

And soon a new expression passed into her face; the fixed despair rose into a settled determination, a firm, active resolution.

"You look as if you were going to do something. What is it?" inquired Gentiliska.

"I am going to give myself up! I am guiltless, and I will not longer act the part of a guilty person!" said Sybil, firmly.

"Your misfortunes have turned your head. You are as mad as a March hare!" exclaimed Gentiliska, in consternation.

"No, I am not mad. On the contrary, it seems to me that I have *been* mad, or I never could have borne the fugitive life that I have been leading for the last two months! I will bear it no longer. I will give myself up to trial, come what will of it. I would even rather die a guiltless death than lead an outlaw's life! I will give myself up!"

"After all the pains we have taken, and risks we have run, to rescue you?" exclaimed Gentiliska, in dismay.

"Yes, after all that! And yet I thank you all the same. I thank you all, that you have set me at liberty, and by so doing have given me the opportunity of voluntarily delivering myself up."

"Just as if Captain Inconnu would let you do it. I tell you he has his own reasons for saving your life," angrily retorted the girl.

"And I have my reasons for risking my life upon the bare chance of rescuing my good name," said Sybil, firmly; "and your captain would scarcely detain me here as a captive, against my will," she added, smiling strangely.

"Well, may be he would, and may be he wouldn't! but here he comes, and you can ask him," said the girl, as the galloping of a horse's feet was heard in the front yard.

A moment passed, and then the robber chief, with three or four of his men, entered the room, bringing with them the mail bags and other booty taken from the stage-coach.

"Good-evening, Mrs. Berners! You are welcome back among your devoted slaves!" was the greeting of Captain Inconnu, as half in deference, half in mockery, he raised his cap and bowed low before the lady.

For an instant Sybil was dumb before the speaker, but she soon recovered her self-possession and said:

"I ought to thank you for your gallantry in rescuing me from the custody of those rude men; especially as the freedom you have given me affords me the opportunity of voluntarily doing that which I should not like to be forced into doing."

Captain Inconnu bowed in silence, and in some perplexity, and then he said,

"I am not sure that I understand you, madam, as to what you would do."

"I would go freely before a court of justice, instead of being forced thither," explained Sybil.

"I trust you would never commit such a suicidal act!" exclaimed the captain, in consternation.

"Yes, I would, and I will. I care nothing for my life! I have lost all that makes life worth the living! All is gone but my true honor—for its mere semblance has gone with everything else. I would preserve that true honor! I would place myself on trial, and trust in my innocence, and in the help of Providence," said Sybil, speaking with a stoical firmness wonderful to see in one so young.

Captain Inconnu, who had listened in silence, with his eyes fixed upon the ground, now lifted them to her face and replied:

"Sleep on this resolution before you act, Mrs. Berners; and to-morrow we will talk further on this subject."

"I must of necessity sleep on it before acting," said Sybil, with a dreary smile, "since nothing can be done to-night; but also I must tell you that nothing can change my resolution."

"Thus let it stand over until to-morrow," replied the captain. Then with a total change of tone and manner, he turned to Gentiliska and said:

"Now let us have supper, my little princess, and afterwards we will open the mail bags and see what they have brought us."

Gentiliska clapped her hands together, to summon the old woman of the band, who quickly made her appearance at the door.

"Supper immediately, Hecate!" said the girl.

The woman nodded and withdrew. And in a few moments she reappeared and summoned them in to the evening meal.

The supper was served in the rudest possible fashion. There was neither table nor chairs. A fine table-cloth not too clean was spread upon the floor, and on it were arranged a few plain articles of food such as could be quickly prepared.

"You will excuse our imperfect housekeeping, I hope, Mrs. Berners. The fact is we have just moved in, and have not got quite comfortably settled yet," laughed the captain as he folded his own cloak as a seat for Sybil, and led her up and placed her on it, and sat himself down by her side.

Other members of the band joined them at the meal, and Captain Inconnu and Gentiliska did the honors.

Fortunately there was nothing stronger than wine set before the men, and not much of that; and upon those who had been accustomed to strong brandy, and a great deal of it, this lighter beverage had but little effect. So, to Sybil's great relief, she perceived that they continued sober to the end of their repast.

"Come in now, and let us take a look at the contents of the mail bags! That may afford some amusement to our lady guest," said Captain Inconnu, when they all arose from the supper.

They passed into the front parlor, where the robber chief with his own hands opened the mail bags, and turning them up side down, emptied all their contents in a heap in the middle of the floor.

The robbers came and sat down around the pile, and began to seize and tear open the letters.

"Hallo, there, my men! When you open a letter with money in it, hand over the money to Gentiliska; she will gather and keep it all until we have gone entirely through this pile, and then we will divide it equitably, if not equally, among you," commanded the captain as he himself took a seat in the circle and began to assist in "distributing the mail." He also set the example of scrupulously handing over the money he found in the letters he opened, to the keeping of Gentiliska, who collected it all in a little pile on her lap.

Some of the letters he read aloud to the company for their amusement, such, for instance, as sentimental letters from city swains to their country sweethearts, begging letters from boys at college to their parents and guardians on the plantations, and dunning letters from metropolitan merchants to their provincial customers. Of these last mentioned, the captain said:

"Look sharp, boys! Here are the New Year's bills coming down! They won't be answered by return mail this time; but they will be sent down again. After which remittances will begin to go up! We must keep a bright look-out for the up coaches about New Year's time! And we shall bag some neat thousands!"

"If we are not all bagged ourselves before that!" growled Moloch.

"Oh, raven! hush your croaking! If we should listen to it long, we would never venture upon an enterprise of spirit! Halloa, what's this? Something that concerns you, Mrs. Berners!" exclaimed the captain, breaking off his discourse with his band and turning to Sybil, who was sitting quietly apart; and he held in his hand an open letter, from which he had taken a bright ribbon.

"Something that concerns me!" echoed poor Sybil, as a wild, irrational hope that the letter might contain news of her husband flashed across the dark despair of her soul.

"Yes," answered the captain. "This letter is from Miss Beatrix Pendleton to her brother. It acknowledges the safe receipt of her valuable India shawl, and sends love and thanks to *you* for recovering it from *us* and dispatching it to *her*. Moreover she sends kind remembrances and this gay ribbon to some old nurse of the name of Margy! Here is the letter! Would you like to read it?" he laughingly inquired, as he offered it to Sybil.

"No!" she answered, in strongly marked disapprobation; "that letter is a private one! not intended for my perusal, nor for yours!"

"No? And yet you see I read it! Here Gentilly! here is a

"'Bit of bright ribbon

To bind up your bonny black hair!'"

laughed the captain, tossing the gay remnant to the girl, who caught it up and immediately twisted it in coquettishly among her ebon locks.

It occupied the band for nearly an hour to open and examine all the letters. When they had done so, and had taken everything that was valuable out of them, they gathered the whole refuse mass of papers together, and ruthlessly committed them to the flames.

Then they divided the money among themselves, the captain and his men having each an equal, instead of a graduated share.

"And now," said Captain Inconnu, "we will bid each other good-night, and try to get some rest. Princess, take our guest up-stairs to the large room immediately over this. She, you, and the other women will occupy that room to-night. Hecate has had my orders to that effect, and I hope you will find that she has made the place as comfortable as circumstances will permit."

And so saying, he stuck a stump of a tallow candle in a scooped-out turnip and handed it to Gentiliska, and motioned her to conduct their guest from the room.

Sybil very willingly left the company of the robbers, and followed her hostess to the chamber above.

It was a large bare room, warmed and lighted by a fine wood fire, and furnished only with a few pallets made of dried leaves, with blankets thrown over them.

The old crone called Hecate and the pale girl nicknamed Proserpine stood basking before the blaze of the fire.

Sybil felt pleased to know that she might sleep in peace that night, protected by the presence of other women.

"This is the new lady's bed, this best one in the corner here by the fire," old Hecate explained, pointing to a pallet that, in addition to its dried leaves and warm blankets, was graced with clean sheets and pillow-cases.

Sybil thanked the old woman for her favor; and being very weary, took off her upper garments and laid down to rest, committed herself to the kind care of Heaven, and soon sank into a deep sleep, that lasted until morning.

CHAPTER XI.

RAPHAEL.

I might call him

Something divine, for nothing natural

I ever saw so noble.—SHAKESPEARE.

When she woke up, the sun was streaming in at the unshaded windows, and by its blaze of light she saw that two of the women had left the room, and left no one with her except Gentiliska.

The girl was up, and was making what shift she could to wash her face with the aid of a tin basin, a stone ewer, and a crash towel, all of which, for want of a wash-stand, were placed upon the bare floor.

When she had finished washing, she carefully emptied the contents of the basin out of the window, and refilled it again with fresh water for Sybil. Then, happening to turn around, she discovered that her guest was awake.

"You rested well," she said, with a smile.

"Yes, for I was worn out. This is the first night in four that I have laid down, and the second night in eight," answered Sybil.

"My gracious goodness! How could you stand it? You cannot be rested yet. You had better lie a bed longer."

"No, I would rather get up," said Sybil, rising.

As on a former occasion, the girl attended the lady at her rude toilet, rendering the assistance of a dressing maid.

Just before they left the room, Gentiliska, chancing to look out of the window, uttered an exclamation of surprise and delight.

"What is it?" inquired Sybil.

"The captain's son! Oh! a beautiful boy, Mrs. Berners! An angel among devils! He has been gone so long! And now he has unexpectedly come back again. Look, Mrs. Berners! Oh! how I do wish somebody would deliver this boy from this band! would save this pure young soul alive!" exclaimed Gentiliska, with more feeling than Sybil had ever seen her display.

Following the glance of the girl's eye, the lady looked from the window.

Prepared as she had been by Gentiliska's praise to behold a boy of rare beauty, she was really startled by the angelic loveliness of the lad before her.

The charm was not alone in the soft bright golden hair that shone like a halo around the fair, open forehead, nor in the straight brown eye-brows, nor the clear blue eyes, nor the sweet serious mouth, nor in the delicate blooming complexion; it was also in the expression of earnest candor and trusting love that beamed from every feature of that beautiful face.

"Yes, indeed; he looks like a seraph. What is his name?" inquired Sybil, in a burst of admiration.

"It is Raphael."

"'Raphael!' an appropriate name. So might have looked the child-artist Raphael, in his brightest days on earth. So may seem the love-angel Raphael, to those who see him in their dreams," said Sybil, gazing, as if spell-bound, on the beauty of the boy.

"There, he has passed in. Now let us go down to breakfast, where we shall meet the little darling again. But look here! let me give you one warning; take no notice of that child in his father's presence. Captain Inconnu is intensely jealous of his beautiful boy, and visits that black passion upon the poor lad's head," said Gentiliska, as they went below.

"Jealous of a boy of fourteen? (and the lad cannot be more;) what a wretch!" cried Sybil, in honest indignation, as she followed her conductress down stairs.

Breakfast was served in the back parlor, in the same rude style as the supper of the night before had been.

As Sybil and Gentiliska entered the room, the captain left a group of men among whom he had been standing, came forward, bade the lady good-morning, took her hand and led her to a seat—not at the table, but at the table-cloth, which, lacking a board, was laid as on the evening previous, upon the bare floor. The captain seated himself beside his guest, and the other members of the band took their places at the meal.

Sybil noticed that young Raphael was among them. But Captain Inconnu vouchsafed neither word nor glance to his son, and no other one presumed to present him to the lady guest.

Yet at that breakfast Sybil made a most innocent conquest. The boy, who had seen very few young girls in his life, and had never seen so beautiful a woman as Sybil, at first sight fell purely in love with her, for the sake of whose sweet face he felt he could die a thousand deaths, without ever even dreaming of such a reward as to be permitted to kiss her hand!

What woman does not know at once when a life has been silently laid at her feet? Sybil surely knew and felt that this fair boy's heart and soul were hers for life or death. "He loved her with that love which was his doom."

And what beautiful woman of twenty years old, is not careless and cruel in her dealings with her boy worshipper of fourteen? She may perceive, but she never appreciates the pure devotion.

Sybil, the most magnanimous among women, was perfectly incapable of any other selfish act, under any other circumstances; but yet she coolly resolved to improve her power over this fair boy, and to use his devotion for her own purpose of escaping from the band and delivering herself up to the authorities—never once thinking of the pain and peril she would bring upon her young votary.

But she was very cautious in her conduct towards him. She kept in mind the warning that had been given her by Gentiliska, and took care to bestow neither word nor look upon the lad, while in the company of Captain Inconnu.

When breakfast was over, all the band dispersed about their various business, with the exception of Raphael, who, with pencil and portfolio, strolled about the forsaken grounds, or sat down on fragments of rock to sketch picturesque points in the scenery, and Captain Inconnu, who intercepted Sybil as she was going to her room and requested a few moments' private conversation with her.

Sybil thought it the best policy to grant the Captain's request. So she permitted him to lead her into the unfurnished front parlor, where for the want of a chair or a sofa, he put her in the low window seat.

"I had the honor of telling you yesterday, madam, that if you should be pleased to do so, we would talk further, to-day, upon the subject of your return to the world," began the rather too courteous captain.

Sybil bowed in silence.

"I am here now, at your orders, for that purpose."

Again Sybil bent her head in acknowledgment of this politeness.

"And first I would inquire," said the captain, with a singular smile, "whether, after having slept upon the question, as I advised you to do, you are still in the same mind?"

"Not exactly," replied Sybil, truthfully but evasively; for though she was still firmly resolved to give herself up to justice, she had changed her plan of proceeding.

"Ah!" commented the captain, with an expression that proved how much he had mistaken the lady's meaning—"ah! I thought a night's repose and a morning's cool reflection would bring you to a more rational consideration of the question."

Sybil answered his smile, but left him in his error, and presently said to him:

"Captain, I have a question to ask you."

"Proceed, madam! I am entirely at your commands," said the captain with a bow.

"Supposing that I had remained in the same mind that I was in yesterday, and that I still persisted in my purpose of leaving your band, and giving myself up to take my trial, would you have assisted me, or would you have hindered me?"

"Mrs. Berners, your purpose was a suicidal one! Your question means simply this: If you were bent upon self-destruction, would I help you or hinder you in your determination? Of course there can be but one answer to such a question. I should employ every power of my mind and body to prevent you from destroying yourself."

That was all Sybil wanted to know. She felt now that her only hope was in the boy.

Smilingly she arose and excused herself to the captain, who soon after left the room.

But not until she knew that he had mounted his horse and ridden away from the house, did Mrs. Berners begin to put her plan in practice.

She was playing a desperate game, and she knew it. The heaviest stake was that fair boy's fate.

She knew that the robber captain would never permit her to take what he chose to term the "suicidal" step of delivering herself up to justice. She therefore knew that she must act without his knowledge, as well as without his help.

But she did not know her present locality, or even its bearings in relation to the county seat, Blackville; and therefore, before she could set out to seek that place, she must enlist the sympathies and services of some one who would be able to guide her to that town.

There was no one to be found for such a purpose but Raphael, the captain's son, and her own adorer. Regardless of all consequences to him, since it was to save her own honor, she resolved to enlist the boy.

And to effect her purpose, she felt that she must begin at once. So she walked out upon the neglected and briar-grown grounds, and strolled around until, "accidentally on purpose," she came upon the boy as he sat sketching. He started up, confused and blushing, and stood with downcast eyes, before the goddess of his secret idolatry.

"Please take your seat again, and I will sit beside you," said Sybil, in a gentle tone.

Raphael was a very perfect little gentleman, and so he bowed and remained uncovered and standing, until Sybil took her seat. Then, with another bow, he placed himself beside her.

"You have been sketching. Will you permit me to look at your sketches?" inquired the lady.

With a deferential bend of the head, the boy placed his specimens in her hand.

They were really very fine, and Sybil could praise them with sincerity as well as with excess.

"You are an enthusiast in art," she said.

"*Until to-day*," replied Raphael, with a meaning glance. "Until to-day, my one sole aspiration in life was to become an artist-painter!"

"And why until to-day? How has to-day changed your purpose?" softly inquired Sybil.

The boy dropped his eyes, blushed, and shivered, and at length replied:

"Because to-day I have a loftier aspiration!"

"A loftier aspiration than for excellence in art there cannot be," said Sybil, gravely.

The lad could not and did not contradict her. But she understood as well as if he had explained, that his "loftier aspiration" was to serve and to please herself.

She carefully examined his sketches, and praised his natural genius. And he listened to her commendations in breathless delight.

At length he ventured to ask her:

"Do you, madam, who so much appreciate my poor attempts, do you also sketch from nature?"

"Ah, no," answered Sybil, with a heavy sigh; "since my captivity here, I have lost all interest in my own work! My only aspiration is for freedom!"

Raphael looked up at the lady, amazement now taking the place of the deep deference of his expression.

"You seem surprised," said Sybil, with a smile.

"I am very much astonished," replied the lad. And his eloquent and ever-changing countenance said, as plainly as if he had spoken, "I knew the captain was an evil man, but I did not know that he was a base one."

"Were you not aware that I am a captive of this band?" next inquired Sybil.

"No, madam; I thought that you had been rescued by our men from the officers of the law. I thought that you were in refuge with us, from a false and fatal charge."

"Your thoughts were partly correct. I was rescued from the bailiffs by Captain Inconnu's band. And I do suffer under a false charge. But, Raphael, what think you? Do you not think that a false charge should be bravely met, answered, and put down? Would not you, if you were falsely charged with any criminal act, bravely go forward to answer it in your innocence, rather than run away from it as if you were guilty?"

"Oh, indeed I would!" answered the youth, earnestly.

"I knew it. Your face assures me that you would neither commit a dishonorable act, nor rest one moment under a dishonoring charge."

The lad thrilled and glowed under the lovely lady's praise, and felt that he must do all he could to merit it. He could find no words good enough to reply to her, but he lifted his cap and bowed deeply.

"You understand me, Raphael! But I will confide still further in you. I will tell you that when that terrible tragedy was enacted at Black Hall, and I was so deeply compromised by circumstances in the crime, I wished to stay and face out the false charge; but I yielded to the persuasions of those who loved me more than life, and sometimes I think more than honor! And I fled with my husband. Since that first flight, Raphael, I have led the hiding and hunted life of an outlaw and a criminal! Raphael, my cheeks burn when I think of it! Raphael, I am a Berners! I can live this life no longer! Come what will of it, I wish to give myself up to justice! Better to die a martyr's death than live an outlaw's life!"

"Oh, madam—!"

It was all the boy could bring out in words. But he clasped his hands, and gazed on her with an infinite compassion, deference, and devotion in his clear, candid, earnest blue eyes.

Sybil felt that she had gone a step too far in talking of her "martyr's death" to this sensitive young soul. So she hastened to add:

"But I have no fear of such a fatal consummation. The charge against me is so preposterous that, on being fairly met, it must disappear. And now, my young friend, I must tell you that I do thank Captain Inconnu and his men for rescuing me from the bailiffs, since it prevented me from suffering the ignominy of being forced to go to trial, and will give me the opportunity of going by my own free will. But I do *not* thank them for detaining, me here to the detriment of my honor, when I wish to secure that honor by frankly giving myself up to justice. I am sure you comprehend me, Raphael?"

"I do, madam; but still I cannot conceive why the captain should oppose your wish to go to trial."

"It is enough that he does oppose it," replied Sybil, who could not tell this lad that his father, being the real criminal, was unwilling that she should suffer for his crime.

"You are certain, madam, that he would do so?" inquired the boy dubiously.

"I am quite certain; for I put the question to him this morning."

"Lady, what would you like to do first?"

"To escape from this place, go to Blackville, give myself up to the judge, and demand to be cleared from this foul charge by a public trial."

"But are you sure that such a trial would result in your complete vindication, and restoration to your home and happiness?"

"As sure as innocence can be of acquittal!"

The boy suddenly got up and knelt at her feet.

"Lady, what would you have me to do? Command me, for life or for death."

"Thanks, dear young friend, you are a true knight."

"But what would you have me to do?"

"Help me to escape from this place, escort me to Blackville, and attend me to the judge's house."

"I will do so! When shall we start?"

"Let me see—how far is Blackville from this place?"

"About five miles."

"And how is the road?"

"As bad as a road can be."

"Could we reach the village on foot?"

"Better on foot than in a carriage, or on horseback; because the foot way is shorter. By the road it is five miles; by a foot-path that I know, which is almost a bee-line, it is not more than half that distance."

"We will go on foot, then," said Sybil, rising.

"When?" inquired the lad, following her example.

"Now. We will set out at once! No one notices our position now. If we were to return to the house, we might be observed and watched."

"I am ready," said the boy, closing his portfolio, and hiding it under a flat piece of rock, where he thought it would be equally safe from trespassers and from the elements.

"Let us go," said Sybil.

"This way then, madam," replied the lad, leading the way to the woods.

"I have another reason for haste," Sybil explained as they went on. "I know that the court is now in session at Blackville, and that the judge has rooms at the hotel. I know also that the court takes a recess at one o'clock. It is now eleven; if we make moderate haste, we can reach the village in time to find the judge and secure an immediate interview. Do you not think so?"

"Oh yes, madam, certainly."

"Does this path become more difficult as we descend?" inquired Sybil, as they threaded their way along an obscure, disused foot-path, leading down the narrow thickly wooded valley.

"Oh, no, madam, not more difficult, but much less so. It is a very, very gradual descent down to the outlet of the valley. By the way, did you ever observe, Mrs. Berners, how much all these long, narrow, tortuous vales between the spurs of the mountains, and leading down to the great valley, resemble the beds of water-courses emptying into some great river?" inquired the boy artist, looking with interest into the face of his companion.

"Oh yes, and many geologists declare them to have been really such," replied Sybil.

In such discourse as this, they beguiled the hour and a half that they spent in walking down this hidden valley to its opening near the ferry-house, on the Black river, opposite to Blackville.

Here, while waiting for the boat, which was on the other side, Sybil drew her thick black veil closely over her face, and whispered to her companion:

"I would not, upon any account, be recognized until I get before the judge. So I will keep my face covered, and my lips closed. You must make all the necessary inquiries, and do all the talking."

"I will do anything on earth to serve you, lady," replied the lad, lifting his hat.

"And now here it comes," whispered Sybil, as the ferry-boat touched the shore.

He handed her in, and placed her on a comfortable seat.

After that Sybil never removed her veil or opened her lips. But the boy talked a little with the ferry-man until they reached the opposite shore.

They landed, and went immediately up to the hotel.

"Is Judge Ruthven in?" inquired the lad.

"Yes, sir," answered the waiter.

"Is he disengaged?"

"I will see, sir. He has just finished luncheon," answered the man.

"Tell him that a lady wishes to speak to him on important business," said the boy.

The waiter left the room, and after an absence of five minutes returned to say that the judge would see the lady, and that he, the waiter, would show her up.

"This may be my last hour of freedom in this world!" murmured Sybil to herself, as, preceded by the waiter and attended by her escort, she went up stairs.

The door of a private parlor was thrown open, and Sybil Berners entered and stood before her judge.

CHAPTER XII.

A WISE AND GOOD OLD MAN.

A just judge; by the craft of the law,

Ne'er seduced from its purpose.—SOUTHEY.

The room was a private parlor, furnished something like a lawyer's office.

In an ample cushioned chair, beside a large desk laden with books and papers, sat a venerable old gentleman of a portly form, fine features, fresh complexion, and long silvery white hair. He was dressed in jet black cloth and snow-white linen. His whole appearance expressed great power, benevolence, and equanimity.

This was Judge Joseph Ruthven, the learned jurist and eminent philanthropist, who had succeeded the lately deceased judge, on the bench of the criminal court.

He arose, with a suave and stately courtesy, to receive his lady visitor.

As the waiter withdrew and closed the door, Sybil approached the judge, and lifted her veil.

"Sybil, my child! Mrs. Berners!" he said, suppressing with his habitual self-control, the exclamations of astonishment that arose to his lips.

He had been the life-long intimate friend of her father. He had known her from her birth, and in her childhood he had held her on his knee a hundred times. It was horrible to see her there before him, and to *foresee* what must follow. Who can blame him, if at that moment he wished her thousands of miles away from him, with the ocean rolling between them?

"I have come, your honor, to give myself up to justice, trusting that justice indeed may be meted out to me," said Sybil, as she sank trembling into the chair that he placed for her. He was scarcely less agitated than herself.

"I am guiltless of the crime with which I stand charged; and I can no longer bear the hiding and hunted life of a criminal! I now freely offer myself for trial, come what will of it! It is better to die a guiltless death than to live an outlawed life!" Sybil repeated, her flesh trembling, but her spirit firm.

Still the judge did not speak, but gazed on her with infinite compassion.

"It is a painful office, I know, Judge Ruthven," said Sybil, her eyes filling and her lip quivering, "a painful office, to consign your old friend's child to a prison, and a more trying duty may follow; but there is no help for it, you know."

"My poor child! my poor child!".

These words almost unconsciously escaped the lips of the judge, as he laid his hand upon her head.

"You are sorry for me," said Sybil.

"From the bottom of my heart."

"And you believe me guiltless? Oh, if you can say that, you will give me so much strength and comfort," she pleaded.

How could he answer her? What could he say to her? He would have given much to be able to reply that he fully believed her to be guiltless.

But, though he had known her intimately, from her infancy up, and saw her standing there looking him frankly and honestly in the face and declaring her innocence, and challenging a trial, and pleading for his trust in her, he could not tell whether she were guilty or innocent.

He could not forget the fierce passions and fearful deeds of her race; nor hide from his judgment the probability that this girl, inheriting the fiery temper of her fathers, and driven to desperation by jealousy, might, in a moment of frenzy, have slain her rival. Thus poor Sybil was an instance of that natural law by which children suffer for the sins of their fathers.

While the Judge dropped his venerable head upon his chest in sorrowful thought, Sybil waited for his answer; and the longer it was withheld, the more impatient she became to have it.

"You surely do not believe me guilty, then?" she pleaded, clasping her hands and trying to catch and meet his eyes as he raised his head.

"My child, whatever I may or may not believe, I must express no opinion here, or to you," he answered, evasively.

"Oh! I suppose not; for you are to be my judge and preside at my trial, and so it would never do for you to give an opinion," said Sybil with a sad smile, as, woman-like, she jumped to this conclusion.

The judge committed himself by no direct reply to her words, but said:

"I trust in Heaven, my child, that all will be well!"

"But, Judge Ruthven, although you may not be able to express an opinion as to my innocence or guilt, yet I earnestly wish that you may hold one—that you may believe me innocent; and so—please look into my eyes!"

The old man, who had been rather shunning her glance, now raised his head and met the honest gaze that was seeking his.

"Judge Ruthven," she re-commenced, "although the men and women of my line have been cursed with fierce and cruel tempers, and have some of them done ruthless and fearful deeds, yet not one of them was ever debased with a false and lying tongue, not one of them ever stooped to deny his or her deed to avert the worst consequences that might befall. And, Judge Ruthven, if in my rage I had slain my rival, if I had been bad enough to do that deed, I should have been brave enough to avow it! I have never stained my hands with blood, and never sullied my lips with falsehood, and so, when I tell you that I am guiltless of the death of Rosa Blondelle, Judge Ruthven, I call upon you to believe me!"

Her eyes were fixed on his, and through them poured her spirit's strength and purity and truth, inspiring his soul with full faith in her.

He arose from his seat, his fine old face tremulous, yet beaming with emotion.

"Give me your hands, my child! I *do* believe you—I believe you!" he fervently exclaimed, taking and pressing her hands.

"Thank Heaven! Now I can bear the rest!" earnestly answered Sybil, bending her head. "And now, Judge Ruthven! do your duty! The quicker it is done and over, the better for us both!"

"Patience, patience, my child! I have now to return at once into the court to preside at a trial now in progress. In the mean while do you remain here. The necessary forms shall be gone through. I will send you counsel. You must be committed for trial; but you will immediately apply through your counsel to be admitted to bail. Remain here until you hear from me. All will be right for the present, and Heaven grant that all may be well in the end!"

"Admitted to bail! Not have to go to prison! Oh, thank you! thank you! But I thought cases like mine were not bailable."

"That is somewhat at the discretion of the court. The fact that you have voluntarily come forward to give yourself up to trial, pleads loudly in your favor."

"And I may go home! Go home perhaps even to-night! Oh! home! home! home! Oh! how blessed to be able to go home! Oh, thank you! thank you! thank you!" cried Sybil, bursting into tears of joy.

"Compose yourself, my child. It is very possible that you may sleep at home to-night, and many nights. But there are certain legal forms that must be observed. I will see that they are properly attended to, and with as little distress to you as may be consistent with their due observance. The case that is now going on will close this afternoon, I think. But I will still keep the court open to as late an hour as possible, to wait for the application of your counsel for bail. Remain here in peace until I send for you," said the judge kindly, pressing the hand of Sybil as he withdrew.

As soon as Judge Ruthven had left the room, Sybil turned triumphantly towards her young escort, who, since his entrance, had remained modestly standing near the door, and she said:

"Dear Raphael! did you hear that? I am to go home and rest in peace until my trial comes on! Oh, Raphael, what joy! And, dear boy, take notice! I did well to come here and give myself up! and this blessed prospect of going home is the fruits of that well-doing! Mind, Raphael, always be sure to *do* well, and you will also be sure to *fare* well!" she concluded, mindful to give her young companion a lesson in morality.

"Oh, madam! I am so glad of this, for your sake!" said the boy, earnestly.

"Thank you, Raphael! And I do not forget that I owe very much of this satisfaction to you. But for your help, I could not have escaped from the band, or found my way through the mountain passes to this place. But now, my boy, you have been long away from your companions. Your absence may be noticed, and may bring you into trouble. So with my best thanks, dear boy, I will bid you good-bye, and send you home," said Sybil, holding out her hand.

But the lad did not take it.

"'Home?'" he echoed sadly, "'home?' Ah, lady, what is my home? A robber's den! No, madam, I will never go back to the band! Here in the village I may get work as an errand boy, or on some farmer's field as a laborer; but even if I do not, though I should perish, I will never go back to the band!"

"Say you so, my boy? Then you shall even go home with me, and be my little brother; and my husband—Ah! my dear Lyon, how do you fare now?—my husband shall be your guardian, and send you to some good school of art where your fine talent may be cultivated," said Sybil, earnestly, again offering her hand.

He took it and raised it to his brow, and said:

"You should be a queen, lady!—a queen, to do your royal will towards all whom you wish to elevate. How can I thank you?"

"By accepting, in simplicity of heart, all that I and all that my noble husband will do for you. For Mr. Berners will also be very quick to recognize and prompt to reward your services to me."

Poor Sybil! in the generous exultation of her soul, she almost lost sight of the sorrows and dangers that still encompassed and threatened her.

She, in her young matronly pride and dignity, feeling ever so much older and wiser than her juvenile worshipper, took upon herself to give him much good counsel as to his conduct through life, and was still engaged in this way when two gentlemen opened the door and entered the room. They were both old acquaintances of Mrs. Berners. The first was a Mr. Fortescue, an elderly man, and a wealthy planter of the neighborhood, now holding the office of high sheriff of the county. The other was a Mr. Sheridan, a brilliant young barrister, often associated with Mr. Berners in the same lawsuit. Both these gentlemen had been frequent guests at Black Hall, both in the time of her father and of her husband.

Mr. Fortescue took off his cap, and bowed to his sometime hostess, as he said:

"Mrs. Berners, if I have come in person to serve this warrant, you will, I am sure, understand that I have assumed an unpleasant duty purely for your sake, to save you unnecessary pain."

"I comprehend and thank you, sir," answered Sybil.

"And you will at once accompany me to the magistrate's office."

"Yes, I am ready; let us go," said Sybil, rising.

"And here is Mr. Sheridan, offering himself as your counsel until you can procure better," said the high sheriff, presenting the young lawyer.

"I shall not be likely to find better, I am sure. I shall be very glad to retain Mr. Sheridan," said Sybil, frankly offering her hand to the young man.

"It is not a pleasant visit, Mrs. Berners, this one to Mr. Hawkin's office; but it will only be a preliminary examination, and I will do what I can to make it a brief one," explained Mr. Sheridan, as he offered his arm to his client to conduct her from the room.

Sybil drew her veil over her face, and leaning on the arm of her counsel, was about to follow the sheriff, who had gone before, when she happened to think of her devoted young worshipper, who was standing disconsolately near the judge's desk.

"Stay here until I return, dear Raphael," she said, with a pleasant smile, and then passed from the room.

They took her to an office under the hotel, where the sitting magistrate was ready to hear the case.

A few witnesses were there—persons who had been present at the mask ball, and had observed the marked attentions of Lyon Berners to Rosa Blondelle, and the jealous rage of Sybil, and who had afterwards been drawn to the scene of the tragedy by the cries of the victim, and had arrived in time to hear the fatal charge of the dying woman, as well as to behold her death.

When Sybil saw these people, she shivered and turned pale—not with fear of their testimony, for she had nerved herself to meet that, but with the sudden recollection of the appalling circumstances under which she had last met them, and which their appearance now called up in all its first horror.

The magistrate's clerk now handed Sybil a chair. She then raised her veil, bowed to Squire Hawkins, and took her seat.

The proceedings were commenced.

The witnesses for the prosecution were one after the other duly sworn and examined; and they deposed to the fatally condemning circumstances attending the murder of Rosa Blondelle as they are already known to the reader.

This examination occupied about an hour. At its close the magistrate turned to the accused lady, and inquired what she had to say in defence.

Sybil arose, and answered by giving the explanation that she had already made, on the night of the murder.

The magistrate heard her through, but then instructed her that her unsupported assertion was no evidence, and would not be received as such, and called upon her to produce her witnesses.

Sybil was about to answer that she had no witnesses to produce, when a look from her counsel arrested her speech.

He respectfully took her hand, replaced her in her seat, and then standing up, he said:

"My client has given a true explanation of the facts that have led so many persons to a false conclusion. But all further defence, we reserve for a higher tribunal."

And having said this, he sat down. He knew that no amount of defence would now save Sybil from being committed for trial, and his object was therefore to shorten this ordeal.

The magistrate then directed his clerk to make out the mittimus. When the instrument was ready, he signed it and looked around for some officer to execute it.

"I will take charge of the warrant and the lady," said the high sheriff, interposing.

"You, Mr. Fortescue!" exclaimed the magistrate, in surprise at the condescension of the high sheriff.

"Yes, I," coolly answered the latter.

"But Mr. Magistrate, we are prepared to offer bail," put in Sybil's counsel.

"Not a bailable case, Mr. Sheridan, as you, being a lawyer, should be very well aware. No case in which the prisoner is arrested upon the charge of a capital crime can be bailed."

"I believe you speak of a rule. I speak of an exception. This lady was not arrested. She came forward, in the consciousness of innocence, and gave herself up, fairly challenging a trial! It is not likely, therefore, that she would run away, if released upon bail."

"Quibbles, sir! quibbles! I know of no exceptions to this rule! Mr. Sheriff, remove the prisoner."

Mr. Fortescue drew Sybil's arm within his own, and whispered to her:

"I will take you back to the Judge's room, where we will remain while Sheridan goes before the Court and puts in an application for bail."

Sybil drew her veil again before her face as she was led from the magistrate's office back to the Judge's room, where she found her young escort, still anxiously awaiting her.

"It is all right, Raphael," she said, "or rather it will be all right very soon! Will it not, Mr. Fortescue?"

"I trust and believe so, madam."

"The magistrate insisted that my case was not a bailable one, and indeed I knew that much myself; but the Judge said that he would admit me to bail, and he can do so, can he not?" anxiously inquired Sybil.

"The magistrate told you the truth; and besides, he had no power to act in the matter of releasing you on bail; but your case is a very exceptional one, Mrs. Berners, and the judge has very great discretionary powers, which I am sure he will stretch to the utmost in your behalf."

"I hope without risk to his own position."

The high sheriff smiled.

"Judge Ruthven," he said, "is the most distinguished jurist, as well as the most honored judge and the most popular man that ever presided in our courts. His proceedings become precedents. He can venture to do a great deal. He can afford to risk much!"

While they talked thus together, Mr. Sheridan reëntered the room, with a very cheerful expression on his countenance.

"All will be well," he said, brightly. "Mr. Sheriff, I bear you the Judge's order to bring your charge into court. Mrs. Berners, you will meet some friends there, and will, with them, enter into a recognizance for your appearance at court when called to trial."

Sybil promptly arose and gave her hand to Mr. Fortescue, who drew it within his arm and led her out of the room, and then from the hotel to the court-house.

The court-room was, comparatively speaking, empty. The crowd that had collected to hear a trial for forgery, which was just ended in the acquittal of the prisoner, had dispersed at its close; and no one remained but the presiding judge, the officers of the court, a few lawyers and a group of gentlemen.

As Sybil was led up the aisle, between the rows of benches usually occupied by spectators, one of the gentlemen turned around, and to her joy and amazement, revealed the countenance of Lyon Berners. If the dead had risen before her, Sybil could scarcely have been more astounded. He, from whose bleeding and insensible body, she had been torn away, scarcely five days before, now stood before her, ill, pale, faint, but living. His head was bound up with a white linen bandage as, leaning on the arm of Captain Pendleton, he came to meet her.

"Oh, my dear Sybil!"

"My dearest Lyon!"

These were the words with which they greeted each other.

"Now, my friends, leave all this until you return together to Black Hall. Now we must not keep the court waiting, but proceed to business," said Mr. Sheridan, taking the hand of his client, and drawing it again through his arm, as he led her up to a table that stood before the bar and upon which was spread out a formidable looking piece of parchment heavily engrossed.

"Here is the bond by which you enter, with your husband, with Captain Pendleton and Miss Beatrix Pendleton, into a recognizance for your appearance at court when called to trial. The amount of bail is high, fifty thousand dollars! But I fancy you are good for that," said the young lawyer.

Sybil smiled gravely, and when the pen was put into her hand, signed her name.

Her signature was followed by those of Lyon Berners, Clement Pendleton, and Beatrix Pendleton.

And the bond being duly sealed and delivered, Sybil was informed that she was free to depart.

Free to depart! No more need of flying and hiding! Free to go home, to sit down in peace by her own dear fireside, to lie down and repose on her own comfortable bed! Free to depart! Free to go home! Oh, joy! Sybil, in her delight, forgot that the darkest thunder-cloud of fate still lowered in the sky, threatening to break in destruction on her head!

Disregarding all forms, she was about to go up to the bench to pour forth her thanksgivings to her old friend Judge Ruthven, when her husband laid his hand upon her shoulder and stopped her, whispering:

"Remember, dearest, that we are in court, and govern yourself. We shall see the Judge at the hotel."

So Sybil merely courtesied to the bench, and gave her hand to her husband, who pressed it warmly, and then passed it over to Mr. Sheridan, who led her from the court-room.

Lyon Berners, supported by Captain Pendleton, and Beatrix on the arm of old Mr. Fortescue followed.

And thus they all returned to the judge's room in the hotel.

"Lyon, dearest! there is my little friend and deliverer. Come here, Raphael, and get acquainted with my husband," said Sybil, as her eyes fell upon her young escort.

The boy came at her call, and she presented him to Mr. Berners, who received him with some surprise, but much condescension.

"I will tell you all about Raphael when we get back to Black Hall. In the mean time, you must take him upon trust, for he is to go home with us," said Sybil.

And before another word could be spoken, the door was thrown open, and Judge Ruthven entered.

All arose and stood up, as the venerable old man went around and shook hands with each one.

Sybil held his hands between hers, and with the tears filling her eyes, warmly thanked him for restoring her to her home; though it might be only for a season, she said, it would give her strength to bear all that might come afterwards.

"Heaven grant, my dear Sybil, that your full and perfect acquittal and vindication may come afterwards, as I entirely believe they will. Your trial may not come on at this term of the court, and if not, there will be a considerable interval of time, during which your counsel must busy himself in hunting up evidence in your favor, and if possible tracing this mystery to its solution. Heaven bless you! There, don't weep," said the judge, shaking both her hands, and then relinquishing them.

And they all sat down and talked hopefully over the subject, until the door was again opened and the waiter appeared to announce that the carriage ordered for Mr. Berners was waiting.

"Come, dear Sybil, let us bid good-by to our friends, and go," said Lyon Berners to his wife.

And both took an affectionate and respectful leave of the judge, and were about to do the same by the Pendletons, when the Captain said:

"No; Beatrix and myself prefer to go down to the sidewalk, and take leave of you at the carriage door."

"And the only reason why we do not go all the way home with you is, because we know that you have some mutual explanations to make, and would rather be alone to-day. But to-morrow we shall go to see you, and if you will let me, I will make you a long visit," added Beatrix Pendleton.

"Oh, Beatrix, dearest! always true and brave!" exclaimed Sybil, suddenly kissing the young lady, while Lyon warmly grasped the hand of her brother.

Both the husband and wife understood and appreciated the motives of these devoted friends.

They went down stairs, attended by the Pendletons, Mr. Sheridan, and Raphael.

When the Berners with Raphael were in the carriage, Clement and Beatrix Pendleton took leave, reiterating their intention to visit Black Hall the next day.

"And I also must be with you at an early hour, Mrs. Berners; for it will be necessary to begin at once to prepare your defence. I would also like to learn, Mr. Berners, whom you intend to associate with me in counsel," said young Sheridan, as he took leave of the lady and gentleman.

"We will settle all that in the morning, Sheridan, and of course I myself must be with you in the defence," replied Lyon Berners.

And they shook hands for the last time, and the young lawyer ordered the coachman to drive on.

"The old ladies at the Hall will be prepared to receive you, Berners. I took care to dispatch a messenger to them two hours ago, to announce your coming," said Captain Pendleton, calling after them.

Lyon stretched his head out of the window, and nodded and waved his hand, as the carriage passed out of the village.

CHAPTER XIII.

HOME.

There blend the ties that strengthen

Our hearts in hours of grief,

The silver links that lengthen

Joy's visits when most brief!—BERNARD BARTON.

"Dear Lyon, how came you here so soon after your dreadful accident, and at such a risk to your life?"

"My dearest Sybil, what led you to give yourself up?"

These questions were simultaneously asked of each other by the husband and wife, as soon as they were fairly upon their journey.

Then their eyes met, and despite the gravity of their position, both smiled.

"Whose question shall be answered first?" inquired Lyon.

"Oh! mine! mine!" exclaimed Sybil; "tell me, dear Lyon, how it is that you are able to be here at all. The bailiffs indeed told me that you were not dangerously injured; if it had not been for that assurance, I should have died with anxiety; but still I had every reason to suppose that you were very seriously injured. How could you get up so soon? How could you bear the stage-coach journey? Are you sure that it has not endangered your life?"

"My dearest Sybil, no," said Mr. Berners, answering her last question first. "On the contrary, it has saved it; for if I had remained in Baltimore in that terrible state of anxiety about you, I should certainly have fallen into a brain-fever. My injuries were not nearly so severe as they seemed. The blow stunned me, and cut my scalp in a glancing way. It bled very profusely, so that the great flow of blood probably saved me from a fit of illness, at the least."

"But the jarring journey by the coach?"

"I did not come that way. I came by water."

"Oh! I forget that you could come so. Go on."

"After you were taken from me, I was laid upon a sofa, where I found myself when I recovered consciousness. The stage-coach that had carried you off had been gone an hour, and no other was to start until the next morning. To hope to overtake you was vain. But to meet you on your arrival at Blackville was practicable, by taking the steamer that was to start at noon. So I ordered a carriage, threw myself into it, and was driven to the pier, where I took passage in the Falcon, bound for Richmond."

"But, oh, Lyon! how could you have borne even so much exertion as that, so soon after your accident?"

"Not very well, to tell you the truth. For as soon as I got on board, I had to turn into my berth, and lay there with ice on my head and mustard at my heels, until the boat arrived at Richmond. But I was then well enough to leave the steamer and embark, on board a schooner, bound up the river. At the mouth of the Black River I got into a small fishing smack, that brought me to Blackville."

"And you reached the village—"

"Only this morning. I expected to find you in the hands of the authorities, when, to my amazement, I heard that you had been rescued from the bailiffs by that band of road robbers. I had scarcely recovered from that astounding intelligence before I met Sheridan hurrying from the hotel towards the court-house."

"To get my bail; but go on."

"He was surprised to see me, of course, but drew my arm in his own and begged me to go with him. On our way thither he told me of the almost incredible news that you had given yourself up to justice; that there had been a preliminary examination, and that you were detained in honorable custody by the high sheriff, until he, as your counsel, should apply to the court to have you released upon recognizance. I went with him to the court-room, where I found Pendleton and his sister. It seems that Pendleton had come to Blackville to meet Beatrix, who was returning from her visit to the city; but on hearing what was afoot they had gone into court to tender their services in case they should be needed."

"Oh!" burst forth Sybil in enthusiasm, "what a noble pair is that brother and sister! What man in this world is worthy to marry Beatrix, or what woman to be the wife of Clement?"

"Yet I hope they both will be happily wedded, for all that," observed Lyon. "And now, dear Sybil, you know the rest. You know that Judge Ruthven 'took the responsibility' of releasing you upon our united recognizance for your appearance at court! And now, as I have told you all I have to tell, I would like to hear all that has befallen you since we parted, and above all, what induced you to give yourself up."

"Stay! tell me; did I not *right* in giving myself up?"

"Yes, dear Sybil. Being separated from me, and in the hands of outlaws, you did right to yield to law. But tell me the immediate motive of your action."

Being so pressed, Sybil commenced and related all that happened to her from the time that she had been so rudely torn from the side of her wounded husband to the moment that she met him again in the court-room. And she did not fail to give due credit to young Raphael, her devoted worshipper and brave deliverer.

At the close of the narrative, Lyon Berners turned towards the boy, saying:

"Give me your hand, young friend! Henceforth you are our son, to share our home and hearts, and to be cared for as long as we all shall live!"

Raphael bowed low over the hand that was extended to him.

And no more words were then spoken, for the carriage was just turning in to the elm avenue leading up to Black Hall.

But when Sybil came in sight of her home, she suddenly turned to her husband, and asked:

"Oh, Lyon! what has become of my little Nelly? You know we left her locked up in our chamber that morning we started out for a walk, and was stopped by the sheriff's officers in the hall of the hotel. What has become of her; do you know?"

"She is safe. I brought her from Baltimore to Blackville with me. But then— I am very sorry; but in the rush of other events I forgot her, and left her in the hotel. However, she will be well taken care of, for the people know her."

"I am so glad to hear she is safe. We will send for her to-morrow," smiled Sybil.

The carriage rolled on to the house, and drew up before its doors.

Sybil looked out from the window, and saw Miss Tabitha Winterose at the head of all the house servants, standing on the porch to welcome her. Among them was her little Skye terrier, held in check by Joseph. But as soon as Nelly saw her mistress' face she broke loose, and with almost human cries of frantic delight and impatience, scampered forward, and climbed into Sybil's down-stretched arms.

"The first to welcome me home, you faithful little friend! But how did you come here, Nelly?" asked Sybil, taking the little creature on her lap, holding its head between her open hands, and looking down into its loving brown eyes.

But for all answer Nelly suddenly darted up and kissed her mistress on the chin.

"Welcome home, Miss Sybil! Oh, Lord be thanked as I have lived to see this blessed day!" blubbered Joe, coming forward, and laughing and sobbing with delight under the full conviction that all his mistress' sorrows were now over.

"Welcome back, Mrs. Berners, my dear child! a thousand welcomes back!" whimpered Miss Tabby, pressing forward to meet her.

"And me too, Miss Sybil," added Dilly, rather irrelevantly.

"Now, Lord, let thy servant depart, for I have seen the desire of my eyes," said old Abraham, reverently lifting his hat from his white head, and slightly misquoting the Scriptures.

Sybil had by this time alighted, and was shaking hands right and left with her attached servants.

But now a touching sight met her view—a little delicate baby boy, with fair curling hair, clear blue eyes, and a pink and white complexion, hiding behind Miss Tabby, clinging to her skirts, and peeping out with a look half shy and half confiding.

"Oh, you poor child!" said Sybil, tenderly raising him in her arms and pressing him to her bosom, while her tears fell fast upon his head. "You poor, poor child! If I had done what they said, could I ever have looked in your sweet eyes again?"

"Don't cry, poor lady, don't cry," said the child, lifting up his little apron and trying to wipe her eyes.

"Ah, you poor baby! But you shall never want a mother while I live," continued Sybil, still weeping for pity.

"Don't cry, Cro' will be a good, *good* boy," coaxed the child; softly stroking her face with his little hand.

"Cro' will give you his mudic box, and all his p'ay things. Don't cry," begged the child, and as a last resort, he put his arms around her neck, and added, "Cro' will love you."

"Come, my dear Sybil! come into the house," said Mr. Berners, who, having paid and discharged the hired carriage, now turned to offer his arm to his wife.

But Sybil covered the child in her arms with kisses, and pressed him warmly to her bosom, before she relinquished him to the care of Miss Tabby.

Then she turned to her husband, who still held out his arm to her.

"Poor Lyon!" she said. "You are scarcely able to stand, yet you wish to escort me in. Joseph!"—she called to their faithful servant—"come here. Don't you see your master's state?"

Joe came and looked upon his "sovereign lord," and his eyes and mouth gradually opened in a growing consternation, as he gazed upon the bandaged head.

"Lor save us, marse Lyon; has you been blowed up agin, or has you got you'sef inter a—" Joe paused in respect.

"Row, would you say, Joe? Something like it, I must confess; and a very disreputable appearance I present, no doubt! But there, Joe, I will take your arm into the house, for I do feel rather light-headed still," said Lyon, with a smile, as leaning on his servant, he went up the porch stairs. Sybil followed, attended by Raphael, Miss Tabby and little Cromartie, Delia, and all the servants.

"Come up into your own room, my darling Miss Sybil, Mrs. Berners I mean, which it is all well aired, and nice and warm and ready for you," said Miss Tabby, leading the way up-stairs, followed by Sybil and her maid Delia.

"Oh, how good it is to be home once more! Oh, how delightful to enter one's own bed-room again," sighed Sybil, with the sense of a great relief, as she sank into her own luxurious easy-chair, beside the bright wood fire.

"Let me take off your bonnet, my pet," said the affectionate old maid, untying with trembling fingers the hat of Sybil.

"Miss Tabby, how came little Nelly here?" inquired Mrs. Berners, as the little dog, who had followed her up stairs, jumped into her lap.

"Why, lors, Miss Sybil, the groom from the livery-stable who brought the news of your coming, fotch the dog too. I b'lieve he said as Capting Pendleton found him running round loose, and sent him home."

"Oh, Miss Tabby, sometime when you and I are sitting by our winter evening fire, I can tell you such stories of what I have gone through, and the best story of all is that of little Nelly," said Sybil caressing her tiny four-footed favorite.

"Surely!" exclaimed Miss Tabby, who, having relieved Sybil of her bonnet and shawl, now sat down for a quiet little talk, while waiting for dinner to be announced. She had little Cro' on her lap.

"Miss Tabby," inquired Sybil, suddenly, "where is that child's nurse? I notice that you seem to have him all the time."

"Where is his nurse, is it Miss Sybil? Ah, the brazen, piece! She's gone and got married to Saundy McGruder the livery-stable keeper—master of him who brought the news of your 'rival! *Ugh!*" exclaimed Miss Tabby in strong disgust. *She* had never taken upon herself to get married, and she set her face steadily against all such improprieties in the young servants that were under her control.

"And so she deserted her charge? Poor baby! Hard to lose his mother and his nurse at the same time," said Sybil, compassionately. Suddenly she changed the subject, and inquired:

"Miss Tabby! did *you* ever believe I did that?"

"Did which, honey?"

"What they accused me of?"

"Now I wish you hadn't axed me that there question, Miss Sybil! I do so! for it looks just as if you had a doubt on me, as never doubted you," exclaimed the faithful creature, with an injured look.

"Heaven bless you, good soul! Then you *don't* believe it!" cried Sybil, in delight.

"Now look here, honey! I've nursed you ever since you was a month old, and how *could* I believe you would do a thing like that! Though the good Lord knows as you had aggravation enough to drive you out'n your seventeen senses, and into anything! But you never did that! I'd stake my soul on to it. Why, see here! When that ignorant nigger, Dilly, as was a crying and a howling after you, fit to break her heart, when she axes me, 'Oh, Miss Tabby, do you think as my mistress *did that?*' I fetches her sich a box of the years, as I shouldn't wonder if they ring yet, though that was a matter of nigh two months ago!"

"Thanks, dear old friend, for your faith in me. And now, dear Miss Tabby, did you notice that fair boy whom we brought home with us?"

"I never see such a heavenly looking boy in all my days. To be sure I noticed of him. Wherever did you pick him up, Miss Sybil?"

"On my travels, old Tabby. I will tell you all I know about him, when you and I sit down together to gossip by that winter evening fire we spoke of."

"And, oh, how much you'll have to tell me, my child. I looks to have my hair bristle up on ind!"

"Then wear a strong cap, and tie the strings under your chin tightly, that it may not be lifted from your head," laughed Sybil. "But about the boy; he is to make his home with us; and so I want you to have one of the best bedrooms prepared, and a plate always put on the table for him; and to instruct the servants that they are to treat him in all respects as a son of the house," answered Sybil.

"Lor' bless me! Is that so!" exclaimed the old maid, as her eyes opened in amazement. "Well, Miss Sybil, I have heard of ladies afore now, being so angelable as to pervide for their husband's unnateral relations; but that you should do sich a thing I never would a believed. You're a wery good child! but your goodness don't lay into that toleratin' line, that I know."

"What on earth do you mean, Tabby?" sharply demanded Sybil. "I'm shocked and disgusted at you, that I am."

"Why, what for? You said the boy was to be respected as a son of the house; and then ag'in, they've both got light hair and blue eyes, and fair skins," said Miss Winterose, in dismay.

"Tabby, as far as I understand you, I am quite ashamed of you. That boy is the son of a man who calls himself Captain Inconnu, but whom I believe to own another name; but no matter about that now; that will figure in some of the stories that I shall tell you by our evening fires—Well, what do you want?"

This last question was addressed to a colored boy, who opened the chamber door and looked in.

"Please, ma'am, I wanted to tell Miss Tabby as dinner was on the table," said the child.

"And didn't you know better, you little brute, than to open a lady's door without knocking? Go down to the kitchen with yourself, this very instant!" exclaimed Miss Tabby, indignantly.

"Don't scold the child this first day of my return," pleaded Sybil.

"And, lor', now here I have been a keeping on you, child, a-satisfyin' of my old woman's curiosity, and not even a leaving of you time enough to dress for dinner," said the old maid, regretfully.

"Dress for dinner!" echoed Sybil, lifting her eye-brows. "I had almost forgotten such a piece of propriety! I have not dressed for dinner for nearly two months!"

But for all that, she got up, and went to her toilet glass and smoothed her hair, and washed her hands, and put on a clean collar.

"That will do for to-day. Now don't look hurt, you good old Tabby, and I'll promise to-morrow to 'dress up to the nines!'" said Sybil, laughing, as she tripped out of the room. She was in such good spirits at being home again, she had for the moment forgotten that she was only there on sufferance.

"And I had such a splendid dinner got for her, too! With all the silver-gilt and cut-glass out, and some of the old wine them devils happened to leave when they robbed the cellar. I haven't told her about that robbery yet! I don't want to tell her no bad news the first day as she gets home," ruminated Miss Tabby, as she sat over the fire with little Cromartie in her arms.

Of course Miss Winterose could not guess that Sybil had heard of the raid upon her cellars.

Sybil ran down stairs, at the foot of which she found Mr. Berners and Raphael waiting for her.

"I have been taking a nap on the parlor sofa, and my young friend here has been mousing among the books in the library," said Lyon Berners, as he met his wife.

"I hope you feel refreshed," said Sybil.

"Very much," answered Lyon. "Raphael, my boy, give Mrs. Berners your arm in to the dinner-table."

The lad blushingly obeyed, and they went in to dinner.

There was one little affectionate mischievous thought darted through Mr. Berners' brain; "I will show my wife that I can trust her with this pretty page who is in love with her, better than she could trust me with the beautiful widow who was not in love with me," he said smilingly to himself, as he followed them in to the dining-room.

This may be said to be the re-commencement of Sybil Berners' happy home-life. Of the awful cloud that overhung her fate, she scarcely thought at all this evening. When dinner was over she led the way into her own bright drawing-room, which had been that day "swept and garnished" for her reception. Fresh snow-white lace curtains were at the windows, contrasting finely with the warm, bright hues of the crimson satin hangings, the crimson velvet parlor set, and the crimson Brussels carpet. A brilliant sea-coal fire was glowing in the grate, and vases filled with fragrant hothouse plants stood on every white marble-top table and stand.

Like a child home for the holidays, Sybil roamed about in delight from object to object, and fondly opened her disused piano, to try if it was still in tune. She was surprised and pleased to find that its tone was perfect. She had been absent but two months or less, and she knew it, yet she felt as if two years must have elapsed since she had touched her piano. She sat down and played some of her favorite airs, and sang some of her favorite songs, to the great entertainment of Mr. Berners and Raphael.

But this evening she was too happy and too restless to keep to any one thing. So she soon left the piano, and called Raphael to follow her to a book-stand in the corner, where she showed him some fine engravings from the old masters—a volume containing master-pieces from Guido, Correggio, Leonardo, Murillo, and others. With all this wealth of art the poor child-artist was delighted.

"But here is something better still, my boy! Here is a volume of the rarest gems," she said, opening a book of Raphael's Madonnas and laying it before him.

He uttered a cry of delight, and then checked himself, blushed, and apologized.

Meanwhile Lyon Berners reclined upon the sofa. He was still weak from his accident, and from the imprudent journey that had followed it. He lay there, watching Sybil, content that she should be amused, until the wife herself suddenly lifted up the volume she had been examining with the boy, and calling Raphael to follow her, went over to her husband, and kneeling by his side, with the book resting on the edge of the sofa, she turned a page, and said:

"Look here, dear Lyon! I want you to notice this amazing resemblance," and she pointed first to an engraved head of the artist Raphael occupying the centre of the title-page, and then to the living head of the boy Raphael bending by her side.

"It is a likeness," said Lyon.

"Likeness! It is a portrait! If I had known this boy before, and had seen this picture anywhere else, I should have supposed it had been taken for him," said Sybil, earnestly.

Lyon closed the book, and asked her to play and sing a certain beautiful evening hymn which was a great favorite with them, after which he suggested they should retire.

So passed the first evening of Sybil's recovered home.

The next morning, after she had breakfasted, she took another school-girl's holiday frolic. She ran all over the house, renewing her acquaintance with every room.

She had scarcely finished her pleasant tour, when old Joe came after her to say that Marser Sheridan, from Blackville had called to see her.

Her counsel!

The announcement of this visitor awoke Sybil from her pleasant dream of home and safety.

With trembling hands she arranged her dress, and went below to the parlor, where she found Mr. Berners entertaining the lawyer.

Both arose at her entrance, and Mr. Sheridan shook hands with her, saying:

"I do not know a better place to get up my brief for the defence, Mrs. Berners, than here on the scene of the tragedy and the imputed crime."

The tone and manner of the lawyer were very cheerful, and at once restored Sybil's composure.

"I have heard your explanation of the circumstances that led you to the bed-side of Rosa Blondelle, at the moment in which her murderer had left her, but I heard it at second hand. I would now hear it from yourself," said Mr. Sheridan.

Sybil began and related the whole story, which the lawyer took down from her lips.

"Now," he said, "Mr. Berners, I would have your statement, commencing from the moment the deceased rushed into the library."

Lyon Berners related the circumstances attending Rosa Blondelle's death, as far as he knew them.

"And now I would like to minutely examine the room in which the crime was committed," said Mr. Sheridan.

"Come, then," answered Lyon Berners. And he led the lawyer to the rooms lately occupied by Rosa Blondelle.

"A man might easily have escaped by these windows an instant after having committed the crime. They close with a spring catch. The fact of their having been found fastened when the room was examined, proves nothing whatever against my client. The murderer could in an instant unfasten one of them from within, jump through, and clap it to behind him, when it would be as fast as if secured by a careful servant within," said the lawyer, after the examination was complete.

Then they all returned to the library, where Mr. Sheridan summed up his brief for the defence.

"Give yourself no uneasiness, Mrs. Berners," he said. "Your case lies in a nut-shell. It is based upon your own explanation of your attitude at the bed-side of the victim, and upon the fact, which I shall undertake to prove, that the assassin had escaped from the window at the foot of the bed."

The lawyer spoke so cheerfully that Sybil's spirits rose again.

He then, as a precautionary measure, he said, to give them the help of the greatest bulwarks of the bar, advised that they should write to Washington to engage the services of the celebrated Ishmael Worth, who, in a case like this, would apply in the regular way to be admitted to plead.

Mr. Berners accepted this advice, and said that he would lose no time in following it.

Then the lawyer took his leave.

He had scarcely got out of sight before Captain Pendleton and his sister Beatrix drove up to the door.

"I have come to stay with you as long as you will let me, my darling," said Beatrix, as Sybil hastened to welcome her.

"Then you will stay with me forever, or until you are happily married, dearest," answered Sybil, hospitably, as she led her friend up to a bedroom to lay off her bonnet.

Captain Pendleton, meantime, was taken care of by Mr. Berners.

"Clement!" said the latter, when he had taken his guest to his dressing-room, "we are old, tried friends, and need not fear to speak the truth to each other. Tell me now, frankly, has not the action of the judge, in admitting Sybil to bail, been very much censured? Will it not injure him and affect his position, even to the risk of impeachment?"

"Oh, no! There is a great deal of talk, to be sure. Malcontents complain that he has exceeded his prerogative, that he has overstepped the law, that he has tried to establish a dangerous precedent, and so on, and so on."

"And what does Judge Ruthven say to all this?"

"Nothing, nothing whatever! Do you suppose for an instant he is going to condescend to defend himself to such asses? He says nothing."

"But his friends! his friends! surely *they* defend him?"

"They do. They tell the donkeys that a judge has certain discretionary powers to modify the severity of the law when justice requires it; that these modifications become precedents for other judges to follow, and finally they become laws that none may dispute; that in this case Judge Ruthven has followed the spirit of the law, if not its letter; that he based his act upon the fact that the accused lady, being perfectly safe from the officers of the law at the time, voluntarily came forward, delivered herself up, and challenged a trial; and that therefore she was a worthy object of the privilege of bail."

Honest Clement Pendleton was no lawyer, and he had spoken a trifle unprofessionally; but it was no matter. Lyon Berners understood him, and was satisfied.

Sybil and Beatrix came down to join them; and then they all adjourned to the dining-room, where they had luncheon.

Then Captain Pendleton went home, leaving Beatrix with Sybil.

A few days after this the Court adjourned, and Sybil knew that she would not be brought to trial until the spring term. In that long interval, what discoveries might not be made to save her? Her hopes rose high.

"But oh!" she thought, with a shudder, "if these months had to be passed in prison!" And in the depths of her grateful heart she again thanked Providence and Judge Ruthven for her restoration to home and friends.

Then Christmas came. Under the circumstances they preferred to spend it very quietly. Beatrix was still with them, and Clement was invited to come and dine on Christmas-day.

Sybil took great delight in delighting. And if good taste forbade her now to indulge in the lavish hospitality and gay festivity that had always been customary in Black Hall at this season, she determined to indemnify herself by making unusually handsome presents to her servants and dependants, as well as the most liberal donations to the poor—and so to be happy in the happiness she should bestow.

With this intention she put a small fortune in her longest purse, and went in her roomiest carriage to Blackville, intending to empty the purse and fill the carriage before her return.

The day being Christmas eve, the village was full of people, come there to shop for the holidays, and poor Sybil was brought to a sense of her condition by the treatment she received—silence, rude stares, or injurious whispers greeted her as she passed. But they were only pin thrusts, which she soon forgot in the interesting errand upon which she had come.

She loaded her carriage with bundles, boxes, and baskets, and returned home in time to separate the treasures, and write upon each one of them the name of the person for whom it was intended.

The next morning Captain Pendleton arrived early, to assist in the distribution of the presents. No one was neglected; every body was made happy with several valuable gifts.

Little Cro' went to paradise in the corner of the room, with his cap full of toys.

That day also Sybil's dependents enjoyed as good a dinner as was set for herself and her friends. So, after all, in spite of fate, they kept their "Christmas, merry still."

When it was generally known that Sybil Berners had returned to Black Hall, there was much discussion among the ladies as to whether they should call on her.

Some declared that she was a murderess, whose face they never could bear to look on, and therefore of course they never would go near her. Others, who said that they believed her guiltless and wished her well, added, that they felt the same delicacy in going or in staying away—as in the first case Mrs. Berners might consider their call an intrusion from motives of curiosity, and in the second case she might construe their absence into intentional neglect. And between these two extremes there was every shade of opinion as to Sybil's culpability, and every sort of reason for not going to see her just yet.

And so it followed that Sybil passed a whole, good, peaceful fortnight in the company of her husband, her three devoted friends, her faithful servants, and her little pets.

But at length, early in January, sympathy on the one hand and curiosity on the other prevailed over every feeling and reason, and Sybil's neighbors, both detractors and defenders, began to call on her.

But Mrs. Berners had penetration enough to know her friends from her foes, and so she felt no hesitation and made no mistakes when she welcomed the visits of the first and declined those of the last mentioned.

So the winter slipped away peacefully enough, and Sybil seldom remembered what her friends tried to make her forget—the heavy cloud that still hung over her fate.

She was reminded of it only when her counsel came to consult with her; but then they always wore cheerful countenances, and spoke hopeful words that inspired her with confidence and courage.

Sometimes indeed, the recollection of the awful crisis that could not be shunned, that must be met, would come to her in the middle watches of the night, and fill her soul with horror; but with the first beams of the morning sun, this darkness of her spirit, like the darkness of the hour, would pass away.

It was in all the reviving life and budding beauty of early spring, that the Criminal Court resumed its sittings at Blackville.

The case of Sybil Berners, charged with the murder of Rosa Blondelle, was the very first upon the docket.

It was a day as bright, beautiful, and glorious as any day that ever dawned, when the summons came that called Mrs. Berners up to the court to be put upon trial for her life.

CHAPTER XIV.

THE TRIAL FOR LIFE.

If you condemn me, fie upon your law!

There is no right in the decrees of judges

I stand for justice! Answer! Shall I have it?—SHAKESPEARE.

The awful contrast that there was between her appearance of the fairest freedom and her reality of the darkest bondage!

But she scarcely realized such a contrast until that morning, when she arose and threw open her south window and looked out upon her own beautiful home valley, now fresh with the verdure of early spring, and radiant with the light of the young day. A luminous haze like sifted gold-dust hung around the mountain tops; a dewy freshness sparkled on their wooded sides; and the river lay like a clear mirror below.

"Must she leave all this for the terrors of the court-room?" she inquired, with a shudder of her shrinking heart. And for a moment she felt that even the gloom of the prison might have better prepared her to meet the horrors of a trial for life, than this peaceful, bright home staying had done.

Yes, the contrast between her surroundings and her impending ordeal seemed an awful mockery of fate!

She knew that the court would open for the spring term that day; but she did not know that she would be wanted so soon.

They were all at breakfast that morning in the cheerful front parlor.

Mr. and Mrs. Berners, their protégé Raphael, their little adopted baby-boy Cromartie, who always sat in a high chair beside his benefactress, Beatrix Pendleton who was resolved to stay with Sybil to the last, and Tabitha Winterose who sat at the head of the table to serve out the coffee and tea, because Sybil had said that everything tasted better coming from "Old Tabby's" hand—these were all gathered around the table, when Sheriff Fortescue was announced and entered the room.

"You have come for me!" said Sybil, in a low, terrified tone, as she arose from her seat before any one else could move or speak.

"Resume your seat, Mrs. Berners, and finish your breakfast. There is no hurry," answered the old gentleman, as calmly as he could.

Then he saluted the party, shook hands with Mr. Berners, and accepted the seat offered him by Joe.

"She is wanted this morning?" inquired Mr. Berners, in a low voice.

The sheriff bowed gravely in assent.

Sybil had been kindly pressed to resume her seat and finish her breakfast. She sank back into her chair indeed, but could not eat another morsel. Nor could any one else at the table, not even poor little Cro', who saw by the faces of all around that something terrible had happened, or was about to do so.

The meal was at an end. The breakfast party arose in trepidation.

"Is she wanted now, immediately?" hastily inquired Lyon Berners.

The sheriff again bowed in assent, but added:

"I do not wish to hurry her."

"I will not keep you waiting, Mr. Fortescue," said Sybil, trying to steady her voice, as she prepared to leave the room.

But here little Cro', who had been watching every body anxiously, found out by some process of his own that the terrible thing which was going to happen threatened Sybil, and he slid down from his high chair at the risk of breaking his limbs, and ran to her and clung to her dress.

"Take him away, Miss Tabby! Sybil is going to Blackville, Cro', and she will bring Cro' some candy, when she comes back," she said, tenderly placing the child in Miss Winterose's arms.

Mr. Berners told Joe to have the carriage brought around and to prepare to drive it, and then he gave his arm to Sybil, who really needed its support in going up to her chamber.

Beatrix followed her.

Raphael walked up and down the length of the breakfast-room, in uncontrollable agitation.

Miss Tabby clasped the child to her bosom, and rocking him and herself to and fro, wept and sobbed bitterly.

"And as for me, I feel like a hangman," muttered old Mr. Fortescue to himself as he stood looking moodily out of the window.

Mr. Fortescue had not been high sheriff very long, and was new to the ghastly duties of his office, to be sure, he might have easily deputed this irksome task to another, but he chose to perform it himself, lest that others should not do it so kindly.

In a few moments Sybil returned, ready for her drive.

She was dressed—her dress was afterwards minutely described in the county paper, and also in many others that reported the trial—she was dressed then in a light gray suit throughout, bonnet, mantle, and gown being of the same material, and even gloves and veil of the same hue; a pale blush rose relieved the neutral shade of her bonnet, and a ribbon of the same delicate tint fastened her small linen collar.

Beatrix Pendleton, in a black silk suit, with a black lace bonnet and shawl, followed her.

Beatrix, with the warm approbation of her brother, had determined to sit in the dock, beside Sybil. She, the falsely accused lady, should not go there unsupported by the presence of another lady.

"Good-bye, Raphael! good-bye, Miss Tabby! I hope to be back this evening. Good-bye, dear little Cro'! Sybil will bring you something good, when she comes," said Mrs. Berners, with all the cheerfulness she could command.

But Raphael turned pale as death when he silently gave her his hand.

Miss Tabby could not speak, for hysterical sobs.

Little Cro' cried outright.

To shorten this trying scene, Mr. Berners drew his wife's arm within his own and led her to the carriage. He had just settled her in the back seat, when little Nelly rushed past everybody, and ran up the steps, and crouched breathless and palpitating at the feet of her mistress.

"Yes; let her stay, Lyon," said Sybil, lifting the faithful little creature to her lap.

Mr. Berners next helped Miss Pendleton to a seat beside his wife, then entered the carriage and took his place opposite Sybil, while Mr. Fortescue got in and sat down in the fourth seat, facing Beatrix.

And Joe got his order to drive on towards Blackville.

Scarcely a word was spoken for the first mile. It was Sybil who broke the silence.

"Will my counsel meet me at the court, Mr. Fortescue?" she inquired.

"They are waiting for you, Madam. Mr. Worth has arrived, and is in earnest consultation with Mr. Sheridan," gently replied Mr. Fortescue.

"How long do you think the trial will last, Mr. Fortescue?" tremblingly inquired Sybil.

"It is quite impossible to form an opinion, madam," replied the Sheriff.

"My dear Sybil," said Lyon Berners, "let us hope and trust that the trial will be short, and the result acquittal. Keep up your courage."

But he who gave her this advice found his own heart fast failing him. He could fearlessly have met his fate in his own person; but in the person of his beloved wife—

Fortunately for our unhappy party, it was not generally known that the accused lady would be put on trial this day; so when they drove into Blackville, they found no more than the usual little crowd about the hotel and the court-house.

The carriage was drawn up before the last-named building.

The two gentlemen got out and assisted their companions to alight.

As they were about to enter the court-house, Sybil lifted her hand to draw her gray veil before her face; but Beatrix stayed her.

"Don't do it, my dear Sybil. You have no reason to veil your face, or bend your head, or even lower your eyes, before the gaze of any one alive!" she said, proudly, for her friend.

Sybil felt the force of these words, and indeed her own pride seconded their advice.

"I will take you first to my room, where your counsel are waiting to speak with you," said old Mr. Fortescue, drawing Sybil's hand through his arm, and leading her, followed by her husband and her friend, into the sheriff's office.

There they found Mr. Sheridan standing at a long table covered with green baize and laden with papers.

With him was a gentleman whose grandeur and beauty of person and manner must have deeply impressed any beholder, under any circumstances. "The form of Apollo and the front of Jove," had been said of him; and if it had been added that he possessed the intellectual power of a Cicero, and shared the divine spirit of Christ, it would have been equally true.

"Mr. Worth, late of the Washington Bar, now admitted to practice here for your benefit, Mrs. Berners," said Mr. Sheridan, presenting his colleague, after he himself had greeted the party.

Sybil lifted her glance to meet the gaze of the pure, sweet, strong spirit that looked forth on her from Ishmael Worth's beautiful eyes.

Sybil Berners might have been presented to half the weak-minded kings and vain queens on their mouldering old European thrones, without the slightest trepidation; but before this glorious son of the soil, this self-made man of the people, this magnate of the American Bar, this monarch of noble Nature's crowning, this magnificent Ishmael Worth, her spirit bowed in sincere homage, and she lowered her eyes and courtsied deeply, before she offered him her hand.

Holding that little hand between his own, he spoke a few strong, reviving words to her.

He told her, in the first place, that he had spent the whole night in making himself master of her case; that his firm faith in her innocence would give him great power as her advocate; that he would do his best for her sake; but that while doing his best, they must lean on Divine Providence for support and deliverance, who, in his own good time—later, if not sooner—would vindicate the innocent.

And as he uttered these words, looking down in her face, he infused into her soul comfort and courage, and patience to meet the worst this first day of trial might bring.

But no one knew better than Mr. Worth the almost utter hopelessness of the cause he had undertaken to defend; and that was no small sacrifice for an eminently successful barrister like Ishmael Worth, who had never in the course of his professional career lost a single case, to withdraw himself from his own bar and business, and take much trouble to get admitted to practice at another, for the sake of defending an utter stranger, in whose case there seemed not more than one chance in a thousand of success.

But if there had not been even that one slight chance, still the magnanimity and tenderness of Ishmael Worth's nature would have brought him to the accused lady's side, her defender to the death.

Something like this passed through the mind of Lyon Berners as he grasped the hand of Mr. Worth, and warmly thanked him.

And then the sheriff drew Sybil's arm within his own to lead her on. Lyon Berners offered his arm to Beatrix Pendleton, and followed them. The counsel brought up the rear.

Thus the little procession entered the court-room. The presiding judge, Joseph Ruthven, sat on the bench, with two associate judges, the one on his right hand, the other on his left. A few lawyers and law officers sat or stood around in groups. On the judge's extreme right, a little below the bench, two long seats were occupied by witnesses for the prosecution; on the extreme left was the jury-box; in the intermediate space in front of the bench, stood the prisoner's dock, the witness's stand, and the counsel's tables. The remaining portion of the room, nearest the front doors, was filled up with the spectators' seats. But very few spectators were present; only some dozen villagers who had nothing better to do than to loiter there, and some score of farmers who had that morning come to market, and had dropped in to see what might be going on at the court.

Great was their excitement when they saw Mrs. Berners led in by the sheriff, and followed by her friends. They had not expected her trial would come on so soon. Indeed, an absurd rumor had prevailed that she would not be brought to trial at all. But now here she was, sure enough, and they stared at her with dilated eyes and open mouths.

Sybil impulsively put up her hand to drop her veil; but remembering Beatrix Pendleton's words, she refrained, and turned and swept her proud eye round upon the gazers, whose lids fell under her glance.

She was not put into the dock, but offered a chair at the table with her counsel. She bowed to the bench before taking her seat. On her right sat her husband; on her left, her friend Beatrix Pendleton, near her counsel. She was very much agitated, but a pressure from the hand of her husband, a glance from the eyes of Ishmael Worth, helped to reassure her.

Nor must the fidelity of another friend, a poor little four-footed friend, be forgotten. Little Nelly had faithfully followed her mistress, and now lay curled up at her feet.

Meanwhile the preliminary forms of the trial proceeded. The jurymen were sworn in and took their seats. Then Mr. Sheridan touched his client's hand to call her attention, while the clerk of arraigns, standing up with an open document in his hands directed the accused to listen to the reading of the indictment.

Sybil raised her head and became attentive, while that officer read aloud the terrible instrument, setting forth that Sybil Berners of Black Hall, in the county of Blank, being instigated thereto by diabolical agency, did, with malice aforethought, on the night of the thirty-first of October ultimo, feloniously break into the chamber of Rosa Blondelle, then residing at Black Hall, in the county of Blank, and there did unlawfully and maliciously stab, kill, and murder the said Rosa Blondelle, etc., etc., etc.

During the reading of this indictment, charging her with a crime at once so base and so atrocious, Sybil's emotions were all revolutionized. No longer unmerited shame and terror had power to bend her soul. The fiery spirit of her race arose within her; the "burning blood" boiled in her veins; a fierce indignation flashed from her dark eyes, like lightning from a midnight cloud; bitter scorn curled her beautiful lips.

When told to stand up, to hold up her hand, and to answer whether she were guilty or not guilty of the felony laid to her charge, she answered haughtily:

"Not guilty, of course, as every one here knows, or should know. No more guilty than were many of the queens and princesses of old, who were martyred for crimes that we in these days know they never committed."

She had exceeded the forms of law, and said more than was necessary; but her heart was on fire, and she could not help it; and no one interrupted her.

"How will you be tried?" proceeded the clerk of arraigns, trying to avoid the beautiful, terrible eyes that were gazing on him.

"By God and—my peers, if indeed I have any peers here," answered this arrogant young Berners, sweeping her full eyes scornfully over the rustic occupants of the jury box, and then resuming her seat.

Her words and manner did her no good; their only effect upon the jury was to convince them that Mrs. Berners had inherited all the furious passions of her forefathers, and that she was an excessively high-tempered and high-spirited young lady, quite capable of doing a very rash deed.

"Patience, patience, my dearest one," whispered her husband, as he passed his arm behind her.

"I cannot be patient or prudent, Lyon, under such insults. I cannot, if they kill me," she fiercely whispered back.

"Hush, hush," he said, softly patting her shoulder.

And then both became quiet, while the business of the trial proceeded.

The State's Attorney, Charles Coldman, took the bill of indictment from the hand of the clerk, and proceeded to open the case. Mr. Coldman was not the friend of the accused, neither was he her enemy. He did not belong to the old aristocracy of the State, neither had he distinguished himself in any manner. A successful lawyer he was, in so far as he had attained his present position, but no farther. He had never been admitted within the exclusive circles of Black Hall, or shared its hospitalities. And if this exclusion did not make him the enemy of the lady of that manor, it certainly did not embarrass him with any of those old associations of friendship and intimacy, such as might have distressed him, had he been, like nearly all the other members of the Blackville bar, the frequent guest of her father and her husband.

Thus the State's Attorney could deal with the lady of Black Hall, as he would deal with any other person on trial at that court.

He opened the indictment, and gave the theory of the crime. Here was no complication, he said, and no uncertainty. The case was so clear, that it need occupy the court but a little time. He then, in a grand, eloquent, and highly colored style, described the murder. He drew a moving-picture of the lovely young victim, whose fair image many who were present, he said, would recall with tears of pity; he described her accepting the invitation of the jealous mistress of Black Hall, and drawn within its dread doors, as a bird is enticed into the trap which is to be its destruction. He showed her on that fatal Hallow Eve reposing in her chamber, sleeping the sleep of innocence in fancied security. He painted, in lurid colors, the form of the murderess stealing down the stairs that led to her victim's room, "in the dead waste and middle of the night," creeping to the innocent sleeper's bedside, and plunging the fatal dagger in her peaceful, unsuspicious bosom. He described the startled look and cry of the victim, shocked from calm repose by a violent and bloody death; the scene of confusion, horror, and terror that ensued; the dying words of Rosa Blondelle, charging Sybil Berners with her death. He adverted to the guilty flight of the murderess and the desperate means she and her friends had taken even to the immolating of other lives, to secure her escape; until at length, unable to hold out against the authorities any longer, she had surrendered at discretion, and made a merit of giving herself up to justice. All this, he concluded, he should undertake to prove to the gentlemen of the jury.

He then proceeded to call the witnesses for the prosecution. The first witness called to the stand was—Sybil's best friend, Captain Clement Pendleton of Pendleton Park.

He came forward slowly, with a pale, stern face. He would rather have lost his power of speech, than have used it for her detriment. But he was known to have been present at the death of Rosa Blondelle, and he was therefore subpoenaed to attend the trial as a witness for the prosecution.

Being duly sworn, he testified that he had been startled by loud screams from the room below his chamber; and that on rushing down into that room, he had found Mrs. Rosa Blondelle bleeding from a wound in her chest, and supported in the arms of Mr. Lyon Berners, who was in the act of bearing her across the room to the sofa, on which he then laid her.

"Was there any one else in the room?" inquired the prosecuting attorney, seeing that the witness had paused.

"Mrs. Berners was there."

"Describe her appearance."

"She was very much agitated, as was quite natural."

"Had she anything in her hand?".

"Yes," answered Clement Pendleton, who never added a word against Sybil that he could honestly keep back.

"Witness, you are here to tell the *whole* truth, without reservation. What was it that the prisoner held in her hand?"

"A dagger—the dagger," added poor Clement Pendleton recklessly; "with which the unknown assassin had killed Mrs. Blondelle."

"Stay, stay! we are going a little too fast here. Are you prepared to swear that you know, of your own knowledge, that some person other than the prisoner at the bar 'killed Mrs. Blondelle?'"

Captain Pendleton was a soldier and no lawyer, yet he saw at once how his faith in Sybil's innocence had led him to the false step of stating inferences for facts. So he explained:

"I spoke in accordance with my own firm convictions."

"Ah, but I fancy your own conviction will not prevent that of the prisoner," commented the State's Attorney, with a grim humor.

"And now, Captain Pendleton," he continued, "as you are sworn to tell the truth, the whole truth, and nothing but the truth, I must trouble you to answer the questions here put to you, by stating exactly such facts as came under your personal observation only."

And then he resumed the examination of the witness, and drew from him a relation of all the fatal circumstances that occurred in the library at Black Hall, on the night of the tragedy, among them the guilty appearance of Sybil Berners with the reeking dagger in her crimsoned hand, and the dying declaration of the murdered woman, charging Sybil Berners with her death.

He would have gone on and told Sybil's own explanation of her appearance, but was stopped there by the State's Attorney, at whose request the presiding Judge instructed him that such declarations on the part of the accused, could not be received in evidence.

And so he was told to withdraw.

I will not weary my readers with any detailed account of this trial. A slight sketch of the principal points will he sufficient for our purpose.

There were some half dozen more witnesses who had been present at the death of Rosa Blondelle, and who, being duly sworn, corroborated the testimony of Captain Pendleton.

Then the Scotch nurse, Jennie McGruder, was called to the stand.

Her testimony bore very heavily upon the accused.

She told how, on the night of the murder, she had, according to her custom, carefully searched both the bed chamber and the nursery that constituted Mrs. Blondelle's apartments; that finding no intruder there, she had securely fastened all the windows and all the doors of the two rooms, with the exception of the door leading to the staircase communicating with Mrs. Berners' apartments, which were immediately above those of Mrs. Blondelle. This door was always left unfastened, as it was thought perfectly safe to leave it so.

She told how, while she was with the child in the nursery that same night, she was startled by hearing piercing screams from the adjoining bedroom; that she had rushed there in time to see the deceased Rosa Blondelle running wildly from the room, followed by the prisoner, Sybil Berners, who had a dagger in her hand.

She also corroborated the testimony of the other witnesses as to the fatal words of the dying woman charging the prisoner with her death.

After this witness came a number of others who testified to the ill-feeling which existed between the prisoner and the deceased.

These witnesses were all in turn severely cross-examined by the counsel for the defence, but, as the State's Attorney had said, their testimony was so clear and simple that it was impossible to involve them in any self-contradiction.

The State's Attorney had also been very careful to call the attention of the jury to each condemning point of the fatal evidence against the accused.

And here the examination of witnesses on the part of prosecution closed, and the court adjourned.

Sybil was conducted into the sheriff's room, where refreshments were provided by that kind-hearted officer for herself and her friends, and where everything possible was done and said to support her under the terrible ordeal of her trial. Being still under bail, as she would be to the end of her trial, she was then permitted to return home with her friends for the night.

One little touching event must be recorded here, as it showed the thoughtful tenderness of her nature. Even in the midst of her anguish of anxiety in regard to the awful issues in the result of this trial, she remembered baby Cro' and his small interests; and she stopped in the village to procure for him that "something good" which she had promised.

But to do the orphan justice, he was gladder to see Sybil than to get what she brought him.

Miss Tabby caught her in her arms, and wept over her.

Raphael did not weep, nor even speak; but he clasped her hands, and looked at her with a silent grief more eloquent that words or tears. It was a period of agony to all concerned; and Sybil was indebted to opium for all the sleep she got that night.

CHAPTER XV.

THE VERDICT.

'Tis not ever

The justice and the truth o' th' question carries

The due o' th' verdict with it.—SHAKESPEARE.

At an early hour the next morning the court was opened, the Judges resumed their seats, and the accused was conducted back to her place.

Ishmael Worth opened for the defence.

I shall not even attempt to give so much as an epitome of his speech. I should never be able to do justice to the logic, eloquence, pathos, and power of his oratory. I shall only indicate that the points upon which he dwelt most were, the magnanimous nature of his client, which rendered her utterly incapable of committing the atrocious crime with which she stood charged; the fatal fallibility of circumstantial evidence, which he illustrated by direct reference to many recorded cases, well-known to the legal profession, in which parties had been convicted and executed, under the strongest possible circumstantial evidence, and had afterwards been discovered to have been guiltless; the facility with which a murderer might have concealed himself in that bedroom occupied by the deceased on the night of the murder, have eluded the search of the sleepy nurse, and after committing his crime, being frightened by the screams of his awakened victim, should have escaped through the window and slammed the shutter to, from the outside, when it would fasten itself with its spring bolt; the perfect naturalness of the circumstance that the accused, on hearing her guest scream, should have flown down those communicating stairs to her assistance, and should have drawn from her wounded bosom the dagger left there by the flying murderer. This, and much more than can even be touched upon here, he said, and then proceeded to call witnesses for the defence.

These were some of the old friends and neighbors of the accused lady, who warmly bore witness to the generosity and nobility of her nature, which placed her in their estimation so far above the possibility of committing a crime so heinous.

Then came the white servants of her household, who described the situation of Rosa Blondelle's rooms on the first floor of Black Hall; the easy entrance into them from the grounds below, and the insecure spring fastenings of the windows, which might be opened from without by a thin knife passed under the latch and lifted.

All felt how small the amount of material was, out of which even the most learned and eloquent advocate could make a defence for Sybil Berners.

The examination of the witnesses for the defence closed.

Mr. Sheridan then made his last effort for his client, and was followed by Mr. Worth, both of whom exerted their utmost faculties in the hopeless cause of their unhappy client.

But ah! no eloquence of theirs, of any one's, could do away with the damning evidence against the accused lady.

The State's attorney, in a final address to the jury, pointed out this fact, and then sat down.

The venerable Judge Joseph Ruthven arose to sum up the evidence and charge the jury. We know that he believed in the innocence of the pure and noble young lady, whom he had known from her earliest infancy. Such a belief under such circumstances must have swayed the judgement and affected the action of the justest judge under the sun.

Judge Ruthven palpably leaned to the side of the prisoner. After summing up the evidence for the prosecution rather briefly and coldly, he urged upon the jury the value of a good name in the case of an accused party; the excellent name of the accused lady; the unreliability of circumstantial evidence; the fallibility even of the testimony of the dying, when such testimony was given in the excitement of terror and the agony of death; of how such testimony, however sincerely given and believed in, had often been utterly disproved by subsequent events; and finally, that if a single doubt, however slight, remained in their minds of the guilt of the prisoner, it was their bounden duty to give her the benefit of that doubt by a full acquittal. And so, praying Divine Providence to direct their counsels, he dismissed them to deliberate on their verdict.

The jury left the room in charge of a sheriff's officer.

And then the tongues of the spectators were loosened. The charge of the judge had given great offence.

"It amounts to a positive instruction to the jury to acquit the prisoner!" fiercely whispered one malcontent.

"And when the testimony has so clearly convicted her!" added another.

"Nothing but partiality! He and her father were old cronies," put in a third.

"A partial judge ought to be impeached!" growled a fourth.

And so on the disapprobation rumbled through the court-room in thunder, not loud, but deep.

And then all became still as death.

Meanwhile the judge sat calmly on the bench, the only evidence of his strongly suppressed anxiety was the extreme paleness of his venerable face. What was passing in his mind during this time of awful stillness and waiting, in which the earth seemed arrested in her orbit, the sun stopped in his course? The dread question, should he, with more than Roman courage, be obliged to pass sentence of death on that child of his old friend, that young high-born, refined, and beautiful woman, whom from the depths of his soul he believed to be perfectly innocent?

Meanwhile Sybil Berners, her face bloodless, her frame almost pulseless, breathless as with suspended animation, leaned upon her husband's breast and waited for the verdict that was to give her life or death.

Both pale as herself, her husband and her friend sat, the first on her right side and the second on her left, as they sit by the dying, supporting her as best they might, her husband's arm around her waist, her friend's hand clasping hers.

The hour wore slowly on. The room grew dark. But the judge did not adjourn the court. He thought, most likely, it was better for all concerned to end the agony that night if possible.

At length the lamps were lighted, and their beams fell upon the pallid group of friends, upon whom the doom of death seemed already to have descended; and further on, upon the "sea of heads" that now filled the court-room and—waited for the verdict; for the crowd had greatly increased since the commencement of the trial.

At length the hush of silence was stirred by a motion near the door of the jury-room.

Sybil's weary head still rested on her husband's bosom; he gathered her in a closer embrace, that she might not look up until she should be compelled to do so.

She was too inexperienced to know what that little stir that moved the stillness meant.

The door of the jury-room was thrown open by the deputy-sheriff, and the jury filed into the court, and stood in a group near the bench.

All hearts stood still. The face of the venerable judge turned a shade paler.

The clerk of arraigns arose, and addressing the jury, inquired:

"Gentlemen of the jury, have you agreed upon your verdict?"

"We have," solemnly answered the foreman, on the part of his colleagues.

"Prisoner, stand up and look upon the jury," proceeded the clerk, addressing Sybil.

"Rise, my darling, rise!" said the heart-broken husband of the lady, as he helped her to her feet.

Sybil stood up, still leaning on his arm.

"Look on those men there!" whispered Lyon Berners.

"Where? Where?" inquired Sybil, in perplexity, for the court-room was but dimly lighted, and her brain was half dazed with horror.

"There, my darling, there!" muttered Lyon Berners, pointing to the jury.

"Prisoner, look upon the jury!" repeated the clerk.

Sybil turned her glazing eyes towards the group.

"Jurymen, look upon the prisoner!" continued the clerk.

They looked, and some among them must have seen that the doom they were about to pronounce in _ verdict could never be carried into effect.

The clerk proceeded.

"How say you, gentlemen of the jury; is the prisoner at the bar guilty or not guilty of the felony laid to her charge?"

CHAPTER XVI.

CONDEMNED.

And in that deep and utter agony,

Though then, than ever, most unfit to die,

I fell upon my knees and prayed for death.—MATURIN.

"Guilty!"

The word tolled like a knell through the air.

Silence like death followed.

Some one passed to the judge a glass of water. His hand shook so that he spilled it.

Then he arose, trembling so much that he leaned for support on the stand before him. Yet he did his duty—the last duty he was ever to do on that bench.

"Prisoner at the bar, stand up."

She was raised to her feet, and supported in the arms of her husband.

"Sybil Berners! What have you to say why sentence of death should not be pronounced against you?"

Nothing. She had not understood the question. She did not answer it. There is a point in suffering at which the soul becomes insensible of it. While waiting for the verdict, Sybil had gradually passed into an abnormal state, which, without being a dream, resembled one. Her spirit was snatched away from the present scene. She was in the village church, and not in the court-room. The Judge on the bench was her old pastor in his pulpit. He was preaching, she thought; but something ailed her head, for she could not understand the drift of his discourse. And the church was so crowded, that she felt half-suffocated in it.

Amid the breathless, pulseless silence, the doom of death was spoken.

Not one word of it all did Sybil comprehend. But she felt as if the evening service was over, and the people were rising to leave the church.

"Come, Lyon," she breathed, with a deep sigh, "it is over at last, and oh! I am so tired! Take me home."

Take her home! Alas for the heart-broken husband! He would have given his own body to be burned to death, if by doing so he could have taken her home. But he knew that, in all human probability, she could never go home again.

"One moment, darling," he whispered, and sat her down again to await the action of the sheriff.

Mr. Fortescue soon came up.

"Mr. Berners," he said, in a broken voice, "I am an old man, and I had rather die than do my present duty."

"Oh, do what must be done, do it at once, do it yourself, for no one else would do it so kindly," answered Lyon Berners.

"You know where I must take her?"

"Certainly."

"Then draw her arm through your own and follow me. She will go more quietly with you than with me," said the sheriff.

They had spoken in a very low tone, in order to spare Sybil, though they scarcely needed to have taken the precaution; for she was paying no attention to anything that was passing around her. She sat leaning back, with a look of utter weariness and stupor on her beautiful, pale face.

He raised her up, drew her hand through his arm, and whispered:

"Come, my darling, we are going now."

This roused her a little. She looked around for her party, and saw Beatrix Pendleton sitting with her face buried in her handkerchief, as she had sat since the rendering of the verdict.

"Look, she is asleep. I don't wonder; it is very tiresome, and I'm almost asleep myself," murmured Sybil, wearily gazing on her friend.

At that moment Captain Pendleton came up.

"Wake her, Clement, and bring her after us. You will both come home and take supper with me," said Sybil, as she was about to be led away.

Captain Pendleton did not answer her, but gazed on her as if his heart was about to break.

"Don't look at me so, Clement. You must think I am sick; but I am not— only tired and stupid. I hope Tabby will have supper ready when we get home," said Sybil, with a faint smile, as they led her off.

Captain Pendleton followed quickly, and touched Lyon Berners on the shoulder.

They exchanged glances.

"Oh, Heaven! Is this so?" whispered the captain, with a glance towards Sybil.

"It is so," answered Lyon Berners.

"This affliction added to all the rest!"

"It is better, much better thus. She does not suffer now. Thank Heaven for this veil of insanity drawn between her and the horrors to come! Pray heaven that she may never come to her senses while she lives in this world," muttered Lyon Berners.

Captain Pendleton stepped back and gave his sister his arm.

"You will go with her to the prison?" he inquired.

"Yes, and stay with her there, if I may be permitted," answered Beatrix, who was weeping bitterly.

"My dear, my noble sister! how I admire and thank you!" fervently exclaimed Clement Pendleton, as he led her after Sybil.

A storm had been gathering all the afternoon. It had not been noticed by the people, whose attention had been swallowed up in the absorbing interest of the trial. But now, as they reached the open doors, the storm burst in thunder on the air, and the rain fell in torrents.

Many of the people retreated into the court-room to wait until the weather should be clear, or they should be able to procure umbrellas.

But our unhappy party went boldly out into the rain.

Sybil's carriage had been waiting, as on the preceding evening, to take her home. It was to be employed now to take her somewhere else.

"I am glad of this storm," said Mr. Berners, after he had put his wife into her seat, and while he was holding the door open for Beatrix, whom her brother had just led up. "I am very glad of this storm."

"Why?" inquired Captain Pendleton.

"Because it will enable me to humor the delusion of my poor Sybil."

"How?"

"By persuading her that the storm makes it necessary for us to stop at the house of an acquaintance," hastily explained Lyon Berners, as he put Beatrix into the seat next Sybil.

Then he took the third seat and Mr. Fortescue, as the custodian of Sybil, took the fourth.

Captain Pendleton mounted the box beside the coachman, who had received his directions where to drive, but who could scarcely see his way, for weeping.

The storm came down in fury. The lightning glared, the thunder rolled; the rain swept the mountain sides like a flood.

"We shall never be able to reach Black Hall to-night, my darling. We must stop at some house," said Lyon Berners, artfully.

"Yes? that's bad," answered his wife, who with an evident effort roused herself to reply, and then sank back into her seat, in an attitude of weariness, and began slowly to pick at the fringe of her parasol, in an absent-minded, quiet manner.

The county prison was at the lower end of the village, at the junction of the Black river and Bird creek. It was a plain, rude structure, built of the iron-gray stone dug from the quarries of the Black mountain. It did not look like a prison. But for the grated windows it might have been taken for a commodious country house. And but for its well-cultivated grounds and stone fence, it might have been taken for a store-house. It comprised within its four walls the home of the warden and his family, as well as the lodgings for the turnkeys, and the cells of the prisoners.

Old Father Martin, the warden, found his office almost a sinecure. There were never many inmates of the prison, at any period. And sometimes for months together it would be quite vacant, so that in rainy weather its corridors and cells would be the play-ground of the warden's grandchildren.

Now however, there were some ten or twelve petty offenders confined there, who were waiting trial for such comparatively small offences as disorderly conduct, assault, etc.

Sybil had never in her life seen even the outside of this prison.

So when the carriage drew up before the outer gate, and Mr. Berners alighted and handed her out, and said that they would be obliged to stop here at Mr. Martin's until the storm should be over, she silently acquiesced, and permitted herself to be led, under the shelter of the sheriff's umbrella, up to the door of the building.

At the sheriff's ring, it was opened by the turnkey in attendance.

The sheriff immediately led his prisoner into the warden's office.

They were followed by Mr. Berners and the two Pendletons.

"I was expecting of this here," said the warden, as he drew forward a chair for the lady.

Sybil sank into it, weary, stupefied, apathetic, and utterly unconscious of her real situation.

Beatrix Pendleton sat down by her side and took her hand. Lyon Berners hung over the back of her chair. The little Skye terrier, who had followed the party, jumped upon her lap and coiled itself up there. Sybil noticed no one, but sat curiously contemplating the tips of her gloved fingers.

Meanwhile the sheriff and the warden went off to a writing desk that stood in one corner of the office, and where the sheriff formally delivered up his charge into the keeping of the warden.

"You will find some decent place to put her in, I hope, Martin. You will extend to her every indulgence consistent with her safe custody," said the sheriff, when the business was concluded.

The old warden scratched his gray head, reflected for a minute, and then said:

"The cells is miserable, which I have represented the same to their worships time and again, to no purpose. But if you'll take the responsibility, and back me up into doing of it, I can lock her up in my daughter's bedroom, where she will be safe enough for one night; and to-morrow we can have a cell fixed up, if her friends will go to the expense."

"Certainly, do all that; and if you should be as kind and considerate of her as may be consistent with your duty, her friends will be sure to reward you handsomely," answered Mr. Fortescue.

"Well, I'd do that any way, I think, for any poor woman in such a depth of trouble, reward or no reward," replied the kind-hearted warden.

The two men then went up to the young prisoner.

"I will take you up to your room now, ma'am, if you please," said the warden.

This aroused Sybil. She looked up suddenly and said:

"I am afraid we are putting you to much inconvenience Mr.—Mr.—"

"Martin," added the sheriff.

"—Mr. Martin; but the suddenness of this thunder-*storm, you know. And we were all at church, and—"

She lost the connection of her ideas, ceased to speak, put her hand to her forehead in perplexity for a moment, and then relapsed into apathetic reverie.

"Good gracious!" exclaimed the old warden, in dismay. "Why, she's a losing of her mind, an't she?"

"Yes, thank Heaven!" answered Sybil's husband earnestly.

"But—but—in such a case they will never carry the sentence out?" inquired the warden, in an eager whisper.

"Yes, they will; but she will never know what hurts her," grimly replied Captain Pendleton.

The old warden sighed. And then he warned the visitors that it was time for them to go, as he wanted to lock up the prison for the night.

"Is it not possible that I remain with my wife to-night? You see her condition," said Lyon Berners, appealing to the sheriff and the warden, and pointing to poor Sybil, whose wildly dilated eyes were fixed upon vacancy, while her fingers idly played with the gray curls of the little Skye terrier on her lap.

"Mr. Berners, my heart bleeds at refusing you anything in this hour of bitter sorrow; but—" began the sheriff.

"I see! I see! You cannot grant my request! I should have known it and refrained from asking," interrupted Lyon Berners.

At this point Beatrix Pendleton, who had been sitting beside Sybil, deliberately took off her gloves, bonnet, and lace shawl, and laid them on a table near, saying quietly,

"I shall stay with my friend. Mr. Martin, I don't think you will turn me out in the storm to-night. And, Mr. Sheriff, I *know* that women-friends are often permitted to be in the cell with women prisoners."

"Miss Pendleton," said the sheriff, before the warden could speak, "there is not the slightest objection to your remaining with your friend, if you please to do so. Women in her sad position are always allowed a female companion in the cell. It is usually, however, a female warder."

"Thank you, Mr. Fortescue! I will be Sybil's warder, or her fellow-prisoner, as you please, that is, with Mr. Martin's consent. He has not spoken yet," said Beatrix, appealing to the warden.

"My dear young lady, I would no more turn you out in the storm, as you call it, then I would turn my own daughter out. Of course you will stay if you please, though, bless my heart, the trouble is usually to keep people here, not to send them away. They come unwillingly enough. They go away gladly," said the old man.

"My dear Beatrix, you do well! you do nobly!" whispered her brother, pressing her hand.

"Miss Pendleton, how shall I thank you? May the Lord, who makes up all our shortcomings, reward you infinitely!" said Lyon Berners, fervently pressing her hand.

"I think we had better end this interview now," whispered the sheriff.

Lyon Berners turned to look at his wife. She was still sitting in the same dreamy, abstracted, unconscious manner.

"Sybil, my darling, good-night," he said, stooping and kissing her.

"Why," she exclaimed, with a nervous start, "where are you going?"

"Listen, dear," said Lyon, gently. "Mr. Martin has got but one spare room, and that must be appropriated to you and Beatrix. Clement and myself will have to find accommodations somewhere in the village."

"Oh," she said. And then, "Yes." And so she relapsed into apathy.

Lyon Berners kissed her, and turned away to conceal the tears that rushed to his eyes.

Captain Pendleton pressed her hand in silence. And then they both took leave of Miss Pendleton, and went away with the sheriff.

Sybil and Beatrix were left alone with a warden in the office.

Mr. Martin had been the overseer of Pendleton Park in old Mr. Pendleton's time; and he owed his present position as warden of the county prison mainly to the influence of Captain Pendleton. So that he was well acquainted with Miss Pendleton, whom he had every grateful reason for serving.

He came to her now, saying apologetically:

"I am sorry I can't offer my old employer's daughter better accommodation; but I will give her the best room in the house."

"Thank you, Mr. Martin; but I wish to stay in the cell with my friend," answered Beatrix.

"My dear young lady, I thought you understood that you were to stay with her, but not in a cell; I thought you knew that you were to occupy a room together. But oh! now I recollect, it was only with the sheriff that I talked of it," explained the old man; and as he spoke the door opened, and a middle-aged woman appeared, and said:

"Father, the room is ready."

"Come, then, Miss Pendleton, follow us," said the warden, as he took Sybil's hand, drew it under his arm, and walked on before.

He led them up a flight of stairs to a good-sized and neatly furnished bed-chamber, with nothing about it to remind its inmates that they were in a prison.

Here the warden, after seeing that the windows were carefully secured, left the friends together, taking the precaution to double lock and bolt the door upon them.

Beatrix turned to look at her companion. Sybil was sitting twirling her fingers, and gazing down on the little dog that lay upon her lap.

"Come, darling!" said Beatrix, tenderly, "let me help you to undress. That bed looks clean and comfortable. You must lie down on it and go to sleep."

Sybil made no answer, and no resistance. Beatrix undressed her, and then remembered that they had no personal conveniences for the night whatever, neither bed-gowns nor combs nor brushes; but the weather was warm, and so some of these necessaries might well be dispensed with until the morning.

She led Sybil to the bed, and urged her to lie down. But the force of habit was omnipotent; and in spite of her waning sanity, Sybil suddenly recollected a duty never omitted, and said:

"Let me say my prayers first."

So she knelt down.

Beatrix Pendleton waited and watched for some time, for so long a time, at last, that she suspected Sybil had fallen asleep. She went and looked at her attentively, and then called her by name, and touched her, and so finally discovered that she had, in the midst of her prayers, relapsed into that fearful lethargy that was undermining her reason.

"Come, Sybil, dear, get into bed," said Beatrix, taking her hand and lifting her up.

"Yes," said the docile creature, and immediately did as her friend directed her.

There was no surer or sadder symptoms in Sybil's insanity, than the perfect docility of her who had once been so difficult to manage.

She went quietly to bed.

Beatrix prepared to follow her.

But Miss Pendleton was faint from long fasting. Neither she nor Sybil had tasted anything since their luncheon at two o'clock that day, when the court had taken a recess. They had reached the prison sometime after supper had been served; and in the awful crisis of Sybil's fate, no one had thought of food. Sybil did not seem to require it; she lay in a quiet lethargy, like death. But Beatrix was half-famished when she went to bed.

Her hunger, however, was soon forgotten in the great anxiety of her mind; and the sharpest point of it was this:

What effect would the night's repose have on Sybil's state? Would it bring back her lost senses, and with them the consciousness of her awful condition? Beatrix prayed that it might not—prayed that the shield of insanity might still cover her from the surrounding and impending horrors of her position.

At length both the friends fell asleep, and slept until nearly nine o'clock the next morning.

CHAPTER XVII.

THE MERCIFUL INSANITY.

> Every sense
>
> Had been o'erstrung by pangs intense,
>
> And each frail fibre of her brain,
>
> (As bowstrings when, relaxed by rain,
>
> The erring arrow launch aside,)
>
> Sent forth her thoughts all wild and wide.—BYRON.

They were awakened by the drawing of bolts and turning of locks outside their door, and by the voice of the warden, saying:

"Go in, Kitty, and see if they are up. I will stay outside and guard the door."

And then the same middle-aged widow whom they had seen on the previous night entered the room.

Beatrix being fully awakened, turned anxiously to look at her friend.

Sybil was lying also wide awake, but very quiet.

"What sort of a place is this, Beatrix?" she inquired, and then immediately relapsed into lethargy, as if she had forgotten her question.

"Thank Heaven!" fervently exclaimed Sybil's friend, "she is still shielded."

"Which of you two ladies is in for it?" inquired the warden's daughter, coming forward.

"We are both 'in for it,'" answered Beatrix, a little scornfully, "and one of us is about as guilty as the other."

"Oh, I didn't know that," muttered the woman, who took the lady's words in good faith. "I didn't know there was more than one concerned; but what I meant to ask was, which is Mrs. Berners? Because there is a trunk come for her, which father thinks it contains clothes and other necessaries that she may need at once."

"Very likely. Let your father push it through the door, and I will see to its contents. And oh! for Heaven's sake, my good woman, let us have some breakfast as soon as possible," entreated Miss Pendleton.

The woman promised to comply with her request, and left the room.

The trunk was pushed in, and the door closed, locked, and bolted again.

Beatrix went to examine the consignment. There was a letter directed to Mrs. Berners, unsealed and tied to the handle, together with the key of the trunk.

Beatrix took both off and carried them to her friend, saying "Here is the key of a box that has come for you, and here is a letter, dear Sybil, from your husband, I suppose; will you read it?"

Sybil opened the letter, gazed at it with dreamy eyes, and followed the lines with her glances, but without taking in their meaning.

Sad enough this would have seemed to Miss Pendleton at any other time; but now, every evidence of her friend's failing mind was welcome to her, and to all who loved the unhappy young wife.

"Shall I read it for you, dear?" inquired Beatrix, tenderly, taking the letter from her hand.

"Yes, read it," answered Sybil, rousing herself, for an instant, to some little interest in the matter, and then sinking back into indifference.

Beatrix read aloud. The letter was only an earnestly affectionate greeting from the husband to the wife, telling her that he had sent her a box of needful articles, and that he himself would come to see her as soon as the doors should be opened to visitors. It was a cautiously written letter, so worded as to humor her hallucination, in case she should still imagine herself to be in a country house instead of the county prison.

As Beatrix ended each sentence, she looked around to see if Sybil was listening.

Ah! no; after the first few lines had been read, her attention wandered, and at the end of the note she astonished the reader, by saying:

"I am very thirsty, Beatrix."

"Then, dear, let me help you to rise and dress; and you shall have some tea. They are rough people we are stopping with, so I requested them to bring our breakfast up here," said Miss Pendleton, artfully, and laying aside the note.

Sybil submitted to the services of her friend. And then for the first time Beatrix noticed that in this victim's case physical weakness was now added to mental infirmity. Body and mind were both failing together. "Well, so best," thought Sybil's true friend.

By the time they were both dressed, there was another sound of turning locks and drawing bolts, and then the warden's daughter brought in the tray of breakfast, while the warden himself stood outside on guard.

Notwithstanding the awful situation, both these young women were able to take a little breakfast—poor Sybil because she was quite insensible of the horrors of her position, and Miss Pendleton because, with all her sorrowful sympathy for her companion, she had the appetite of a healthy young woman who had been fasting some eighteen hours.

Soon after the breakfast was over and the service cleared away, Mr. Berners came. Again bolts and bars were drawn, and the husband was ushered in by the warden to see his wife.

Lyon Berners shook hands with Beatrix Pendleton, and then passed at once to Sybil, who sat in a state of reverie on the side of her bed.

"You have come for me at last, Lyon?" she said. "The people here are very kind, but I am very glad you have come, for I want to go home."

"Dear Sybil," he replied, embracing her, and humoring her delusion. "You are not well enough to go home yet; you must stay here a little longer."

"Yes," she said, looking up for a moment, and then relapsing into silence and reverie.

Mr. Berners exchanged a glance with Miss Pendleton.

At the same moment the warden put his head in at the door, and beckoned Mr. Berners to come out into the passage.

"Well," inquired the latter, when he was outside.

"Well, sir," said the warden, "you know she must go into, a regular cell to-day. I can't help it. I wish I could. I pity the poor lady! I do! I pity her, whether she did it or not! And I can't help *that* either! So please the Lord, I'll do all I can to comfort her and her friends, consistent with my duty to the higher powers. So come along, sir, if you please, and I'll show you a corridor where there is no other prisoner now confined, and you can choose the best cell for her yourself."

Lyon Berners bowed and followed his conductor across the broad passage and down another one which was at right angles with the first. Here all the cells were vacant. The warden unlocked several for inspection.

The last cell opened was at the north-east angle of the building. It was twice the size of the others, and had, beside its door, two narrow grated windows— one on the north, looking out upon the Black river, and the other on the east, upon Bird creek.

"Here, sir, now, is a large, cool, well-aired cell, where we used to confine as many as a half a dozen prisoners together, when we was full. But as you see, there is nobody at all in all this corridor. So we can put her in this, and if you like to go to the cost of having it scrubbed and white-washed, why, I'll have it done this morning. Likewise, if you would wish to put in a comfort or two, in way of furniture, there'll be no objection to that neither. There'll be no objection to nothing that don't interfere with her safe keeping, you understand, sir?"

"Yes, I understand and thank you. Pray, have every article of this furniture removed, have the room thoroughly ventilated and cleansed, and while you are doing that I will go up to Black Hall, and send down all that is necessary to make this room decent for my poor wife. Heaven grant that it may prove her death-room!" added the heart-broken husband to himself.

The warden promised compliance with all these requests, and then the two returned to Sybil's room.

"I must leave you, dear, now, for a few hours, but I will certainly be back at the end of that time," said Mr. Berners, caressing his enfeebled wife as he took leave of her.

In the course of that day, the large north-east cell was transformed into as clean and comfortable a bed-room as money and labor could make it. The floor was covered with straw matting, the windows shaded with white muslin curtains.

Besides the fresh bed and bedding, there was a small bureau, a washstand, a toilet set, book-table, writing-desk, dressing-case, and work-box; a guitar, with some music, and a small choice collection of books.

All these comforts were collected there as much for Miss Pendleton's sake as for Sybil's.

The room did not look in the least like a prison-cell, nor was there any legal necessity that it should.

It was late in the afternoon when Sybil and her devoted friend were transferred to the new quarters.

"What is this for?" inquired Sybil, rousing herself a little, when she found she was about to be removed.

"Oh, you know, dear, that we have been sleeping in the daughter's room, and keeping her out of it, and now she wants her own, and so they have fixed up another one for us," said Miss Pendleton, soothingly, as she drew her friend's arm within her own and led her on after the warden, who walked before them with a large bunch of keys in his hand.

"Why, here are all my things!" said Sybil, startled to unusual interest by the sight of her personal effects arranged in the new cell.

"Yes, dear," whispered Miss Pendleton, as she put Sybil gently down into the rocking-chair—"yes, dear. You know Lyon fears that it will be some time before you are able to go home, and these people are too poor to make you comfortable, so he sent these things for them to fix up this room for you."

"Beatrix," said Sybil, putting her hands up to her temples.

"What is it, dear?"

"My head is very bad."

"Does it ache?"

"No; but it is so queer; and I have had a horrid dream—oh! a horrid, ghastly dream; but I can't recall it."

"Don't try, my darling; you took cold in the storm last night, and you are not well now; so turn your thoughts away from your disagreeable dream, and fix them upon something else," said Beatrix soothingly, although at heart she was very much alarmed, as it was probable that the sight of her favorite little effects had started a train of associations that might bring her back to perfect sanity and to utter agony.

At that moment, too, there was a diversion. Lyon Berners entered the cell, bringing in a basket of fruit and flowers.

"From your own garden and conservatories, my dear Sybil. Until you are well enough to go home, you must have some of your home comforts brought here," he said, as he set the elegant basket down on a stand, and went and embraced her.

"Yes; thank you very much, dear Lyon. When do you think I will be well enough to go home?" she asked, and then, without giving the slightest attention to her husband's affectionate answer, she dropped at once into a deep and dreamy state of abstraction.

Miss Pendleton beckoned Mr. Berners to come to her at one of the windows.

"What is it?" inquired Lyon, anxiously.

"She came very near a consciousness of her position just now, when she first recognized her property, but the peril passed away. And now we must be very careful to foster this merciful insanity that shields her from misery. And as one precaution, I wish you would ask the warden to oil these rusty bolts and bars, and make them work noiselessly. She has never noticed that she is locked and bolted in, and I wish her never to notice it, or to suspect it."

"Thanks, a thousand thanks, dear Beatrix! I will follow your suggestions," said Mr. Berners, warmly grasping her hand.

Then the warden turned to the visitor, and told him that the hour had come for locking up the prison for the night.

Mr. Berners went back to his wife and took an affectionate leave of her.

She let him go, with even less of opposition than on the preceding evening, for it seemed as if her fitful rise towards sensibility had reacted in a deeper fall into apathy.

Lyon Berners returned to his desolate home. Among all who were affected by the condemnation of Sybil Berners, there was none who suffered such agony of mind as that which nearly drove her husband to frenzy. If Sybil's terrible trials and unspeakable sorrows had resulted in a mild and merciful insanity, that vailed her mind from any knowledge of the deep horrors of her position, Lyon's utter anguish of spirit had stung him to a state of desperation that incited the wildest schemes and the most violent remedies.

As he lay tossing in his sleepless bed each night, he felt tempted to go and seek out that band of outlaws, and to bribe them to the half of his fortune to make a night attack upon the prison, and forcibly rescue his beloved wife.

There was, however, a serious objection to this plan; for besides its unlawfulness and its uncertainty of success, it was impracticable, from the fact that no one—not even the most experienced thief-catchers—had been able to find the lost clue to the retreat of the robbers. Since their flight from the ruined house, four months previous, they had never been heard of.

Sometimes, as Sybil's husband lay groaning in anguish on his pillow, he was strongly tempted to procure some drug that would give her a quick and easy death, and save her from the horrors to come.

But Lyon Berners resisted this dark temptation to commit a deadly sin.

More frequently still, when his agony seemed greater than he could bear, he would feel a desperate desire to put a period to his own wretched existence.

But then came the devoted spirit that whispered for *her* sake he must live and suffer, as long as she should have to live and suffer.

All these dark trials and temptations tortured Lyon Berners in those sleepless, awful nights he spent alone in his desolate home.

But in the morning, when he would go and visit Sybil in the prison, he not only exerted all his mental powers of self-control, but he called in the aid of powerful sedative drugs to produce the calmness of manner with which he wished to meet his wife.

Meanwhile, as the days passed, Sybil sank deeper and deeper into apathy.

Her hallucination was now complete. She imagined that, in company with her husband and their friends, she had been at church one Sabbath afternoon, when a tremendous storm of thunder, lightning, rain, and wind came up, and that they had all been obliged to take refuge in a country house for the night, and that she herself had been taken ill from the exposure, and had to remain there until she could get well enough to go home. As the days passed and the hallucination grew, she lost all count of time, and always thought that she had arrived "last Sunday," and was going home "to-morrow!"

Miss Pendleton was permitted to remain with her, and Mr. Berners was allowed to visit her every day.

So some weeks had passed, when one day a terrible event occurred.

It was early in the morning: the prison doors were just opened for the admission of visitors, and Lyon Berners had just entered the lower hall, on his way to the warden's office, to get that old man to conduct him to Sybil's cell, when he was overtaken and accosted by the sheriff:

"On your way to your wife, Mr. Berners? That is well. She will need you at this hour," said Mr. Fortescue, after the usual morning greeting.

"What is the matter?" inquired Lyon Berners hurriedly, and in great alarm.

"For Heaven's sake, compose yourself now! You will need all your self-possession, for her sake, as well as for your own. Come into the warden's office with me. He also must go with us to her cell."

In great distress of mind, Mr. Berners followed the sheriff into the warden's office.

Old Mr. Martin, who was at his desk, came to meet the visitors.

"One moment, Martin. I will see you in one moment. Just now, I wish to speak to Mr. Berners," said the sheriff, as he drew Lyon Berners aside.

"What is it now?" inquired Sybil's husband, in an agony of alarm for her sake.

"Can you not surmise?" compassionately suggested the sheriff.

"I—Oh, great Heaven!—I dare not!" he exclaimed, throwing up his hands and clasping his head.

"You must know that the petition sent up to the Governor for her pardon has been returned with an adverse decision."

"I feared it! Oh, heaven!"

"Oh, try to be firm! I must now tell you the worst. The petition did not come down alone—" The speaker paused an instant, and then added gravely and compassionately:

"There was another document came down with it—a document that I must read to her."

"THE DEATH WARRANT!"

Lyon Berners uttered these words with such a groan of anguish and despair as seemed to have rent his soul and body asunder as he reeled and caught at the window frame for support, and then dropped into a chair by its side.

"Mr. Berners, for her sake! for heaven's sake! bear up now! Martin, a glass of brandy here! quick!"

The warden who always kept a bottle on his desk, hurriedly filled a tumbler half full of brandy, and hastened up with it.

"Drink it! drink it all!" said the sheriff, putting the glass into Mr. Berners' hand.

Lyon Berners drank the strong and fiery spirit, feeling it no more than if it had been water.

A few moments passed, during which Mr. Berners struggled hard for self-control, while the warden in a low voice inquired:

"What is it?"

"*The death warrant!*"

As the sheriff whispered these awful words, the warden clasped his hands, saying fervently:

"*Now may the Lord help them both!*"

Then the sheriff turned to Mr. Berners, who had again sank upon a chair, and was still striving to recover himself, and he kindly inquired:

"Are you ready now to go with us to her cell? She will need your support in this trying hour."

"Heaven give me strength! Yes, I am ready!" said Mr. Berners.

And the ministers of fate went to take the death warrant to the cell of Sybil Berners.

CHAPTER XVIII.

HOW SYBIL RECEIVED HER DEATH WARRANT.

She looked on many a face with vacant eye,

On many a token without knowing what;

She saw them watch her without asking why,

And recked not who around her pillow sat.—BYRON.

The warden unlocked the door and entered the cell, followed by the sheriff and Mr. Berners.

Sybil was dressed, but lying on the outside of her bed.

Beatrix was sitting beside her, engaged in some light needle-work.

"She is very feeble both in mind and body to-day," said Beatrix, in answer to an inquiring look of Mr. Berners, as she arose to give him her seat by the bedside.

"How are you this morning, love?" inquired Mr. Berners, tenderly taking her hand.

"Oh! I am better! Shall we go home to-morrow, Lyon?"

"If it please Providence, dear," answered her husband, putting a strong constraint upon himself. But he saw that though she had asked the question, she scarcely heard his answer; her attention had wandered from the point, and she was idly pulling the curly-haired ears of her little dog, who lay coiled up beside her.

Meanwhile Mr. Fortescue had shaken hands with Miss Pendleton, and was now saying:

"Beatrix, my child, you had better retire from this scene for a few moments."

"Why?" inquired Beatrix, looking her old neighbor firmly in the face.

"Because I have a very painful duty to perform, which will be very distressing to you to witness."

"What is it?" inquired Miss Pendleton, without removing her eyes from his face.

The sheriff stooped and told her in a whisper.

She turned pale as death, caught her breath, and leaned for an instant on the table near her. Then, with a supreme effort, she stood up and said:

"You have known me from my childhood. Do you think me such a dastard as to desert my friend in the hour of her utmost need? No, Mr. Fortescue; I will stand by Sybil to the last. So do your duty! Thank Heaven, you cannot hurt her much!"

"Thank Heaven indeed, if that is so, Beatrix," answered the sheriff, as he made a sign to Mr. Berners, and approached the bed with the death warrant in his hand.

"Sybil, darling," whispered her agonized husband, "here is Mr. Fortescue come to see you."

"Has he? that is kind," she answered, looking curiously at her own fingers, and then forgetting the presence of her visitors.

"How are you, Mrs. Berners?" inquired the sheriff.

"I am better. I am going home to-morrow, and then you must come and—" She broke off suddenly, and began to feel about with her fingers over the white counterpane.

"Good Heaven!" exclaimed the sheriff, looking up into Mr. Berner's face.

Lyon Berners gravely bent his head.

The sheriff hesitated, as if uncertain how to proceed.

Mr. Berners came to his side and whispered:

"If you *must* read that document to her, be merciful and read it *now*, when her mind is dulled to its meaning."

The sheriff nodded, and then said:

"Mrs. Berners, I have something to read to you. Can you listen?"

"Yes. Is it interesting?" inquired Sybil, rousing herself.

Without answering that last question, the sheriff prepared to read the awful instrument of doom. Lyon Berners sat down on the side of the bed, and drew his wife's head upon his bosom.

Miss Pendleton sat pale and still as a statue.

The old warden stood with his eyes bent upon the floor.

Sybil roused herself to listen, and she heard the first few lines of preamble addressed to the sheriff, but after that her attention wandered beyond control; and at the conclusion, she slightly smiled, and turning to her husband, said:

"Lyon, be sure to come early to-morrow. I want to go home in the cool of the morning."

"Yes, dear, I shall be here very early," answered Mr. Berners as steadily as he could speak, with his heart breaking.

Then laying her gently back on her pillow, he touched the sheriff on the shoulder and beckoned him to follow to the window.

"You see," said Mr. Berners, as they stood side by side, looking out.

"I see. I am very much shocked. This should be looked into. A medical examination should be made. Another appeal should be sent to the governor. Has Mr. Worth returned to Washington?"

"No; he has been waiting the issue of the petition to the governor."

"Then I advise you to see and consult him without loss of time. Do it now; this morning," urged the sheriff, as he took up his hat and gloves to leave the cell.

He went to Sybil's bedside to take leave of her.

"Good-morning, Mrs. Berners," he said, holding out his hand.

"Good-morning, Mr. Fortescue. Thanks for your call. When you come again—" she began smilingly, but lost the connection of her ideas, and with a look of distress and perplexity she sent her fingers straying over the counterpane, as if in search of something.

With a deep sigh the sheriff left the cell.

And at the same time Lyon Berners quietly kissed his wife, and withdrew.

Mr. Berners went at once to the hotel where Ishmael Worth lodged.

On inquiry at the office, he found that Mr. Worth was in his room. Without waiting to send up his name first, he desired to be immediately shown up to Mr. Worth's presence.

He found the young lawyer sitting at a table, deeply immersed in documents. He was about to apologize for his unceremonious intrusion, when Mr. Worth arose, and with grave courtesy and earnest sympathy, informed his visitor that he had already heard, with deep sorrow, the adverse decision of the governor.

Mr. Berners covered his face with his hand for a moment, and then sank into the chair placed for him by Mr. Worth.

As soon as he had recovered himself, he entered upon the subject of his visit—the insanity of Sybil, and the use that might be made of it in gaining a respite that should prolong her life for some months, until perhaps she might be permitted to die a natural death.

"Her state, as you represent it, gives me hopes of obtaining not only a respite, but a full pardon," said Ishmael Worth, when Mr. Berners had finished his account.

"I scarcely dared to hope as much as that," sighed Mr. Berners.

"I must speak now from the law's point of view. You and I believe that, sane or insane, Mrs. Berners never committed that murder. But the jury says she did. Now if she can be proved to be insane at this time, her present insanity will 'argue a foregone conclusion;' namely, that she was insane at the time she is said to have committed the crime; and if insane, then she was therefore irresponsible for her action, and unamenable to the laws. Let this be satisfactorily proved, and properly set before the governor, and I have little doubt that the result will be a full pardon."

"You give me hope, where I thought hope was impossible. If we can only obtain this pardon, and get my dear wife out of her horrible position, I will take her at once to some foreign country, where, far from all these ghastly associations, she may live in peace, and possibly recover her reason, and where she may have some little share of earthly happiness even yet," sighed Lyon Berners.

"And if it can be shown that there has been insanity in her family, it will make our argument much stronger. Has such ever been the case?" earnestly inquired Ishmael Worth.

"Ah, no! unless the most violent passions roused at times to the most ungovernable fury, and resulting in the most heinous deeds, can be called insanity, there is none in her family," said Mr. Berners sadly, shaking his head.

"That is also insanity certainly," said the philosophical Ishmael Worth, "but scarcely of the sort that could be brought forward in her favor."

"Nor is it the type of her present mental malady, which is very, very gentle."

"However, we have ground enough to go upon. Our case is very strong. We must lose no time. The first step to be taken will be to procure an order to have the lady examined by physicians competent to form a judgment, and make a report upon her condition. Their report must go up to the governor, with the petition for her pardon. And now, Mr. Berners, if you will go home and seek the rest you need, and leave this business in my hands, I will set about it immediately," said Ishmael Worth, kindly.

"Thank you! I thank you from my soul! I will confidently leave her fate in your hand. I know I could not leave it in any better under heaven! But, tell me, when shall I see you again?"

"To-morrow morning, after your visit to the prison, you can call here if you please, and I shall be able to report some progress," said Mr. Worth, rising from his chair.

Lyon Berners then shook hands with him, and left the room.

Not to go home and rest, as he had been advised; there was no rest for Sybil's husband; there could be none now; he went to wander around and around her prison walls until the day declined and the sky darkened, and then indeed he turned his steps homeward, walking all the way to Black Hall, because in his mental excitement he could not sit still in carriage or saddle. There he passed the night in sleeplessness and horror. Imagination, favored by the darkness, the stillness, and the loneliness of the scene, conjured up all the ghastly spectres of the future, impending tragedies, and nearly drove him into frenzy. He started up from his bed and walked out into the summer night under the shining stars, and wandered up and down the wooded banks of the river until morning.

Then he returned to the house, and after a hasty breakfast, which for him consisted only of a cup of very strong coffee, he set out for Blackville.

He reached the prison before its doors were open to visitors, and he waited until he could be admitted. He found Sybil placid, peaceful, and unconscious of imprisonment and deadly peril of her life, as she had ever been. He spent an hour with her, and then he went to the hotel to see Mr. Worth.

He found the young lawyer in good spirits.

"I have made much progress, Mr. Berners. I succeeded in procuring the order for the medical examination. It is appointed for to-morrow at ten o'clock. Dr. Bright, Dr. Hart, and Dr. Wiseman are the physicians authorized to make it. They have all been notified, and are to meet at the prison at the hour specified," said Ishmael Worth, as he shook hands with his visitor and offered him a chair.

Lyon Berners warmly expressed his thanks, and sank into the seat.

"You look very ill, Mr. Berners; you look as if you had not slept for many nights. That will not do. Let me be your physician for once, as well as your lawyer. Let me advise you to take opium at night. You *must* sleep, you see."

"Thanks; but I think my malady beyond the help of medicine, Mr. Worth, unless it were something that should send me into the eternal sleep," said Lyon Berners, mournfully.

"Come, come; take courage! We have every reason to believe that this medical examination will result in such a report as, sent up to the governor with the new petition, will insure her release. And then you will carry out your purpose of going with her to some foreign country. Gay France, beautiful Italy, classic Greece, good old England, are all before you where to choose," said Ishmael Worth, cheerfully.

Then they spoke of the three physicians who were to conduct the examination: Dr. Bright, who had once had charge of the State Insane Asylum, but who had recently retired to his plantation in this neighborhood; Dr. Hart, who was the oldest and most skilful practitioner in the county, having attended more families, and first introduced more children to their friends and relations, than any other man in the place; and lastly, Dr. Wiseman, the village druggist, who had taken his degree, and was also physician to the county prison.

"Dr. Hart has attended Sybil's family for nearly half a century; he has known Sybil from her earliest infancy; his visit will not alarm her, though, for that matter, nothing alarms her now, not even—" He did not finish the sentence; he could not bear to utter the words that would have completed it.

Soon after he arose and took his leave. And he passed the day and night as he had passed the last and many previous days and nights.

CHAPTER XIX.

THE EXAMINATION.

Alas how is it with you?

That you do bend your eyes on vacancy.

And——SHAKESPEARE.

The next morning he was early as usual at the prison, and as usual he had to wait until the doors were opened.

The news of the impending medical examination of the prisoner had been conveyed to the warden on the preceding afternoon. The prisoner and her companion had been notified of it this morning, so that when Lyon Berners was admitted to the cell he found the place in perfect order, and Sybil and Beatrix carefully dressed as if for company.

"See! we are all ready to receive our visitors, Lyon. And oh! I am so glad to be at home again, and to give a dinner party! Like old times! Before we went on our wedding tour, Lyon!"

These were the first words Sybil addressed to her husband, as he entered the room.

Lyon Berners drew her to his bosom, pressed a kiss on her lips, and then signed to Miss Pendleton to follow him to the window.

"What does all this mean, dearest Beatrix?" he inquired.

"If means that her insanity is increasing. She awoke this morning, perhaps with some dream of home still lingering in her mind; at all events, with the impression that she was at Black Hall. I have not combated the pleasant delusion; indeed I have rather fostered it."

"You were right, dear friend. You know of this intended visit of the physicians?"

"Oh, yes; and so does she, only she fancies that they are to be her guests at a dinner party."

As Beatrix thus spoke, there was a sound of approaching footsteps in the corridor, and the cell door was again opened to admit Dr. Hart.

The good physician shook hands with Mr. Berners, who stood nearest the door, and whispering hastily:

"I wish to speak with you apart presently," he passed on to meet Sybil, who, with the courtesy of a hostess, was coming forward to welcome him.

He shook hands with her pleasantly, and inquired after her health.

"Oh, thanks! I am very well since I got home. I took cold. Where did I take cold?" she said, with an air of perplexity, as she passed her thin white hand through her silken black tresses.

"You have been travelling, then?" said the doctor, to try her memory.

"Yes; travelling."

"And saw many interesting sights, no doubt?"

"I—yes; there were caves—the Mammoth Cave, you see; and ships in the harbor; and—and—" A look of doubt and pain passed over her, and she became silent.

"And many, many more attractive or instructive objects met your sight, no doubt?"

"Yes; we were in England just before the Conquest, and I saw Harold the Saxon and Edith the Fair. But 'Fair' was 'foul' then—so foul that the Spirit of Fire consumed her. Oh!—"

She paused, and an expression of horrible anguish convulsed her beautiful face.

"But you are at home now, my child," said the doctor soothingly, laying his hand upon her head.

"Oh, yes," she answered, with a sigh of deep relief as her countenance cleared up; "at home now, thank Heaven! And oh, it is so good to be at home, and to see my friends once more. And then again, you know—"

Whatever she was going to say was lost in the chaos of her mind. She sighed wearily enough now, and relapsed into profound reverie.

The doctor took advantage of her abstraction to leave her side, and beckon to Mr. Berners to follow him to the farthest corner of the cell, so as to be out of hearing of the two ladies.

"What do you think of her case?" anxiously inquired. Sybil's husband, as soon as he found himself apart with the physician.

"She is deranged of course. Any child could tell you that. But, Mr. Berners, I called you apart to tell you that myself and my colleagues, Bright and Wiseman, determined to visit our patient singly, and to make a separate examination of her. Now, for certain reasons, and among them, because I am a family practitioner, we all agreed that I should pay her the first visit. And now, Mr. Berners, I must ask you to go and find out if there is an experienced matron about the house; and if so, to bring her here immediately."

Lyon Berners bowed and went out, but soon returned with the warden's widowed daughter.

"Here is Mrs. Mossop, doctor," he said, introducing the matron.

"How do you do, madam? And now, Mr. Berners, I must further request that you will take Miss Pendleton out and leave Mrs. Mossop and myself alone with our patient," said the doctor.

Mr. Berners gave Miss Pendleton his arm and led her from the room.

One of the under-turnkeys locked the door and stood on guard before it.

Mr. Berners and Miss Pendleton walked up and down the corridor in restless anxiety.

"My brother was here to see me yesterday afternoon, Lyon," she said.

But Mr. Berners, absorbed in anxiety for his wife, scarcely heard the young lady's words, and certainly did not reply to them.

But Beatrix had something else to say to him, and so she said it:

"Lyon, if you should succeed in getting Sybil's pardon, (pardon for the crime she never committed!) and should decide to take her to Europe, do you know what Clement and myself have determined to do?"

"No," said Mr. Berners, with a weary sigh.

"We have decided to go abroad with you and share your fate; whether we go for a year or two of pleasant travelling and sight-seeing, or whether we go into perpetual exile."

Lyon Berners, who had been almost rudely indifferent to the young lady's words until this moment, now turned and looked at her with astonishment, admiration, and gratitude, all blended in the expression of his fine countenance.

"Beatrix! No! I appreciate your magnanimity! And I thank you even as much as I wonder at you! But you must not make this sacrifice for us," he said.

Miss Pendleton burst into tears.

"Oh!" she said amid her sobs; "there can be nothing in the world so precious to us as our childhood's friendships! Clement and I have played with Sybil and you since we were able to go alone! We have no parents, nor sisters, nor brothers, to bind us to our home. We have only our childhood's friends that have grown up with us—you and Sybil. Clement will resign his commission in the army; he does not need it, you know, any more than his country now needs him; and we will let the old manor house, and go abroad with you!"

"But, dear Beatrix, to expatriate yourselves for us!"

"Oh, nonsense!" she said, brushing the bright tears from her blooming face. "You are trying to make this out an act of generosity on our part. It is no such thing. It is a piece of selfishness in us. It will be a very pleasant thing, let me tell you, to go to Europe, and travel about and see all the old historic countries, for a year or so."

"A year or so! Oh, Beatrix! it will not be a year or so, of pleasant travelling! It will be the exile of a lifetime!"

"I don't believe it! I have more faith than that! I believe that

'Ever the right comes uppermost,
And ever is justice done;'

sooner or later, you know! And anyhow Clement and myself have resolved to go abroad with you and Sybil! And you cannot prevent us, Mr. Berners!"

"I am very glad that I cannot; for if I could, Beatrix, I should feel bound by conscience to do it."

"Set your conscience at rest, Mr. Berners! It has nothing to do with other people's deeds!"

"But, dear Beatrix, you are reckoning without your host, Destiny, which now means the report of the medical examiners and the action of the governor upon it! She may not be free to go to Europe."

"I think she will," said Beatrix, cheerfully.

At that moment there was a knock from the inside of the cell.

The turnkey unlocked the door.

Dr. Hart came out alone, and the door was locked after him.

Mr. Berners left the side of Beatrix, and went to meet the physician.

"Well?" inquired Sybil's husband.

"My dear sir, hope for the best. She has yet to be visited by my colleague, Dr. Bright, late of the State Insane Asylum. He is, of course, an expert in cases of insanity. His report will have more weight than mine in regard to her case. But I tell you this in confidence. I ought really not to give any sort of opinion to any one at this point of the investigation."

And with a friendly shaking of hands and a polite bow, Dr. Hart went below.

A few minutes passed, and Dr. Bright, who was a stranger to Mr. Berners, came up and passed to the door of the cell, which was opened for him by the turnkey in attendance.

The "mad doctor," as he was popularly called, remained more than an hour shut up with his patient.

At length he came out, bowed to the lady and gentleman that he saw waiting in the corridor, and went down stairs.

Mr. Berners would have given much for the privilege of questioning the "mad doctor;" but as such a privilege could not be obtained at any price, he was forced to bear his suspense as well as he could.

In a few moments Dr. Bright was succeeded by Dr. Wiseman, the least important of the three medical examiners.

He saw Mr. Berners, came right up to him and grasped his two hands with both his own, and with the tears springing to his eyes, exclaimed:

"I hope to heaven our examination of this lady may eventuate in her release from captivity."

There was something in the delicacy of the physician's words, as well as in the earnestness of his manner, that deeply affected Sybil's husband. He pressed the young doctor's hands as he replied:

"I thank you very much for your earnest sympathy; and I need not say how devoutly I join in your prayer that this investigation may terminate in the release of my dear and most innocent wife."

The physician then passed into the cell, which was opened for his admittance, and then closed as before.

A half hour went by, and he came out again.

"I do not know what conclusion my colleagues have come to, Mr. Berners; but for myself, I do not think this lady is, or has been for some time, a responsible agent," he said, in passing Sybil's anxious husband.

"You hold your consultation immediately?" inquired Mr. Berners.

"Yes, immediately, in the warden's private parlor, which Mr. Martin offered for our use," answered Dr. Wiseman, as he bowed and went down stairs.

Mr. Berners and Miss Pendleton were then permitted to return to Sybil's cell, to remain with her while waiting the result of the physicians' consultation.

They found Sybil so fatigued from the visits that had been made her, that she lay quite still and almost stupefied upon her bed.

Mrs. Mossop was watching by her side; but at the entrance of Mr. Berners and Miss Pendleton she arose and left the cell.

Lyon went to the bedside of his wife, and asked how she felt.

"Tired."

This was the only word she spoke, as with a heavy sigh she turned her face to the wall.

Lyon and Beatrix sat with her all the afternoon, and even until the warden came to the door with the information that the physicians had concluded their consultation, and were about to leave the prison, and that Mr. Worth was below, waiting to see Mr. Berners.

CHAPTER XX.

THE LAST EXPEDIENT.

———'Tis late before

The brave despair.—THOMPSON.

Lyon then took an affectionate leave of his half-conscious wife, shook hands with Miss Pendleton, and with a heart full of anxiety went down stairs.

He met Ishmael Worth coming out of the warden's office.

"The physicians have gone," said the young lawyer, after greeting Mr. Berners—"just gone; but they have left a copy of their report, the original of which they will have to deliver under oath. That original document will have to go with the petition to the governor, which I myself will take up to Richmond to-morrow."

"Thanks! thanks!" exclaimed Mr. Berners, pressing the young lawyer's hand with deep emotion.

"And now, shall we adjourn to my chambers and examine this report?"

"Yes, if you please! But can you not give me some idea of its character?"

"It is favorable to our views. That is all I know. We can soon make ourselves acquainted with the whole matter, however," said Ishmael Worth, as they left the prison and walked rapidly off in the direction of the village.

As soon as they were both closeted together in Mr. Worth's chamber, with the door closed and locked to keep off intruders, the young lawyer broke the seal of the envelope, and they examined the report together.

But ah! that report, though favorable to the prolongation of Sybil's life, was not conducive to its preservation.

The physicians reported the imprisoned lady as having been carefully examined by themselves and found to be insane. But they gave it as their unanimous opinion that her insanity was not constitutional or hereditary: that it was not of long standing, or of a permanent character; that, in fine, it was the effect of the terrible events of the last few months acting upon a singularly nervous and excitable organization, rendered even more susceptible by her present condition, which was that of pregnancy.

At this word Lyon Berners started, threw his hands to his head, and uttered a cry of insupportable anguish.

Ishmael Worth laid his hand soothingly, restrainingly upon him, saying:

"Be patient! Even this circumstance, sad as it seems, may save her life. We do not 'cut down the tree with blossoms on it.' This report, as I said, must go up with the petition to the governor. The petition prays for her full pardon on the grounds set forth in this report. The governor may or may not grant the full pardon; but if he does not, he *must* grant her a respite until after the birth of her child. Thus her life is sure to be prolonged, and may, probably *will*, be saved. For if the governor does not pardon her, still in the long interval afforded by the respite, we may, with the help of Providence, be able to discover the real criminal in this case, and bring him to justice; and thus vindicate her fame, as well as save her life."

"You give me hope and courage; you always do," answered Lyon Berners, gratefully.

"I only remind you of what you yourself know to be facts and probabilities; and would recognize as such, but for the excitement and confusion of your mind. And now, do you know what I mean to do?"

Mr. Berners gravely shook his head.

"I mean to leave for Richmond by to-night's stage-coach, taking with me the original attested medical report and the petition for her pardon. I mean to travel day and night, so as to lay the documents before the governor at the earliest possible moment. And as soon as he shall have acted upon them I shall leave Richmond for this place, travelling day and night until I bring you her pardon or her respite."

"How shall I thank you? What words can express how much—" began Mr. Berners, with emotion; but Ishmael Worth scarcely heard him. He had stepped across the room and touched the bell-pull.

"Send my attendant here," he said to the waiter who appeared at the door.

A few moments elapsed, and a venerable old negro man of stately form and fine features, with a snow-white head and beard, and dressed quite like a gentleman—a sort of an ideal Roman senator carved in ebony, entered the room, bowed, and stood waiting.

"Be so kind as to pack my portmanteau, professor. I go to Richmond by the nights coach."

The "professor" bowed again, and then respectfully inquired:

"Do I attend you, sir?"

"No, professor. I must travel day and night without stopping. Such haste would be too harassing to a man of your age."

The old servitor bowed, and withdrew to obey.

"He," said Ishmael Worth, pointing affectionately to the retreating form of the professor, "is not only my faithful attendant, but my oldest and most esteemed friend."

"He is happy in possessing your esteem and friendship, Mr. Worth, and no doubt he deserves both," said Lyon Berners.

"He deserves much more," murmured Ishmael softly, with one of the old, sweet, thoughtful smiles shining in his eyes.

Then Mr. Berners, who would have liked to linger longer near this sympathizing friend, who was working so zealously in the almost hopeless cause of his imprisoned wife, saw that the young lawyer had many preparations to make for his sudden journey, and but little time to make them in; and so he arose and shook hands with Ishmael Worth, and bade him God-speed in his humane errand, and left the room.

Mr. Berners returned to his most desolate home; took, by his physician's advice a powerful narcotic, and slept the sleep of utter oblivion, and waked late on the next morning more refreshed than he had felt for many weeks past.

He visited his wife as usual, and found her in the same quiescent state of mind and body and still utterly unconscious of her situation, utterly ignorant that within a few days past the dread death warrant had been read to her, which doomed her young life to die in the beautiful month of June, now so near at hand—in the blooming month of roses, her favorite of all the twelve.

Yes, the death warrant had been duly read to her, but not one word of it all had she understood; and that was all that had been done to inform her of her real situation. If it was any one's duty to impress the truth upon her mind, provided her mind could be made capable of receiving the impression, every one shrunk from it, and prayed that to the last she might never know more of her condition than she now did.

As for the rest—the preparation of her soul to meet her Judge—what would have been the use of talking, about salvation to a poor young creature driven to insanity by the horrors of a false accusation and an unjust conviction?

The best Christians, as well as her nearest friends, were willing to leave her soul to the mercy of Heaven.

She was even unsuspicious that she was destined to be a mother.

This circumstance, that so deepened the pathos and terror of her position, also invested her with a more profound and pathetic interest in the eyes of her husband.

Would she live to bring forth her child, even though the governor did spare her life so long? he asked himself, as he gazed fondly on her pale face and sunken eyes.

Would the child—perhaps destined to be born in the prison—live to leave it? And then, what must happen to the mother? And what must be the after life for the child?

And fondly as he loved, he earnestly prayed that both mother and child might die in the impending travail unless—unless the new petition sent up to the governor, and grounded upon the report of the physicians, should get her a full pardon.

Four days of the keenest anxiety crept slowly by.

There was no possible means of hearing how Ishmael Worth prospered in his mission to the governor.

There were but two mails a week from Richmond to Blackville.

Ishmael Worth would go and come with all possible speed, for he must be his own messenger.

It was on the morning of the fifth day, since the young lawyer departed on his humane errand.

Lyon Berners was making his usual morning visit to his wife in her cell.

She was sitting as placidly unconscious of danger as usual, in her harmless hallucination, playing with her little dog, which was coiled up on her lap.

Beatrix Pendleton, who had scarcely left Sybil for an hour since her imprisonment, sat gravely and quietly near, engaged as usual upon some little trifle of needle-work.

And Lyon Berners sat purposely with his back to the light to shade his face, and hide the uncontrollable agitation of his countenance, as he gazed upon his doomed wife, and shuddered to think of the awful issues at stake in the success or failure of Ishmael Worth's mission.

Should this second petition be more fortunate than the first one, and should Mr. Worth succeed in obtaining for her a full pardon, Sybil might go forth this very day a free woman, and her husband might take her far away from these scenes of suffering to some fair foreign land, where she might recover her reason and her peace of mind.

Should Mr. Worth fail in obtaining a full pardon, but succeed in gaining a respite, Sybil would be permitted to live, if she could, long enough to bring forth her child, and then her own forfeited life must be yielded up.

But should her advocate fail also to obtain the respite, Sybil had just one week to live; for on the seventh day from this, she was ordered for death!

And she, shielded by a mild and merciful insanity, was so peacefully unconscious of impending doom!

But to-day he knew that he must hear the best or the worst that could befall her; for to-day the Richmond coach would arrive, and would bring her zealous advocate, Ishmael Worth.

And even while he sat thus gazing with his grief-dimmed eyes upon his fated young wife, the sound of approaching footsteps was heard; the cell door was unlocked, and the warden presented himself, saying in a low tone:

"Mr. Worth has just arrived, and wishes to see you down stairs in my office, sir."

Before the warden had finished his sentence, Lyon Berners had started up and sprung past him.

He hurried down the stairs, threw open the door of the warden's office and confronted Ishmael Worth, who, pale, weary, travel-stained, and troubled, stood before him.

"For Heaven's sake!" cried Sybil's husband, breathlessly—"speak! what news? Is it to be *death*,—or—LIFE!"

CHAPTER XXI.

ISHMAEL WORTH'S NEWS.

Even through the hollow eye of Death

I spy Life peering; but I dare not say

How near the tidings of our comfort is.—SHAKESPEARE.

"Life, or death?" cried Lyon Berners, pallid with intense anxiety.

"It is a respite," answered Ishmael Worth, gravely and kindly, taking the arm of the agitated man and gently leading him towards a chair.

"Only that!" groaned Lyon Berners, as he dropped heavily into the offered seat.

"But that is much," soothingly began Ishmael Worth, "very much, for it is an earnest of—"

"How long?" moaned Mr. Berners, interrupting his companion.

"During the pleasure of the governor. No new day has been appointed for her—*death*!" added the young lawyer, in a low voice and after a short pause, for he could not bear to utter the other awful word of doom.

"Go on!" said Sybil's husband, still violently shaken by his emotions.

Ishmael Worth arose from the seat into which he had sunk for a moment, and he laid his hand on the shoulder of the suffering man and said:

"Try to calm the perturbation of your spirits, Mr. Berners, so that you can hear and comprehend what I am about to communicate to you."

"I will."

"Listen, then. You are aware that the respite, for an indefinite period, of any condemned person, is almost always the prelude to the full pardon."

"Yes."

"Mrs. Berners has a respite for an indefinite period. I consider that respite an earnest of her full pardon. You do not doubt my sincerity in saying this?"

"No."

"Listen yet longer. As no new day has been set for her death, so I think no further action will be taken in the matter until after the birth of her child— and some considerable time after that event. And then, I think, a full pardon will be granted her."

"'Hope deferred!'" began Mr. Berners, with a deep sigh.

"Yes, I know," said Ishmael Worth, with a grave smile; "but hear me out."

"I am listening."

"I had several interviews with the governor, and though he was very reserved in communicating his sentiments, I perceived that he really wished to pardon his petitioner."

"Then why, in the name of Heaven, did he not do so?" demanded Mr. Berners, starting up from his seat.

"Be calm and I will tell you," said Ishmael Worth, gently drawing him down into the chair.

Again Lyon Berners dropped into it with a deep groan.

"If it were not that trouble has so disturbed the clearness of your mind, you would yourself see that men in authority cannot do these things so suddenly. I repeat that I perceived that the governor would gladly have granted the pardon immediately upon the presentation of the petition, founded as it was upon such strong grounds, and he was only deterred from doing so by the fact that at the present point of time such a pardon would be a very unpopular measure."

"That a lady's innocent life should fall a sacrifice to a politician's selfish love of popularity!" bitterly commented Lyon Berners.

Ishmael Worth was silent for a moment, because he felt the injustice of Lyon Berners' remarks, yet did not wish to rebuke them, and then he said, deprecatingly:

"I do not think the governor's course here was directed by any selfish policy. He feels that he must be guided in a great degree by the will of the people, who are now most unjustly certainly, but most violently set against Mrs. Berners. So he sends down the respite, to which, under the peculiar circumstances, no one can object, and sends it as a prelude to the pardon which I believe will certainly follow when the popular excitement has had time to subside."

"Heaven grant it may be so," fervently prayed Lyon Berners.

"And now," said Ishmael Worth, drawing from his breast pocket a sealed parcel directed to the sheriff of the county, "I must take this document to Mr. Fortescue at once."

"I will not detain you, then. A thousand thanks for your kindness! I pray Heaven that some day I may be able to return it," fervently exclaimed Lyon Berners, rising from his chair.

Ishmael Worth took his hand and held it while he looked earnestly in his face, and said:

"You have every good reason now to hope for the best; so much reason not only to hope, but to feel assured of her release, that I should counsel you to begin at once your preparations to leave the country, so as to be able to start on your voyage with her immediately after the pardon arrives."

"Thanks for your words of comfort! Thanks for your counsel! I always leave your presence, Mr. Worth, with new life!" warmly exclaimed Lyon Berners, cordially grasping and shaking the hands that held his own.

Then Ishmael Worth took leave and went away.

Lyon Berners returned to the cell of his wife. He was admitted by the turnkey in attendance.

He found Sybil fast asleep, on the outside of her bed. Beatrix was sitting by her, strumming low, soft notes on the guitar as an accompaniment to a soothing air that she was singing.

"What news?" exclaimed the young lady in half-suppressed eagerness.

"There is a respite for an indefinite period, that Mr. Worth thinks is a certain prelude to a future pardon," answered Mr. Berners, seating himself beside his wife's bedside.

"Thank Heaven!" fervently exclaimed Beatrix. "But why not the full pardon at once?"

Mr. Berners explained the reasons for the delay.

"The people are even more cruel and unjust than the law! But still—oh! thank Heaven for so much hope and comfort as we have!" she said.

"Mr. Worth feels so sure of the pardon, that he advises me to make all necessary preparations, so as to be able to leave the country immediately upon my wife's liberation," added Mr. Berners.

"That will be glorious! Oh! do you know that advice seems so practical that it gives me more confidence than anything else which has been said?" exclaimed Miss Pendleton, eagerly. "I will tell Clement to begin to get ready at once! For you know we are set to go with you!"

"God bless you!" was the only response of Lyon Berners. Then he inquired, "How did my dear wife happen to fall asleep at this hour?"

"She laid down to rest. Then I took the guitar and sang to her and she fell asleep like an infant."

At that moment Sybil awoke with a smile, and greeted her husband pleasantly.

He stooped and kissed her; but said nothing of the respite, because she was still happily unconscious of any necessity for such a thing. Neither did he speak of the possible voyage to Europe; deeming it premature to mention such a hope yet, lest she should, in her innocent ignorance of her real position, chatter of it to her visitors, and so do her cause harm.

He staid with her until the prison regulations for closing the doors at six o'clock in the afternoon, obliged him to take leave and depart.

Then he went home in a more hopeful frame of mind than he had enjoyed for many weeks.

The summer was slipping swiftly away.

Since the arrival of her respite for so long and indefinite a period, it had been deemed proper by the warden to accord to his charge many valuable privileges that she had not enjoyed, nor indeed, in her unconsciousness of her real situation and indifference to all external circumstances, had not missed in her imprisonment.

She was now permitted to walk in the shaded grounds and blooming gardens within the walled inclosure around the prison.

Here, through the influence of fresh air and gentle exercise, her physical health improved very much, though her mental malady remained unmodified.

Here, also, some members of her household from Black Hall, were admitted to see her.

Hitherto Miss Tabby, Raphael, and even little Cromartie had been carefully excluded from her presence, lest the violent emotion of the woman and the youth, or the innocent prattle of the child, should suddenly strike

"The electric chord wherewith we are darkly bound,"

and shock her into a full consciousness of the awful position which her friends were now more than ever anxious to conceal from her knowledge. For they argued, if only this mist of insanity could be kept around her for a little while longer, until the hoped-for pardon should come, then she need never know that she had been the inmate of a prison or stood within the shadow of the scaffold.

It was the opinion of her physician, and the fear of her friends, that her reason would return with the birth of her child; and they prayed that it might not do so until she should be free from the prison.

And so they had guarded her from all associations that might suddenly bring back her memory and her understanding; and therefore had denied the visits of her faithful and afflicted servants and *protégés* from Black Hall.

Now, however, after she had been some weeks enjoying the privilege of daily exercise in the fresh air of the grounds, and her health had gained so much, her harmless hallucination began to take a pleasing and favorable turn.

She now knew that she was going to be a mother; and she fancied that she was staying at some pleasant place of summer resort for the benefit of her health, and that Beatrix Pendleton was also one of the guests of the house; and that Lyon Berners was only an occasional visitor because the duties of his profession confined him the greater part of the time at Blackville.

It happened one morning, when Sybil was taking her usual exercise in the garden, attended by her husband and her friend, she suddenly turned to Mr. Berners and said:

"Lyon dear, I want to see Tabby and Joe. The next time you come to see me, I wish you would bring them with you."

"I will do so, dear Sybil. Is there any one else you would like to see?" inquired her husband, who deemed now that, with proper precautions, her friends from Blackville might be permitted to see her.

"No, no one else particularly," she answered.

"Are you sure?"

"Why, yes, Lyon, dear; I am sure I do not care to see anybody else especially. Why, who is there indeed, that I should care for at Black Hall, except my own faithful servants?" she asked, a little impatiently. She had never once, since her imprisonment, mentioned the name of Raphael or little Cromartie. She had apparently forgotten them, as well as all other persons and circumstances immediately connected with the tragedy at Black Hall and the trial at Blackville.

And Mr. Berners would not venture to remind her of their existence.

"Very well, dearest, I will bring your friends to see you to-morrow," said Mr. Berners soothingly.

CHAPTER XXII.

HOPE.

One precious pearl, in sorrow's cup,

Unmelted at the bottom lay.

To shine again when, all drunk up,

The bitterness should pass away.—MOORE.

But if Sybil in the chaos of her mind, had lost all memory of her two protégés, *they* had not for a moment forgotten her.

Raphael, who was perfectly well aware of Sybil's situation, was breaking his heart at Black Hall. And every morning when little Cro' was set up in his high chair beside Mrs. Berners' vacant place at the head of the breakfast table, he would ask piteously:

"If 'Sybil-mamma,' was coming home to-day?" And every morning he would be answered, evasively:

"May be, to-day or to-morrow."

The day succeeding his promise to his wife, Mr. Berners informed Miss Tabby that he should take her to the prison to see Sybil, and requested her to get ready at once to go. And at the same time he sent a message to Joe to put the horses to the carriage and prepare to drive them.

Miss Tabby, at the prospect of meeting Sybil, whom she had not seen for some months, burst into a fit of loud hysterical sobbing and crying, and could not be comforted.

Mr. Berners had patience with her, and let the storm take its course, knowing that it would be followed by a calm that would best prepare the poor creature to meet her lady.

When Miss Tabby was composed enough to listen to him, Mr. Berners very impressively said to her:

"You must remember Mrs. Berner's mental derangement, that renders her utterly unconscious of her imprisonment, and unconcerned about her future, and you must be very cautious neither to betray any emotion at the sight of her, nor to make any allusion to the murder or the trial, or to any person or event connected with either; for she has forgotten all about it."

"That is a wonderful blessing indeed, and I would bite my tongue off sooner than say anything to disturb her," said Miss Tabby, with a few subsiding sobs.

The same admonition which he had administered to Miss Tabby was also emphatically impressed upon the mind of Joe. And the old man was even more ready and able to understand and act upon it than the old maid had been.

When Raphael and little Cro' found out that Mr. Berners was going to take Miss Tabby to see Mrs. Berners, they both pleaded to go with him also.

But this could not in either case be permitted.

To Raphael Mr. Berners explained the case of his wife, and sent the boy away more sorrowful, if possible, than before.

To little Cro' he gave his gold pencil and his new blank note-book from his pocket, that the child might amuse himself with drawing "pictures," and he promised to take him to see "Sybil-mamma" at some future day.

It was yet early in the forenoon when the carriage from Black Hall rolled through the prison gates, and drew up before the great door of the building.

Miss Tabby groaned and sighed heavily as she followed Mr. Berners into the gloomy hall.

They were met by one of the turnkeys, who informed Mr. Berners that Mrs. Berners and Miss Pendleton were taking the air in the walled garden behind the building.

Preceded by the turnkey and followed by Miss Tabby, Lyon Berners went through the hall out at the grated back door, and through the walled back yard, and through another heavy gate into the strongly enclosed and well-shaded garden, where he found his wife and her friend sitting under the trees.

This was so much better than anything Miss Tabby had expected to see, that her depressed spirits rose at once as she hurried after Mr. Berners to meet Sybil, who, with Beatrix, had arisen to receive him.

Mr. Berners had scarcely time to embrace his wife and shake hands with Miss Pendleton, before Miss Tabby rushed past him, caught Sybil in her arms, and forgetting all Mr. Berners' cautions and her own promises, fell to sobbing and crying over her foster-child, and exclaiming:

"Oh, my lamb! my baby! my darling! And is it here I find you, my darling! my baby! my lamb!" etc., etc., etc.

"Why, you foolish old Tabby, what are you howling for now? Haven't you got over your habit of crying for every thing yet, you over-grown old infant?" asked Sybil, laughing, as she extricated herself from the clinging embrace, and sat down.

"I know I'm an old fool," whimpered Miss Tabby, as she wiped her eyes, and leaning up against the bole of the tree.

"To be sure you are! Everybody knows that! But you are a dear, good old Tabby, for all; and I am delighted to see you. And now aren't you going to speak to Miss Pendleton?"

"Oh, yes! how do you do, Miss Beatrix? inquired the old woman, as she courtesied and offered her hand to Miss Pendleton.

"I am well and glad to see you, Miss Tabby," answered the young lady, cordially.

"And oh, Miss Beatrix, I do pray the Lord to bless you every night and morning of my life! For surely you do deserve blessings for staying with Miss Sybil in this here awful—"

An admonitory pressure of Miss Tabby's shoe by Mr. Berner's boot arrested her speech for an instant, and then modified it:

"In this here commodious and sillubrious watering place!" she added, with a knowing nod towards Mr. Berners, which happily escaped Sybil's notice.

Sybil had many questions to ask about Black Hall and its inmates, and its surroundings; but first she asked the general question:

"How are all at home, Miss Tabby?"

"Oh, all are well, my dear child!" answered the old woman, "as well as can be, considering your—Oh, there I go again!" she exclaimed, suddenly breaking off in alarm.

"All are well, you say, Miss Tabby?" inquired Sybil.

"Oh yes, honey, all well, the servants and the cattle and the pets and all the other animyles, and Raphael and little Cromartie—Oh, my goodness! there I go again, worse than ever."

"Who? Raph—Cro'?" began Sybil, passing her hand in perplexity to and fro across her brow. "Who are they? Did I dream of them, or read of them somewhere? Raph—Cro'. Oh, dear me, my head is so queer! Did I read or dream?"

"No, my dear," exclaimed Miss Tabby, hastening to retrieve her error. "You did not read, nor likewise dream of any sich. They's peacocks, honey; nothing but peacocks, as was bought to ornament the lawn, you know."

"Oh yes, I know! peacocks!" said Sybil with a smile, readily adopting the explanation that had been made to her. "But I dreamt a strange dream about those peacocks. I dreamt—Oh, I can't remember what I dreamt!" she continued, contracting her brows with an expression of pain and perplexity.

"Never mind, my darling, what it was. Dreams are profitless subjects to employ the mind upon," said Beatrix Pendleton, taking Sybil's hand, and lifting her up. "Now come with me. I have something pleasanter to talk about," she added, as she drew Sybil down one of the shaded garden walks.

There was one subject among others upon which Sybil was quite sane; her own approaching maternity. Beatrix knew this, as she led her to a distant garden seat, and made her sit down upon it, while she said:

"Now, darling, that Miss Tabby is here, had we not better commission her to buy some flannels and lawns and laces for the wardrobe of the coming child? She can bring them when she comes next time. And you and I can amuse ourselves with making them up."

"Oh yes, yes, indeed! That will be delightful. How strange I never thought of that before! Why, I do believe I would have let the little stranger arrive without an article to put on it, if you hadn't reminded me—and I a married woman, who ought to know better, and you only a girl, who ought to know nothing! Well, I do declare!" exclaimed Sybil, turning and staring at her companion.

"Never mind, darling; it is only because you have been ill, and I have been well, that you have forgotten this necessary provision, while I have remembered it," said Beatrix soothingly.

"Well, I won't forget it again!" exclaimed Sybil, starting up and running towards her husband, and followed by Miss Pendleton.

"Lyon!" she said, breathlessly. "How much money have you got about you?"

"I don't know, dear. You can have it all, if you wish, be it little or much; for it is all your own, Sybil," replied Lyon Berners, putting his purse in her hands.

"Oh, no, I don't want that; but you must give Tabby as much money as she may require, to make some purchases for me."

"Yes, certainly," said Mr. Berners, taking back his pocket-book.

"Me! me make purchases for you, my lamb? La! whatever can you want in this awful—There I go again!" exclaimed Miss Tabby in dismay.

"You have too much curiosity, you good old soul. But here, come with me, and I will tell you what to buy for me—after you have instructed me as to what I shall want," said Sybil, laughing archly, as she led the way to a rude arbor at a short distance.

"Now, Tabby, what I want you to buy for me, is everything in the world that is needed for a bran, spic and span new baby!"

"La! Miss Sybil; whose baby?" inquired the astonished housekeeper, with her mouth and eyes wide open.

"Tabby, don't be a goose!"

"But, Miss Sybil, I don't know what you mean!"

"Tabby, I'm not 'Miss Sybil' to begin with! I'm Mrs. Berners, and have been married more than a year, and you know it, you stupid old Tabby!"

"But, Miss Sybil, or ratherwise Mrs. Berners, if I must be so ceremonious with my own nurse-child, what has that to do with what you've been a-asking of me to buy?"

"Nothing at all," answered Sybil, half-provoked and half-amused at the dullness of the old housekeeper. "Nothing whatever. But you must go out and buy everything that is required for the wardrobe of a young child; and you must find out what *is* necessary, for I myself haven't the slightest idea of what that is."

The housekeeper looked at the lady for a moment, in questioning doubt and fear, and then, as the truth slowly penetrated her mind, she broke forth suddenly with:

"Oh, my good gracious! Miss Sybil, honey! you don't mean it, do you?"

"Yes, I do, Tabby; and I thank heaven every day for the coming blessing," said the young wife, fervently.

"But oh, Miss Sybil, in such a place as this—There I go again!" exclaimed the housekeeper, breaking off in a panic, and then adding, "I an't fit to come to see you; no that I an't. I'm always a forgetting, especially when you talk so sensible!"

"What's the matter with you Tabby? Are you crazy? you never thought I was going to stay *here* for such an event, did you? In a public resort like this? Tabby, I'm shocked at you! No! I shall be home at Black Hall to receive the little stranger, Tabby," said Sybil, making the longest and most connected speech she had made since her reason had become impaired.

"Ah, Lord! ah, my Lord!" cried the old woman, on the verge of hysterics again.

"Now, Tabby, don't begin to whimper! You whimper over everything though, I know. You whimpered when I was born, and when I was christened, and when I was married; and now you whimper when I am going to be crowned with the crown of maternity. Oh, you old rebel!" cried Sybil, contradicting all her sarcastic words by caressing her old friend.

"No, I don't mean to! but if you knowed! Oh! if you knowed!" exclaimed Miss Tabby, suppressing and swallowing her sobs.

"Now, then, let us go back to Lyon. Lyon will give you what money you may need for the purchases; and I beg that you will make them as soon as possible, and bring them to me here," said Sybil, as she arose and walked back to the spot where she had left her husband and her friend.

After a little general conversation, in which Sybil sometimes joined naturally, and from which she also sometimes wandered off at random, Mr. Berners proposed to call in Joe to pay his respects to his mistress.

Sybil sprang at the proposal, and Joe was duly summoned from his seat on the box of the carriage before the door.

He came into the garden hat in hand, and bowed gravely before his unfortunate mistress.

And when she asked him many questions about that department of the domestic economy of Black Hall that fell under his own supervision, he answered all her questions satisfactorily, without ever once falling into the unlucky blunders that had marred Miss Tabby's communications.

"Your favorite mare, Diana is in prime order, ma'am, and will be so whenever you come home again to take your rides in the valley. And your coach horses Castor and Pollux, ma'am, couldn't be in better trim. I shall take pride in driving of you to church behind them, ma'am, the first Sunday after you come home, which we all at Black Hall hopes, as the waters of this here cilibrated spring may soon restore your health, and send you back to us strong and happy," said Joe, at the conclusion of a very long address.

"Thanks, Joe! I know that you are very sincere and earnest in your good wishes. Many thanks! But, dear old soul, how came you to be so lame?"

Joe was taken by surprise, and stood aghast. He knew of course that his mistress was slightly insane; but he was utterly unprepared for such a lapse of memory as this. He looked at his master in distress and perplexity.

"Oh!" answered Lyon Berners for his man, "Joe was thrown from his horse, and had his ankle sprained."

"Poor Joe! You must be very careful until it gets quite well," said Sybil, compassionately.

And soon after this her visitors, master and servants, took their leave.

CHAPTER XXIII.

SYBIL'S CHILD.

But thou wilt burst primeval sleep,

And thou wilt live my babe to weep;

The tenant of a dark abode,

Thy tears must flow as mine have flowed.—BYRON.

Summer ripened into autumn. Sybil and her faithful friend employed the golden days of September and October in the graceful and pleasing feminine work of making up garments for the expected little stranger.

But meanwhile, outside the prison walls, a cloud, black as night, was gathering over the young prisoner's doomed head.

The rumor got abroad that the Governor meant to follow up the long respite with a full pardon.

His course in this matter was canvassed and commented upon severely in every bar-room, grocery, street corner, political meeting, and elsewhere.

The press took up the matter, and vindictively reprobated the course of the Governor, putting his conduct upon the motives of partiality for the aristocracy.

Had the murderess been a woman of the people, it said, her life would have paid the forfeit of her crime.

But she was a lady of the county aristocracy, a daughter of the house of Berners; and however notoriously that house had been cursed with demoniac passions, and however deeply dyed with crime, its daughter, however guilty, was not to be held amenable to the laws!

Was such outrageous worship of the aristocracy by partial judges and venal governors to be endured in a country of freemen?

No! the voice of the people would be heard through their organ, a free press! and if not listened to, then it would be heard in thunder at the polls in the coming autumn elections!

Such was the spirit of the people and the press in regard to Sybil.

It was strange how the people and the press clamored for the sacrifice of Sybil Berners' life—the "female fiend," as they did not hesitate to call her, "daughter of demons," "the last of a race of devils, who should have been exterminated long before," they declared.

It was because they honestly ascribed to her a nature she did not possess, and imputed to her a crime she had not committed, thus making her innocently suffer for the sins of her forefathers.

Of course there were honorable exceptions to this general and unmerited reprobation of a guiltless young creature, but these exceptions were mostly among Sybil's own set, and were too few to have any force against the overwhelming weight of public sentiment.

And it was the general belief that, if the Governor should outrage public opinion by pardoning Sybil Berners, he would be politically ruined. Sybil Berners could not be permitted to live. She must die before the Governor could be re-elected by the people. And the election was coming on in the ensuing November.

Would he purchase success by the sacrifice of this young sufferer's life?

Ah! her best friends, asking themselves this question, were forced to answer, "Yes!"

This state of affairs had a most depressing effect upon Sybil's husband, especially as he had sustained a great loss in the departure of her zealous advocate, Ishmael Worth.

The young lawyer, soon after he had brought down Sybil's respite from the Governor, had been called away on business of the utmost importance, and had eventually sailed for Europe. He had gone, however, with the most confident expectations of her liberation.

How these expectations were destined to be defeated, it was now plain to see.

It required all Mr. Berners' powers of self-control to wear a calm demeanor in the presence of his unsuspicious wife. He had carefully kept from the cell every copy of a news-*paper that contained any allusion to the condemned prisoner and her circumstances, and he did this to keep Beatrix, as well as Sybil, ignorant of the impending doom; for he wished Beatrix to preserve in Sybil's presence the cheerful countenance that she never could wear if she should discover the thunder-cloud of destruction that lowered darker and heavier, day by day, over the head of her doomed companion.

But Sybil herself was losing her good spirits. The autumn had set in very early; and though now it was but October, the weather was too cool and often also too damp to make it prudent for the poor prisoner to spend so many hours in the prison garden as she had lately been permitted to do. She sat much in her cell, sad, silent, and brooding.

"What is the matter with you, my darling?" inquired Beatrix Pendleton one day, when they sat together in the cell, Beatrix sewing diligently on an infant's robe, and Sybil, with her neglected needle-work lying on her lap, and her head bowed upon her hand, "What is the matter with you, Sybil?"

"Oh, Beatrix, I don't know. But this autumn weather, it saddens me. Oh, more than that—worse than that, it *horrifies* me so much! It seems associated with—I know not what of anguish and despair. And I want to leave this desolate and gloomy place. It is so lonely, now that all the visitors have gone but ourselves. How can you bear it, Beatrix?"

"Very well, dear, so long as I have your company," answered Miss Pendleton, wondering that Sybil should miss the throng of visitors that had existed only in her own imagination.

"But I am homesick, Beatrix. Oh, Beatrix! I am so—so—homesick!" said Sybil, plaintively.

"Never mind, dear. Try to be patient. It would not do for you to undertake the journey now, you know," said Miss Pendleton, soothingly.

"Oh, but, Beatrix, I did so want to be at *home* to welcome my first dear child! There was never a Berners born out of Black Hall since the building was first erected," she pleaded.

"Never mind, dear. Everything now must give way to your health, you know. We could not endanger your health, by taking you over all these rough roads to Black Hall just now," said Miss Pendleton, gently.

"Ah, well! I will try to content myself to stay here in this gloomy place. But, oh! Beatrix, after all, I may die, and never see my home again. My dear home! Oh, if I should die here, Beatrix, I should be sure to haunt my home!"

"But you will not die. You must put away such gloomy fancies!"

As Miss Pendleton spoke, the cell door was opened, and the warden appeared bearing in the tray containing the supper service for the two ladies. It was not usual for the warden to wait on them in person; and so, to Miss Pendleton's silent look of inquiry, he answered:

"You must excuse my daughter for this once, ma'am, as she has gone to a merry-making in the village—this, you know, being Hallow Eve."

"*Hallow Eve!*" echoed an awful voice.

Both the warden and the young lady started, and turned around to see whence the unearthly sound came.

They beheld Sybil fallen back in her chair, pallid, ghastly, and convulsed.

Beatrix seized her vial of sal volatile and flew to the relief of her friend.

"What is it, dear Sybil? can you tell me?" she anxiously inquired, as she held the vial to the nostrils of her friend.

"*Hallow Eve! Hallow Eve!*" she repeated in a terrible tone.

"Well, dear, what of that? That is nothing."

"Oh yes, yes, it is horrible! it is horrible!"

"Hush, hush, dear! try to be composed."

"Black night! fire! blood! Oh, what a terror!"

"It was only a dream, dear. It is over now, and you are awake. Look up!"

"Oh, no! no dream, Beatrix! an awful, an overwhelming reality!" exclaimed the awakened sufferer. Then suddenly, with a shriek, she threw her hands to her head and fell into spasms.

"For heaven's sake run and fetch a doctor," exclaimed Beatrix, in the utmost distress, appealing to the terrified warden.

He immediately hurried from the room to procure the necessary medical attendance.

Beatrix ran after him, calling loudly:

"Send for her husband and her old nurse from Black Hall, also. I know it is after hours, but I believe she is dying."

The warden nodded assent, and hurried away, leaving Miss Pendleton in attendance upon the agonized woman, who recovered from one convulsion only to fall into another and severer one.

It was midnight, and a sorrowful and anxious group were gathered in Sybil's cell. She lay upon her bed, writhing with agony, and upon the very verge of death.

Near her stood her old family physician Dr. Hart, her old nurse Mrs. Winterose, and her faithful attendant Miss Tabby.

In the lobby, outside the cell door, sat her husband, with his face buried in his hands, wrestling in prayer with heaven.

What was he praying for? That his idolized young wife should be spared in this mortal peril? No, no, and a thousand times no! With all his heart and soul he prayed that she might die—that she might die e'er that dread warrant, which had arrived from Richmond only that morning, and which fixed her execution for an early day, could be carried out!

This agony of prayer was interrupted. The doctor came out of the cell, and whispered:

"It is over. She is the mother of a little girl."

There was no expression of parental joy or thankfulness on the father's part. Only the breathless question:

"And she? Can she survive?"

CHAPTER XXIV.

THE GREAT VALLEY STORM.

"Then hurtles forth the wind with sudden burst,

And hurls the whole precipitated clouds

Down in a torrent. On the sleeping vale

Descends infernal force, and with strong gust

Turns from the bottom the discolored streams

Through the black night that broods immense around,

Lashed into foam, the fierce contending falls

Swift o'er a thousand rearing rocks do race."

"Can she survive?" repeated Lyon Berners, perceiving that the physician hesitated to reply. "If she must die, do not fear to tell me so. I, who love her best, would say, 'Thank God!' Can she survive?"

"Mr. Berners, I do not know. Her situation is very critical. She has had convulsions. She is now prostrated and comatose," gravely answered the doctor.

"Then there is good hope that the Angel of Death may take her home now?"

"There is strong hope, since you choose to call it hope instead of fear."

"Ah! Doctor Hart, you know—you know—"

"That death in some cases might be a blessing—that death in this case certainly would. Yes, I know. And yet it is my bounden duty to do what I can to save life, so I must return to my patient," said the physician, laying his hand upon the latch of the door.

"When may I see my wife?" inquired Lyon Berners.

"*Now*, if you please; but she will not know you," said the doctor, shaking his head.

"I shall know her, however," muttered Mr. Berners to himself, as he raised his hat and followed the doctor into the cell, leaving Beatrix alone in the hall.

It was near midnight, and Miss Pendleton having been very properly turned out of the sick-room, and having been then forgotten, even by herself, had no place on which to lay her head.

When Mr. Berners, following the doctor, entered the cell, he found it but dimly lighted by one of the wax candles with which his care had supplied his wife.

In one corner sat Miss Tabby, whimpering, with more reason than she had ever before whimpered in her life, over the new-born baby that lay in her lap.

Near by stood old Mrs. Winterose, busy with her patient.

That patient lay, white as a lily, on her bed.

"How is she?" inquired the doctor, approaching.

"Why, just the same—no motion, no sense, hardly any breath," answered the nurse.

"Sybil, my darling! Sybil!" murmured her heart-broken husband, bending low over her still and pallid face.

She rolled her head from side to side, as if half-awakened by some familiar sound, and then lay still again.

"Sybil! my dearest wife! Sybil!" again murmured Lyon Berners, laying his hand on her brow.

She opened her eyes wide, looked around, and then gazed at her husband's face as if it had been only a part of the wall.

"Sybil, my dear, my only love! Sybil!" he repeated, trying to meet and fix her gaze.

But her eyes glanced off and wandered around the room, and finally closed again.

"I told you she would not know you," sighed the doctor.

"So best, so best, perhaps. Heaven grant that she may know nothing until her eyes shall open in that bright and blessed land, where

'The wicked cease from troubling,
And the weary are at rest!'"

said Lyon Berners, bowing his head.

But he remained standing by the bedside, and gazing at the pale, still face of his wife, until at length Miss Tabby came up to him, with the babe in her arms, and whimpered forth:

"Oh, Mr. Lyon, won't you look at your little daughter just once? Won't you say something to her? Won't you give her your blessing? Nobody has said a word to her yet; nobody has welcomed her; nobody has blessed her! Oh! my good Lord in heaven! to be born in prison, and not to get one word of welcome from anybody, even from her own father!"

And here Miss Tabby, overcome by her feelings, sobbed aloud; for which weakness I for one don't blame her.

"Give me the child," said Mr. Berners, taking the babe from the yielding arms of the nurse. "Poor little unfortunate!" he continued, as he uncovered and gazed on her face. "May the Lord bless you, for I, wretch that I am, have no power to bless."

At this moment Mrs. Winterose came up, and addressing the doctor, said:

"Sir, I have done all I can do in this extremity. Tabby is fully equal to anything that may happen now. But as for me, sir, I *must* leave."

"Leave? What are you thinking of, woman?" demanded the doctor, almost angrily.

"Sir, I left my poor old husband at the very point of death! I would not have left him, for any other cause on earth but this. And now I must go back to him, or he may be dead before I get there."

"Good Heaven, my dear woman, but this is dreadful!"

"I know it is, sir. But I couldn't help it. My child here ill and in prison, and I called to help her in her extremity, and my husband on his death-bed. Well, sir, I couldn't help my poor old man much, because he was so low he didn't know one face from another, and I could help my poor imprisoned, suffering child; and so I left my dying husband to the care of my darter Libby, and I comes to my suffering child! But now she's over the worst of it, I must leave her in the care of Tabby, and go back to my dying husband. Please God I may find him alive!" said the poor woman, fervently clasping her hands.

"My good soul, here is indeed a most painful case of a divided duty," said the doctor, in admiration.

"Yes, sir; but the Lord fits the back to the burden," sighed Mrs. Winterose, resignedly.

"Have you *two* backs?" wickedly inquired the doctor.

"What was it, sir?" asked Mrs. Winterose, doubting her own ears.

"Nothing. But just see what a storm is coming up! You'll be caught in it if you venture out."

"Law, sir, I'm not sugar, nor likewise salt, to get melted in a little water. And I must go, sir, please, if I am ever to see my old man alive again," said the nurse resolutely, putting on her bonnet and shawl.

"But how are you going six miles through night and storm?"

"Mr. Lyon will not begrudge me the use of the carriage and horses and driver as brought me here, to take me back to my husband's death-bed, I reckon," said the old woman confidently.

"No, indeed; nor any help I can give you, dear Mrs. Winterose," said Mr. Berners, feeling himself appealed to.

"Thanky, sir; I knowed it. And this I say: When the breath is outen my poor old man's body I will come back to my child, holding it always more dutiful to attend to the living as can suffer, rather than to the dead as are at rest. And now, if you please, Mr. Lyon, to see me into the carriage, and order Joe to drive me home, I will be obleeged to you," said the old woman.

Lyon Berners gave her his arm, with as much respect as if she had been a duchess, and led her from the room.

When they reached the outer door, which the warden, in consideration of the necessity, ordered to be opened at this unusual hour, they found the rain pouring in torrents from a sky as black as pitch.

"A wild night to take the road, Mrs. Winterose," said Mr. Berners, as he hoisted a large umbrella over her head.

"I don't know as I remember a wilder one, sir, since the flood of ninety, and that was when I was a young 'oman, which wasn't yesterday. And you'll hardly remember that, sir?"

"No," answered Lyon, hurrying her into the carriage and hastily clapping to the door.

The turnkey on duty that night went with the carriage to unbar the outer gate for it to pass. Notwithstanding his large umbrella he came back drenched with rain.

"Good Lord! an't it comin' down? Another Noah's flood! Bird Creek is boiling like a pot. It is all up in a white foam! so white that you can see it through the darkness; and listen! you can hear it from here!" said the turnkey as he entered the hall, shook himself, making a rain shower around him, and proceeded to bar the entrance again.

"You won't want this door opened again to-night, will you, Doctor?" inquired the man, rather impatiently, of the physician, who had stepped to the door.

Dr. Hart hesitated, and seemed to debate with himself, and then answered:

"I must stay with my patient for another hour, and then, if there should be no change in her condition, I shall have to trouble you to let me out, Mr.

Martin—since you have got no warrant to keep me here," he added, with a smile.

The man put up the last bar with a bang, and looked as if he wished he had the authority of which the doctor spoke.

Dr. Hart returned to the room of his patient whom he found in the same comatose state, watched by Miss Tabby, who was moaning over the young babe that lay across her lap, and by Lyon Berners, who sat beside the bed holding his wife's cold hand.

"Where is Miss Pendleton? I did not see her as I came up the passage," inquired the doctor, after he had looked at his patient.

"The warden's darter came and took her away to sleep in *her* room, and high time too, poor young lady, for she was about worn out," said Miss Tabby.

The doctor took a seat near the head of the bed, where he could watch the sick woman.

And all became very silent in the cell, until at length Miss Tabby spoke.

"What's that roaring? It can't be thunder this time o' year."

"It is the creek swollen by the rain. I understand that it is very high, lashed into a foam," answered the doctor.

"Oh," said Miss Tabby, indifferently; and all became again silent in the cell but for the sound of many waters heard more and more distinctly even through the heavy walls.

At length the doctor arose to go. He made a final careful examination of his quiet patient, and then, turning to her distressed husband, said:

"I must ask you to go out with me, Mr. Berners, to bring back some medicine for your wife, which I wish to put up at my office."

Lyon Berners silently arose and took up his hat. And the two gentlemen left the cell together.

The warden had gone to bed, but had left orders with the night-watch to let the visitors out when they wished to go.

Once more the heavy bars fell, and the thick doors were opened.

"Heaven and earth! what a night!" exclaimed the doctor, as he buttoned his surtout tightly across his breast, and prepared to brave the fury of the storm.

Lyon Berners, scarcely conscious of the state of the weather, followed him.

It was now dawn, and the black sky had faded to a dark gray.

The rain was pouring down as if all "the gates of heaven" had been opened for another deluge.

The river and the creek lashed to fury, were roaring and rushing onward, like devouring monsters.

"Merciful Heaven! Talk of the fury of fire, but look here!" exclaimed the doctor, glancing around. But his voice was lost in the sound of many waters.

Their road, after passing the outer gates of the prison, lay away from the banks of the creek, and down the course of the river, towards the village.

But for the darkness of that stormy dawn they might have seen a fearful sight below. The lower portion of the town was already overflowed, and the waters were still rising. Many of the people were gathered upon the house-tops, and others were out in boats, engaged in rescuing their neighbors from the flooded dwellings.

But for the horrible roaring of the torrents, they might have heard the shouts and cries of the terrified inhabitants shocked and half-frenzied by the suddenness of this overwhelming calamity.

But they heard and saw but little of this as they plunged on through the darkness, in the deluge of rain and thunder of waters. Unawares they were drawing near their fate. They came upon it gradually.

"Good Heaven! what is the matter down there?" suddenly cried the doctor, as he dimly discerned the forms of men, women, and children gathered upon the house-tops, which did not look like house-tops, but like flat-boats floating upon the dark waters.

"I say, Berners, what the deuce is the matter down there? Your eyes are younger than mine—look," anxiously insisted the doctor, peering down into the gloomy and horrible chaos.

"It is a flood. The river is over the town," replied Mr. Berners, carelessly; for he, in his grief, would not have minded if the whole of the Black Valley had been turned into a black sea.

"The river over the town! Good Heaven! And you say that as indifferently as if hundreds of human lives and millions of money were not imperilled," cried the doctor, breaking away from his companion, and running down towards the village.

A terrible, a heart-crushing sight met his eyes!

The doctor's family occupied a beautiful low-roofed villa on the opposite bank of Violet Run, a little stream of water making up from the Black River. The doctor's first thought was of his own home, of course, and he ran swiftly on, through darkness and storm, until he was suddenly brought up on the banks of the run. Here he stood aghast. The pretty rustic bridge that had spanned the run, and led to his own terraced grounds, was swept away; and the run, now swollen to the size of a raging river, roared between himself and his home.

His home!—where was it?

He strained his aching eyes through the murky gloom to look for it, and oh! horror of horrors! his terraced garden and his low-roofed villa had disappeared, and in their place what seemed a raft, with human beings on, floated about at the mercy of the flood.

With a pang of despair, he recognized it as his own house-top, with probably his wife and children clinging to it; and at the same instant the raft, or roof, was violently whirled around, and swept under by the force of the current.

With a cry of desperation, the wretched husband and father flung up his arms to leap into the boiling flood, when he was caught from behind and held fast.

"What would you do? Rush to certain destruction?" said the voice of Lyon Berners, who had just reached the spot.

"My wife! my children!" shrieked the man, dashing his hands to his head.

"Come back, or you will be swept away," said Mr. Berners, forcibly drawing him from the spot just an instant before the water rolled over it.

And still the rain poured down like another deluge, and still the waters roared and the waters rose, and dark night hung over the dawn.

CHAPTER XXV.

THE GREAT VALLEY FLOOD.

The rearing river, backward pressed,

Shook all her trembling banks amain,

Then madly at the eygre's breast

Flung up her weltering walls again.

Then banks came down with ruin and rout,

Then beaten foam flew round about,

Then all the mighty floods were out.—JEAN INGELOW.

Meanwhile the worried and angry prison guard had barred up the doors for the last time that night, to remain barred, as they said, against all comers until the usual hour of opening next day; and then they went to bed, and to sleep, little dreaming of the mighty power that would force an entrance before the light.

Left alone in the prison cell to watch her sleeping patient, Miss Tabby sat and whimpered over the baby, which she still held in her lap.

Sometimes she listened to the roaring of the river outside, and sometimes she muttered to herself after the manner of lonely old ladies.

"Oh, indeed I do wish they would come. One on 'em, at any rate! Oh, it's horrid to be left alone here in this dissolute place, with a dying 'oman, and she my own dear nurse child," she whined, wringing and twisting her fingers, and looking from the face of the sleeping babe to that of the unconscious mother.

"Oh, to think of my own dear father a-dying at a distance, and I never to see him alive no more in this world!" she burst forth, sobbing and crying.

"And oh, good Lord in heaven, what an awful night! I never did see sich a night in my life, with the rain pouring and pouring barrels full in a stream, and the river roaring around the house like a whole drove of lions!" she exclaimed, shuddering from head to foot.

"And an endless night as it is, oh, my goodness! But it must be near morning; I do think it must be near morning," she finally said, as she arose and laid the baby on the bed beside its mother, and then went to the window to look out for the dawn.

She started back with a cry of terror, and sank upon the nearest seat.

The cell, as I told you, was in the angle of the building, and had two windows—the one looking down upon Black River, and the other upon Bird Creek. Miss Tabby had peeped from that one which overlooked Bird Creek.

Day had dawned darkly and dimly, but the solitary woman saw enough to curdle her blood with horror.

The river and the creek, lashed to fury, had swollen so high that they were now merged into one body of water, and had risen nearly to the second story of the building. If Miss Tabby could have put her arm through the grated window, she might easily have reached down and dipped her hand in the rising water, for it was rising so fast that she could almost see it mount.

"Oh, my good gracious alive!" she cried, as she fell back on the chair—"it's a flood! It's a flood like that I heard mother talk about, which carried away the mills in ninety. It's a flood! it's a flood! And we shall all be drownded in this horrid cell, like blind kittens in a tub!"

And made desperate by terror, the old woman started up, and rushed to the barred and bolted door of the cell, and rapped and kicked with all her might, and threw herself against it, and called, loudly and frantically:

"HELP! MURDER! MURDER! HELP! Take us out, or we'll all be drownded in ten minutes!"

But bolts and bars resisted all her strength, and the noise of winds and waters drowned her voice. And the same cause that rendered others deaf to her frenzied cries for help, prevented her from hearing the sounds of terror and confusion that came up from the story below—the groaning and crying of men locked up in their cells; the calling and shouting of warden and watchmen, rushing from corridor to corridor to release the prisoners from their imminent peril; the clattering of feet, the mingling of voices; in short, all the discordant notes that go to make up the infernal concert of a crowd surprised and maddened by sudden and general disaster.

There was also another reason why Miss Tabby's cries for help could not be heard. Sybil Berners was the one solitary prisoner in this long and remote corridor. Her door was barred and bolted fast, and it was not deemed necessary to leave a night watch on duty near it. Thus, if they should happen to be forgotten in the general panic, they would certainly be drowned; for even if the thunder of waters, and the shouting of men, and crashing of timbers, had been less deafening and distracting, Miss Tabby's voice would still have failed to reach the ears of the distant turnkeys.

From her fruitless efforts at the barred door, she rushed in desperation to the grated window. With a fearful shriek she threw her hands to her head, and rushed away again. The surrounding waters had risen within a foot of the window sill! She filled the air of the cell with her shrieks, as she rushed madly about from wall to wall, like a frenzied screaming macaw, beating itself against the bars of its cage.

"To lie drownded here in the cell like a cat in a tub! To be drownded like a cat in a tub!" was the burden of her death song.

And through all this Sybil slept the sleep of coma.

Suddenly the young babe awoke and added its shrill and feeble pipes to the horrible uproar.

The old maid had all a mother's tenderness in her heart. In the midst of her own agony of terror she ceased to scream, and went and took the babe and cried gently over its fate, murmuring:

"Only a few hours old, and to die in this horrible den, my babe! Oh, my babe! And you not even baptized! Oh, my goodness, not even baptized! What shall I do? Oh! what shall I do? Let you die without baptism? Oh, no, no! I never did baptize a child in my life, which I know I'm all unworthy to do it! But—but, I know the church allows any one to christen a child in danger of death. And so, my baby! Oh! my poor baby!" And her voice broke down in tears as she bore the child to a table where there was a pitcher of water.

Very humbly and reverently the old maid performed the sacred ceremony that her faith taught her was essential to the child's salvation. And she gave it the first name that came into her head—"Mary."

"There! now you are ready to go, my baby! Not that—that I really think the good Lord would ever keep you, my innocent one, out of His heaven, merely because you wasn't christened! No, no, I don't believe that either! But still it's best to be on the safe side, when it's so easy as sprinkling a little water and speaking a few words!—HUSH! I do believe they are coming to let us out at last!" exclaimed Miss Tabby, breaking off from her monologue, as through all the general uproar a crashing sound close at hand smote upon her ear!

She hastily laid the child upon the bed, and hurried to the door. No one was there, and the bolts and bars were fast as ever. But before she could turn around the window fell in with a tremendous clatter and bang—glass and grating ringing and shattering upon the floor.

Miss Tabby recoiled and squeezed herself against the wall in the corner. She thought the window had been beaten in by the water, and she expected the flood to follow.

But a tall man in dark clothing leaped through the opening, striking the floor with a rebound, and then stood up and gazed around the dimly lighted cell.

His eyes fell upon Sybil, as she lay in coma on the bed.

"All right, Raphael! You were correct. This is the cell, and here she is. Come!" and he called to some one without.

A second figure, younger and slighter, jumped through the open window into the cell, and stood, like the first had done, peering around through the semi-darkness.

"Haste, Raphael! You were swift-footed enough to bring her here! Try to be almost as swift-footed to bear her hence!" cried the first man, seizing the form of Sybil and wrapping it hastily in the upper quilt.

As he was doing this, something rolled over and cried.

"Hallo! Here's a baby! I never bargained for that!" exclaimed the man in astonishment.

"It is *her* baby, father—the baby for whose sake the governor prolonged her life. Let me take it," pleaded the youth.

"Why the demon didn't you tell me about this before?" angrily demanded the elder, while carefully wrapping up the patient.

"I knew no more than yourself, father. *You* knew, as I and everybody did, that this child was expected, and that the governor respited the mother for its sake; but I didn't know it had arrived until you spoke of it," said the youth.

"Ah! you are more quick-witted than I," laughed the man sarcastically.

"Let me take care of the babe, father," pleaded the boy.

"Why?"

"Because it must be rescued with her."

"Why, again?"

"Because she would break her heart without it."

"How do you know?"

"Oh, father, even a bird loves its birdling; and of course this tender-hearted lady loves her little one."

"She don't seem to love anything now, or even to know anything. She is as stupid and lifeless as anything I ever saw that lived and breathed. She is under the influence of opium, I should think," said the man, who had now the form of the unconscious woman well wound around with the quilt and laid over his breast and shoulder.

"Oh, no, she an't, sir! no, she an't—no sich a thing, sir! But she's been in this here comotious condition, knowing nothing nor nobody, ever since the baby arrove!" said Miss Tabby, coming from her concealment, for she saw in these two men only benevolent individuals who had come to deliver her and her lady.

"Who the demon are you?" demanded the elder, turning sharply towards her.

"I an't no demon, sir! though I am mistreated all as if I was one," whimpered Miss Tabby.

"Then who are you?"

"I'm her poor, faithful, misfortunate nurse, sir," snivelled Miss Tabby.

"Oh, you are!—Raphael, take the child into the boat! Never mind the old woman; let her drown!" said the elder man, laughing savagely.

"Oh, sir, don't you do that! Don't you leave me here to drown, sir! to die such a dismal death in this dark den!" pleaded Miss Tabby, catching hold of the man's coat-tails.

"Go to the devil!" exclaimed the stranger, trying to shake her off.

"But I an't prepared to go, sir, indeed I an't," persisted Miss Tabby, holding on.

"Go ahead, Raphael—I'm coming! And, confound you, so is the water! It will be too late in another minute!" savagely exclaimed the man, succeeding now in shaking himself free.

"Oh, sir! for pity's sake, sir, don't leave me here to drown! How can you resky the mother and child, and leave a poor lone 'oman like me to die? How can you, sir? Resky me, for your own blessed mother's sake! Oh! young gentleman, beg for me! don't leave me!" prayed Miss Tabby, turning from the elder to the younger man.

"Go on, Raphael!" shouted the man.

But the youth hesitated.

"Father," he said, "that old woman was kind to me. Save her! there is room enough in the boat."

"Oh! you darling sweet Master Raphael! Is it yourself that is there?" exclaimed Miss Tabby, delightedly. "Is it yourself indeed? Oh, tell the gentleman what a faithful servant I have been, and how my young lady loved me! and how she'd fret herself to death if I was to be drownded, all through coming to her help in her trouble to-night!" pleaded the poor creature, clasping her hands.

"Father, bring her off, for our sakes, if not for her own," said the boy, diplomatically; "for if we leave her here, and she should be saved by others, she may betray our secret."

"That is true," admitted the elder man. "So we will save the poor old wretch, but only upon conditions. Here, you old devil!" he called, turning to the woman.

"Yes, sir," said Miss Tabby, opening and clasping her hands.

"If I take you off in the boat to-night, and drop you down safe somewhere on dry land, will you promise never to tell any living soul who rescued you?"

"Yes, sir! yes, sir! and swear to it on the Bible! which there is one on the table handy, sir!" eagerly assented Miss Tabby.

"And will you also promise never to speak of our visit to this cell to-night?"

"Yes, sir! yes, sir! and swear to it!"

"And never to mention how Mrs. Berners and her child were saved?"

"Oh yes, sir!"

"Nor even that she was saved at all?"

"Oh yes, sir! and swear to it!"

"And you will never betray the secret, by word or sign?"

"No, sir!"

"But keep it to the day of your death?"

"Yes, sir!"

"Get the book, then, and take the oath. Raphael, take the child to the boat and lay it on the blankets there, and then come back and help the woman off. And, good Heaven! make haste! We must get away from here immediately. I hear footsteps along the corridor! Some one is coming! Haste! We must not allow Sybil Berners to be rescued through the door. That would be worse than being left to drown! Haste, I say!" exclaimed the man, speaking rapidly and excitedly as he caught up another quilt and cast it over Sybil's form, and hurried with her towards the open window.

There was indeed the most pressing need of haste, for more reasons than one: the rising waters were now oozing through the stone walls and covering the floor inside, while outside the flood was almost up to the window sill. In a very few moments it would overflow the place.

Raphael laid the child down where he had been told to put her, and then ran back into the cell to help Miss Tabby, who had faithfully taken the oath required of her.

The elder man laid his insensible burden in the boat, and then climbed in after her.

The last was a difficult feat, for the water was brimming to the window sill, and the boat was above it.

As the man stepped into the boat, his weight caused it to tip so much that it cast a shower into the cell.

Miss Tabby shrieked out that she was going to be drowned, although not a drop of water had touched her.

Raphael soothed her and helped her into the boat, and put her in a seat near the elder man.

"That's the thing! Now do you support this lady's head on your lap, for I shall have to row," said the man, as he transferred Sybil Berners from his own arms to Miss Tabby's, and then took up the oar.

Raphael took up the other oar, and they were rowing away from the prison walls when their attention was attracted by the sound of a dog's whining in the cell. They looked up and saw Sybil's little Skye terrier on the window sill, with her fore-paws in the water. And at the same instant little Nelly struck out, swam towards them, jumped into the boat, and nestled at her mistress' feet.

The rain had ceased, and the clouds were breaking away from the eastern horizon, where the first crimson streak heralded the rising sun.

They rowed swiftly towards the heights, which now appeared not so much like the boundaries of a valley as the hilly shores of an inland sea.

Yes, the Black Valley seemed indeed transformed into a black lake, surrounded with wooded hills, and dotted with wooded isles; but these seeming hills were really mountains, and these seeming isles were the tops of submerged trees.

They rowed to the nearest point of land and stopped the boat, where a little path led up the steep ascent.

"Do you see that path?" inquired the elder man of the old woman.

"Yes, my dear gentleman, I do," said Miss Tabby.

"Do you know where it leads?"

"Yes, my dear gentleman; it leads to a cluster of quarrymen's cottages."

"Then get out of the boat and go up there; there you will find shelter."

"But, my good sir, my sick lady?" inquired Miss Tabby, hesitating.

"Never mind her. She will be a blamed sight better taken care of by us, than she has been lately by any of you! Come, get out with you!"

"But, sir, I daren't desert my sick lady."

"I'm blest, if you don't get out of this boat in double quick time, if I don't pitch your head foremost into the water, and drown you. We have no time to stop here fooling with you till it is broad daylight," said the man, starting to his feet as if about to put his threat into instant execution.

Miss Tabby jumped up and scuttled out of the boat as fast as she could go, without even having stopped to kiss her lady "good-bye."

And this was the last Miss Tabby saw or heard of Sybil Berners for many long years.

CHAPTER XXVI.

AFTER THE DISASTER.

That flow strewed wrecks about the grass;

That ebb swept out the flocks to sea.

A fatal ebb and flow, alas!

To many more than mine and me.—JEAN INGELOW.

The day after the terrible disaster the sun arose upon a scene of awful desolation!

Great was the devastation of lands and dwellings, and the destruction of life and property, by the memorable Black Valley flood!

The Black Valley itself, from its very form, position, and circumstances, seemed doomed to suffer tremendously from such a disaster.

It was a long, deep, and narrow valley, shut in by two high mountain ridges, which, interlocked in rude rocky precipices at its higher extremity, where the Black Torrent, dashing down the steeps, formed the head of the Black River, which, fed by many other mountain springs, ran down the whole length of the valley, and past the village of Blackville at its lower end.

By the fatal deluge of rain, all the mountain springs were raised to torrents, and the Black Torrent was swollen to a cataract, and all poured down vast floods of water into the Black River, which rose and overflowed its banks even to the mountains' side; so that the Black Valley became a black lake.

The advance of the day, and the retreat of the waters, showed at length the full extent of the disaster.

The dwellings in the valley, and in the village at its foot, were nearly all swept away. Only the strongest buildings, and those on the highest grounds, escaped destruction.

The hotel, the court-house, and the church, were each damaged, but not destroyed.

The prison was carried away, and several of the prisoners drowned.

The family of Dr. Hart were saved. Though more than once submerged, they clung to the floating roof, until they were carried down into calmer waters, where they were picked up by the men who were out in boats to rescue the drowning.

The Black Hall Manor suffered severely. The Hall itself was too strongly built, and upon too high ground, to be even endangered; but its detached offices and laborers' cottages were swept away by the flood. Their inmates happily had saved themselves by speedy flight up the mountain side, and were found the next day safe at Black Hall, where they had taken refuge.

But the sunlight also discovered many more wretches made homeless by the flood, and now sitting and shuddering upon the rocks, up and down the mountain sides.

But the dwellings of all those who had been so fortunate as to escape injury by the flood, were freely opened to receive the homeless sufferers.

It was late in the day before the condition of the ground enabled Lyon Berners, attended by some villagers, to seek the site of the late prison.

Not a vestige of the building remained. The very spot on which it had once stood was unrecognizable—a vast morass of mud and wreck.

The warden and his family, with Miss Pendleton and a few of the officers of the prison, were found about a mile beyond the scene, grouped together on a high hill, and utterly overcome, in mind and body, by the combined influences of cold and hunger, grief and horror.

"For the Lord's sake, where is my wife? where is Sybil?" anxiously inquired Lyon Berners, though scarcely knowing whether he hoped or feared she might be alive.

Beatrix Pendleton, who had sat with her head bowed down upon her knees, now raised it and said:

"Heaven knows! I tried to make them go and save her; but they would not! I refused to leave the prison without her, but they forced me on the boat."

"We couldn't have saved her," spoke the warden; "her cell was right at the corner of the building, at the joining of the creek and the river. It was overflowed before we got there, and the water, which must a busted in the window, was a rushing down the corridor and filling up the place so fast, that we had to run up the stairs to the next story to save our own lives."

"Heaven's will be done!" groaned Lyon Berners, who, heart-broken as he was, scarcely understood or believed the warden's explanation, or knew whether he himself were merely resigned, or really rejoiced that his wife had met this fate now, rather than lived to await a still more horrible one.

"And the poor woman who was attending her, and the young child, have also perished?" added Mr. Berners, after a pause, and in an interrogative tone.

Beatrix nodded sadly, and the warden said:

"Yes, sir, of course, which they all three being in the cell together, shared the same fate! And if we could a reskeed one, we could a reskeed all!"

"And where are your other prisoners?" inquired Mr. Berners.

"Some on 'em was drownded, sir, unavoidably. And some on 'em we reskeed by taking of 'em through the windows, and on to the boat; but Lord love you, sir, they give us leg bail the first chance they got; which who could blame them? Most on them as we reskeed has made off up the mountain, sir; and little use it would be to try to catch them, sir, even if we succeeded, seeing as we have got no place to lock 'em up. And as for me, my 'okkerpation's gone,' as the man says in the play! But I'm not thinking of myself, sir. I'm mortal sorry for the poor wretches called so sudden to their accounts," added the warden, brushing the tears from his eyes with the sleeve of his coat.

"Come, Martin," said Mr. Berners, who, even in the midst of his own despair, could not forget the claims of humanity—"Come, Martin! You and your companions in misfortune cannot sit here longer without great danger to health and life! You must get up and come away. The road, though very difficult, is passable, you see, since we come by it. Come away!"

"Come where? To the alms-house, I suppose," groaned the warden, dropping his head in his hands.

"My poor fellow, the alms-house has gone with the rest. There is no alms-house now."

"Then we may as well stay here and die; for there is no other place for us to go," groaned the ruined man.

"There are half a hundred places to go to. Every house that has been spared by the flood has, in gratitude to Heaven, opened its doors to receive those who are rendered homeless by this disaster. Come, my good friend; come with your companions to the village hotel. A number of us who have lost no property by the flood, have already clubbed together for the relief of those who have lost all. Come! if you sit here longer you will surely catch your death."

The warden arose with a groan; and his example was followed by all his comrades.

"My dear Beatrix, take my arm," said Mr. Berners, helping Miss Pendleton to rise.

"My brother! Where is my brother? He was far enough off to be safe from the flood; but why is he not here now."

"My dear Beatrix, he could not possibly get here yet. As soon as the water shall have settled he will come, no doubt," said Mr. Berners, as he led her down the hill towards the village.

The road was very bad. In some places it was nearly half a leg deep in pools of water, or in mud. But they reached the half-ruined village at length. And Mr. Berners, accompanied by the whole party, took Miss Pendleton to the hotel to await the arrival of her brother.

All the sufferers were hospitably received by the landlord's family, who furnished them with dry clothing, warm meals, and good lodging.

But it was not until evening that the subsidence of the waters permitted Captain Pendleton to make his way down the valley to the village, to look after his sister.

The meeting between the brother and sister was very affecting.

Beatrix wept on his shoulder.

"Thank Heaven, you are safe, my dear sister!" were among the first words that he said.

"Yes; I am safe, I am safe, Clement. *But she is lost!* Oh, Clement, *she is lost!*" cried Beatrix, bursting into tears.

Captain Pendleton started, and looked up to the face of Mr. Berners, as if asking for a confirmation or contradiction of these words.

Lyon Berners sorrowfully bent his head, and then turned away to conceal the strong emotion which he could no longer control.

It was not until the next morning that the waters had gone down sufficiently to enable them to go up the valley as far as Black Hall.

And up to this time but few of the dead bodies of the victims had been found; but all these had been easily recognized, and were now prepared for burial.

Mr. Berners engaged special agents to watch for the appearance of Sybil's body, and to advise him the moment it should be discovered; and then, having made every necessary provision, in case of its recovery during his absence, for its reception at the church, and its retention there until his return, he set out for Black Hall, accompanied by the two Pendletons.

As no carriage could possibly pass along the roads in their present condition, our party were forced to go on horseback.

After a heavy and tedious ride through the deep mud left by the flood, they reached Black Hall, which they found half full of refugees; and where they were warmly welcomed by their faithful servants, who, up to the hour of their arrival, had supposed them to be lost.

But then came the question:

"Where is Miss Sybil?" asked almost in a breath by Joe and Dilly and Aunt Mopsa.

And grave and sorrowful faces answered, even before the tongue spoke:

"Lost in the flood!"

Then for a time loud wailing filled the house. But after a while it ceased, and comparative quiet followed.

"Where is Raphael and little Cro'?" at length inquired Mr. Berners.

"Raphael? Bless your soul, Marster, Raphael an't been seen in this house since you yourself left it," answered Joe.

"Then I am very much afraid the poor fellow has been lost," sighed Mr. Berners.

And then, having called Dilly to show Miss Pendleton to a bedroom, and ordered Joe to perform the same service for Captain Pendleton, Mr. Berners went to a back building of the house in which the poor refugees were gathered.

Here he found the people in great distress, mourning over the sudden loss of all their worldly goods.

He consoled them as well as he could; reminded them that, with all their losses, they had lost no members of their families, and promised them that he and his neighbors would rebuild and refurnish their cottages, and finally inviting them to stay at Black Hall until this should be accomplished.

Thanks and blessings followed his words, and then he asked:

"Has any one heard from my old overseer. Winterose? His house stands high, and I suppose that it is safe."

A half a dozen voices answered in a breath:

"Law, yes, sir; his house is safe."

"He's had a stroke, sir."

"They thought he was a dying."

"But he is better now; and his wife, who is a good judge, thinks he'll get over it."

"It gratifies me to hear this, my friends. But although the old man's house is safe, he has met with a much greater misfortune than any of you have in the loss of all you possess," said Mr. Berners, very gravely.

"Law, sir, what?" inquired a dozen voices at once.

"He has lost his eldest daughter," answered Lyon Berners, sadly.

"Who? Miss Tabby? Law, sir, no he an't!"

"She's home, fast enough!"

"She was brought home by a quarryman yesterday morning."

It was the habit of these people to talk all at the same time, so that it required a shrewd listener to understand them.

But there seemed so large an interest at stake in their present communications, that Mr. Berners understood even more than was intended.

"Miss Tabby saved?" he echoed.

"Yes, sir," answered a score of voices.

"AND WHO WITH HER?"

"No one as we know's on, sir."

"No one?"

"No, sir."

"How was she saved?"

"Don't know, sir."

"Nobody knows, sir."

"She don't even know herself, sir."

These replies were all made in a breath.

"Don't even know herself! What is the meaning of that?"

"Yes, sir. No, sir. You see, sir," began half a hundred voices.

"Hush, for Heaven's sake! Speak one at a time. Mrs. Smith, do you answer me. How was Miss Tabby saved?" inquired Lyon Berners, appealing to the oldest and wisest woman of the assembly, and silencing the others by a gesture.

"Indeed we don't know how she was reskeed, sir. She was brought home by a quarryman, but, she was in a cowld fever, and couldn't give no account of herself, nor nothing," replied the old woman.

"Where is she?"

"Up to her father's house, sir. They carried her there."

"I must go there and see her at once," said Mr. Berners, seizing his hat and hurrying from the house.

He walked rapidly through the kitchen garden, vineyard, orchard, and meadow, to the edge of the wood where the overseer's cottage stood.

He found old Mrs. Winterose with her hands full.

Mr. Winterose, who three days before had had a paralytic stroke, that had nearly brought him to the grave, had now so far rallied as to give hopes of his continued life.

He lay sleeping on a neat white bed in the lower front room of the cottage. His wife was the only person with him.

She came forward in great haste to meet Mr. Berners.

"Oh, sir!" she cried, "my child, Miss Sybil! was she reskeed?"

"Ah, Heaven! That is the very question I came to ask you, or rather to ask Tabby," sighed Mr. Berners, dropping into a chair.

"Oh, sir! Oh, sir!" wept the old nurse, "then I can't give you any more satisfaction than you can give me! Tabby don't know nothink! She's in bed up stairs, in a fever, and outen her mind, and Libby is a watching of her."

"Does she talk in her delirium?"

"Talk? Law, sir, she don't do nothink else at all! Her tongue goes like a mill-clapper all the time!"

"Let me go and see her. Perhaps by her rambling talk I may gain some clue to my poor wife's fate."

"I'm 'fraid you won't, sir. *I* an't been able to yet. But you're welcome to come up and see her if you will," said the old woman, rising and leading the way to a neat room overhead, where Miss Tabby lay in bed, babbling at random.

Miss Libby, who was sitting beside her, got up and courtesied, and made way for Mr. Berners, who came forward and bent over the sick woman, spoke to her kindly, and inquired how she felt.

But the old maid, who was quite delirious, took him for the sweetheart of her young days, and called him "Jim," and asked him how he dared to have the "impidince" to come into a young lady's room before she was up in the morning, and she requested Suzy—a sister who had long been dead—to turn him out directly.

But though Mr. Berners sat by her and succeeded in soothing her, he gained no information from her. She babbled of everything under the sun but the one subject to which he wished to lead her thoughts.

At length, in despair, Mr. Berners arose to depart.

"Where does that quarryman live who picked her up and brought her home?"

"Up at the quarries, sir, to be sure."

"But there are fifty cottages up there, scattered over the space of miles."

"Well, sir, it is in the whitish stone one, the nighest but three to the big oak, you know; which his name it is Norriss, as you can find him by that. But, law, sir! he can't tell you no more nor I have," said Mrs. Winterose.

Before she quite finished her speech Mr. Berners ran down stairs and out of the cottage, and bent his steps to the quarryman's hut.

It happened just as the old nurse had foretold.

The man could tell Mr. Berners nothing but this: that Miss Tabby had come to his house just about daylight, having her clothing wet and draggled nearly up to her waist with mud and water, and shaking as with an ague, and sinking with fatigue.

He having neither wife nor daughter, nor any other woman about the house, had no proper dry clothes to offer her; but he made her sit by the fire, while he questioned her as to the manner in which she came to be so much exposed.

She answered him only by senseless lamentations and floods of tears.

When her chill had gone off a high fever came on, and, the quarryman explained, he knew that she was going to be ill, so he offered to take her home; and, partly by leading, and partly by lugging, he had contrived to carry her safe to her father's cottage, which she reached in a state of fever and delirium.

This was all the information that Mr. Berners could get from the honest quarryman, who would willingly have given him more had he possessed it.

Lyon Berners went back to Black Hall, where he found Clement and Beatrix Pendleton waiting for him in the parlor, and wondering at his prolonged absence.

He apologized for having left them for so many hours, and explained the business that had called him so suddenly away, giving them the startling intelligence of Miss Tabby's unaccountable safety; which, he added, left the fate of his beloved wife in greater uncertainty than they had supposed it to be. She was *probably* drowned, but *possibly* rescued. He could not tell. He and they must wait patiently the issue of events.

Wait patiently? Twice more that day he walked up to the overseer's cottage to find out whether Miss Tabby's fever had gone off and she had come to her senses, and he came back disappointed. And again, very late at night, he walked up there and startled the watcher by the sick-bed with the same question so often repeated:

"Has she come to her senses yet?"

"No; she is more stupider than ever, I think," was Miss Libby's answer.

"What does your mother think is the matter with her, then?"

"Oh, nothing but chills and fevers. Only Tabby has a weak head, and always loses of it when she has a fever."

"Well, Miss Libby, as soon as she comes to herself, if it is in the dead of night, send some one over to the Hall to let me know, that I may come immediately; for my anxiety to ascertain my wife's fate, which she only can tell, is really insupportable."

Miss Libby promised to obey his directions, and Lyon Berners returned to Black Hall.

But not that night, nor for many nights after that, did Miss Tabby come to her senses. Her illness proved to be a low type of typhoid fever, not primarily caused, but only hastened by the depressing influences of fear and cold from her exposure to death, and to the elements, on the night of the great flood.

For many weary weeks she lay on her bed, too low to answer or even understand a question.

And during all this time nothing occurred to throw the faintest gleam of light upon the deep darkness that still enveloped the fate of Sybil Berners.

This period of almost insupportable anxiety was passed by Mr. Berners in doing all that was possible to repair the damage done by the disastrous flood.

He was the largest subscriber to, and also the treasurer of the fund raised for the relief of the victims, and passed much time in receiving and disbursing money on their account.

CHAPTER XXVII.

THE VICTIMS.

And each will mourn his own, (she saith,)

But sweeter woman ne'er drew breath

Than that young wife.—JEAN INGLELOW.

The Great Black Valley Flood, as it came to be called, had occurred on Hallow Eve.

Before Christmas Eve many of its ravages had been repaired.

The laborers' cottages had been rebuilt and refurnished. Other dwellings were in process of reconstruction; and the works were only temporarily suspended by the frost. The public buildings were contracted for, to be re-erected in the spring.

All the missing bodies had been recovered, and had received Christian burial, except those of Sybil Berners and her young child, neither of which had yet been found, or even heard of—a circumstance that led many to think that the mother and babe had been rescued and concealed by her friends.

And for many weeks Miss Tabby had lain prostrated in body and idiotic in mind, and thus totally unable to give any account of them.

Lyon Berners' anxiety and suspense gradually settled into deep melancholy and despondency. As a matter of duty, he managed the estate as if Sybil or her child might one day reappear to enjoy it.

It may be remembered that when Lyon Howe, the young barrister, married Sybil Berners, the wealthy heiress, by the conditions of the marriage contract he took her family name, that it might not become extinct.

As an offset to this sacrifice on his part, it was stipulated in the instrument that, in case of his wife dying before him, without leaving children, he should inherit her whole property.

This, in the present state of affairs, gave him all the power he needed in the management of the great Black Valley Manor.

He lived at Black Hall, doing his duty for duty's sake, a very lonely man.

Now that Sybil was gone, the neighbors were all disposed to be too good to him. They visited him, and invited him out. But with a just resentment he declined all visits, and all invitations, except from those devoted friends who had been faithful to his wife in the time of her trouble: Clement and Beatrix

Pendleton, young Sheridan the lawyer, old Mr. Fortescue the sheriff, and Robert Munson the soldier.

Miss Tabby at length rose from her bed of illness, and, to use her mother's words, "was able to creep about the house," but in a state of mental imbecility, which is not an unusual effect of a long, low type of typhoid fever. She was obstinate too, "obstinate as a mule," her sister said. No one could get a word of satisfaction from her upon the mysterious subject of Sybil's fate. When asked by Mr. Berners how *she* was saved, she answered:

"I was picked up by a man in a boat."

"What sort of a man?"

"An or'nary man like any other."

"Did you know who he was?"

"No."

"Where did he pick you up?"

"Not far from the prison."

"Where did he put you down?"

"Close by the quarries."

"What became of Sybil?"

"I don't know."

"When did you see her last?"

"The last time I ever set eyes on her *face*, was when she was lying on her bed in her cell, and I went and laid the baby by her; that was just before the water rushed in. I an't set eyes on *her face* or the *baby's face* since."

And this was literally true, for Miss Tabby had not seen their *faces* in the boat. But those who had not the key to her meaning, could not detect the equivocation.

She was cunning enough in her foolishness to keep her oath, and to leave upon the minds of her hearers the impression that Sybil and her young child were certainly lost.

But Miss Tabby had a tender conscience as well as a soft heart and a weak head, and the keeping of this secret, which she could not divulge without breaking her oath, nor conceal without trifling with the truth, caused her so much distress, that these frequent cross-examinations invariably ended, on her part, in a fit of hysterics.

This was the state of affairs on Christmas Eve following the great flood.

It was the saddest Christmas ever passed at Black Hall.

Mr. Berners had invited no one, not even his most intimate friends, to spend it with him.

But Captain Pendleton and Beatrix had come uninvited, for they were determined that Lyon Berners should not be left alone in his sorrow at such a time.

"We have rejoiced with you in many a Christmas holiday. Shall we not come and mourn with you now?" Beatrix gently inquired, as with her brother she entered the parlor, where Mr. Berners on this Christmas Eve was grieving alone.

He got up and welcomed his friends, and thanked them for their visit.

"I could not find it in my heart to invite any one, even you, true souls; but I am *very, very* glad you have come; though it is another sacrifice on your parts."

"Not at all, Lyon Berners; we love you, and had rather come here and be miserable with you than be merry with anybody else," said Clement Pendleton warmly.

But Mr. Berners was resolved that his generous young friends should not be as "miserable" as they were willing to be in the merry Christmas season. So he wrote a note of invitation for two other guests, and dispatched it by Joe to Blackville that very evening.

The note was addressed to Mr. Sheridan, with a request that he would come, and bring his niece, Miss Minnie Sheridan, to meet Captain and Miss Pendleton at dinner on Christmas-day, at Black Hall.

Now this Miss Minnie Sheridan was an orphan heiress, the daughter of the young barrister's eldest brother. By the death of both her parents, she had been left to the guardianship of her young uncle, who, with his youthful niece, now boarded at the Blackville Hotel.

It was reasonably to be expected that these young people would, on Christmas-day, willingly exchange the hotel parlor and the society of strangers, for the drawing-room at Black Hall and the company of their friends.

Moreover, Mr. Berners had noticed a growing esteem between the brilliant young barrister and the beautiful Beatrix Pendleton, an esteem which he hoped and believed, for their sakes, would ripen into a warmer sentiment. Therefore he invited the Sheridans to meet the Pendletons at the Christmas dinner.

Miss Tabby had, within a few days, returned and resumed her position as housekeeper at Black Hall. Her office was something of a sinecure. She could do little more than fret at the servants. She was not strong enough yet to scold them vigorously.

On the night before Christmas it snowed, but just enough to cover the ground a few inches deep.

Christmas-day broke clear, bright, and beautiful.

Lyon Berners arose early in the morning, to be ready to greet his two friends upon their entrance into the drawing-room.

Although his heart was aching with grief for Sybil, he was resolved to wear a cheerful countenance for the sake of those two loyal souls who had been so devoted to her, and were now so constant to him. He little dreamed how great would be his reward before the day should be over.

Clement and Beatrix Pendleton did not keep him waiting long. They soon came down from their chambers, and greeted him affectionately.

"This cannot be a 'merry' Christmas to you, dear Lyon, but it may be a *good* one. Will you accept this from me? See! with the faith or the superstition of the old Christians, I opened it at random to-day, to find your fate in some text. And this is really what my eyes first lighted on," said Beatrix Pendleton, as she placed an elegantly bound pocket Bible in the hands of Lyon Berners, and pointed to this passage:

"There shall be light at the evening tide."

"Thanks, dear Beatrix! thanks for the sacred gift and happy augury!" said Mr. Berners, as he took the book and read the lines. "'Light at the evening tide,' That, I fancy, means the evening of life. A weary time to wait, Beatrix. Ah! Clement, good-morning. I may wish *you* a merry Christmas, at least," he added, suddenly turning to Captain Pendleton, who had followed his sister into the room.

And they shook hands and went in to breakfast.

There were no more Christmas presents exchanged. No one there, except Beatrix, had thought of giving one; though hers had been graceful and appropriate.

After breakfast they went to church at Blackville. They were drawn thither in the roomiest carriage, by a pair of the strongest horses, with Joe on the box; for they expected to pick up the Sheridans after the morning service, and to bring them to Black Hall to dinner.

The distance between Black Hall and Blackville was considerable, and the road was rough, and so it was rather late when our party reached the church.

The congregation were already in their seats, and the pastor was in his pulpit; so there was no opportunity for our friends to meet until after the benediction was pronounced.

Then, as the people were all leaving the church, Mr. Berners sought out young Sheridan and his little niece, and after paying them the compliments of the season, invited them to take seats in his carriage to Black Hall.

They accepted his offer with thanks, and allowed him to conduct them to the coach, in which the Pendletons were already seated.

There was a merry meeting between the young people, notwithstanding the sadness of some reminiscences.

Youth cannot for ever be sorrowful.

Joe put whip to his horses, and started them at a brisk trot over the snow-clad roads, and under the brilliant sky of that clear December day.

They reached Black Hall in good time.

The splendid Christmas fires were blazing on every hearth in the house.

Beatrix Pendleton took Minnie Sheridan to her own bed-chamber, that they might there lay off their bonnets and shawls and prepare for dinner.

Captain Pendleton went off alone to his room, and Mr. Berners was just about to conduct young Sheridan to some spare bed-chamber, where he could brush his hair, when the barrister laid his hand upon his host's shoulder, and stopped him, saying:

"No; stay here. I have something which I must show you while we are quite alone."

And he shut the doors, and then drew his companion away to the furthest window, out of earshot of any chance eavesdropper.

"What is it?" inquired Mr. Berners, much mystified.

"I do not know; something very important I fancy. But read this first," said the barrister, placing an open letter in his friend's hand.

Lyon Berners in great curiosity examined it. It was addressed to ——— Sheridan, Esq., Counsellor at Law, Blackville.

It contained these lines:

> "Take the enclosed letter to Mr. Lyon Berners on
> Christmas-day, when you find him quite alone. If this

should reach you before Christmas, keep it carefully until that day; then deliver it to its address with secrecy and discretion."

"In the name of Heaven, what is this? Where is the letter? When did you get it?" demanded Lyon Berners, in astonishment.

"It seems to be a mystery. I got the letter only this morning, else in spite of the injunction I should have delivered it to you before. Here it is now," said young Sheridan, placing the mysterious epistle in the hands of his friend.

Lyon Berners examined it in haste and excitement.

It was superscribed:

> "To Lyon Berners, Esq., Black Hall. To the care of ---- Sheridan, Esq. To be delivered secretly on Christmas-day."

Mr. Berners tore off the envelope, when he came to another one, on which was written:

> A Christmas gift for Mr. Berners.

This also he hastily tore off. Then he ran his eyes rapidly over the contents of the letter, and with a great cry—a cry of joy unspeakable—he threw up his arms and sank to the floor.

He who had never been conquered by fear or sorrow or despair, was now utterly vanquished by joy!

CHAPTER XXVIII.

WHAT THE LETTER CONTAINED.

Do you blame me, friend, for weakness?

'Twas the strength of passion slew me.—E. B. BROWNING.

With an exclamation of dismay Sheridan raised his friend, and helped him to an arm-chair, and sat him back in a reclining position on it.

And at the same instant hurrying steps were heard approaching, and some of the servants who had been loitering in the hall, startled by the noise of the cry and the fall, rushed into the room to see what the matter could be.

Lyon Berners had not quite lost his consciousness, and the entrance of the men at once restored his senses.

His first act was to point to the letter which had fallen from his hand to the floor, and say:

"Pick it up and give it to me, and send these people away—quickly, Sheridan, if you please."

The young lawyer immediately went after the intruders, exclaiming,

"Come, come, old Joe, Tom, Bill; what do you mean by rushing in upon us in this way when we are having a good humored rough and tumble wrestling match among ourselves? Be off with you, you barbarians!"

And so with affected mirth, which really deluded the simple darkies, he turned them out of the drawing-room, and locked the door.

Then he went back to Mr. Berners and inquired:

"Now what is it, if I may ask?"

"She is safe! My dear Sybil is safe!—safe beyond all pursuit; beyond all possibility of recapture!" exclaimed Mr. Berners, triumphantly.

"Thank Heaven, with all my heart! But how, and where?" inquired Sheridan, excitedly.

"She was rescued by Raphael! She is on mid-ocean now, in a British ship, under the protection of the British flag, God bless it!"

"Amen! But tell me all about it, or let me read the letter."

"Stop! I must call Pendleton and Beatrix. Those two true friends must hear my secret and share our joy," said Mr. Berners, rising and going to the door.

But there was no need to call, for he had scarcely turned the lock before he heard the light steps of Miss Pendleton approaching.

"What is the matter? Lyon, you are happy or crazy! Which is it? I am sure something delightful must have happened to make you look so! What is it?" demanded Beatrix, as she slided into a seat.

Before Mr. Berners could answer, the door once more opened, and Captain Pendleton entered.

"What is up?" was his first question, on seeing the excited countenances of his friends.

"We have good news. But—where is Miss Sheridan?" inquired Mr Berners, suddenly remembering his youngest guest.

"Oh, Minnie is curling her hair in my room. Her ringlets were so blown by the wind that it was necessary to dress it over again. She wouldn't let me wait for her," explained Beatrix.

"It is just as well," added Mr. Sheridan. "Minnie is a good girl, but she is little more than a child; and though I could answer for her honesty, I couldn't for her discretion."

"Then," said Lyon Berners very gravely, "then let what I am about to read to you remain an inviolable secret between us four."

"Certainly," answered Sheridan.

"Shall we swear it?" inquired Pendleton.

"Yes! yes! if necessary. But, oh! do go on! It is something about Sybil," impatiently exclaimed Beatrix.

"Yes, it is something about Sybil. You need not swear to be secret on this subject. You have given me your words, and that is sufficient. Indeed, I feel sure that without any request on my part or promise on yours, you would still have been secret, for you would still have seen the necessity of secrecy. Now I will read you the letter, which will explain itself," said Mr. Berners, as he unfolded his mysterious epistle, and read:

> "BRITISH   MERCHANTMAN   DELIVERANCE,   }
> "At Sea, Lat. 35 deg. 15 m., Lon. 49 deg. 27 m.,}
> *December 1st, 18—.* }
>
> "TO LYON BERNERS, Esq.: Sir—As you and your set made such a mess of it in trying to save Mrs. Sybil Berners from the injustice of 'justice,' I, who am an outlaw, undertook to take her from out of all your hands.

"The instrument of my work was my dutiful son Raphael. We had intended, with the help of our brave band, to storm the prison, and deliver the fair prisoner by force of arms. But before we were quite ready for that difficult enterprise, the flood came and made all easy. We had only to hire a boat, get into it, and permit ourselves to be lifted by the rise of the waters to the level of her cell window, beat it in, and take her out. We did that and saved her, and also, incidentally, the infant girl and the old maid.

"We put out the woman at the foot of the Quarries, having first bound her by an oath to secrecy as to the means of her rescue and the safety of Sybil Berners—an oath, by the way, of which you hereby have the authority to release her, should you see fit to do so.

"We placed the child at nurse with a woman by the name of Fugitt, who is the wife of the overseer at Colonel Poindexter's plantation, not far from Blackville. The nurse knows nothing of the child, except that she was paid a hundred dollars down for taking care of it, and asking no questions.

"We took the mother to the old ruined wind-mill, where we had a snug room or two. There she was skilfully nursed by our old housekeeper through the dangerous fever that followed her confinement and her exposure. After her recovery and her full restoration to reason, we, avoiding every reference either to her long imprisonment or maternity, both of which events she had forgotten in the delirium of her illness, we took her away to Norfolk, where we went on board the British merchant ship 'Deliverance.' I write this letter from the sea, about half-way across the Atlantic, and I wait to send it by some homeward-bound ship.

"*December 9th.*—The man on the look-out reports a sail in sight, heading this way. If she should prove to be an American-bound ship, her name ought to be 'The Surprise,' for when I send this letter by her she will take you a very great surprise.

"If this should reach you in season, pray accept it as a Christmas gift.

"Mrs. Berners is still improving, though not yet well or strong enough to accommodate herself to the motion of the ship sufficiently to enable her to write to you. Nor will she send any confidential message through me. She will not even see or speak to me. She keeps her state-room, attended by my wife.

"She still resents her rescue, which she calls her abduction, and she feels grief and indignation at being taken away from you, rather than joy or gratitude at being saved from death. But then it is true that she thinks she was only rescued from drowning in the flood. She does not know that she was saved from a still more horrible fate.

"The mild insanity which appeared several months ago, and disappeared at the birth of her child, and which then shielded her from all realization of the horrors of her late position, still saves her from all knowledge of what it was. Although now perfectly sane, she is entirely ignorant that she was ever put on trial for her life, or condemned to death, or sent to prison.

"Nor would I enlighten her on that subject lest the fate of the sleep-walker should be hers—who, having safely walked over the parapet of a bridge above an awful chasm, fell dead with horror the next morning at beholding the peril he had escaped. I would advise you to maintain the same inviolable secrecy on that subject. She does not know the dangers she has passed, and she need never know them.

"They have spoken the ship, and I will go up and see what she is.

"*Later.*—She is not the "Surprise," as she ought to have been. She is the "Sally Ann," of Baltimore, homeward bound, with a cargo of silks. She will lay alongside for half an hour to exchange letters and some provisions.

"A few words more. Don't forget where I told you, you might find your child, and then go and accuse me of stealing it.

"Remember that you have my authority for releasing the old woman from her oath, that she may give you every detail of the rescue. But I counsel you, that as soon as you shall have heard all that she has got to tell you, you will seal up her lips with another oath even more binding than the first.

"The continued existence of Sybil Berners should be kept a profound secret from all others, except those few devoted friends who will follow her into exile; and it should be kept so, for this reason; that sometime, sooner or late, there will be an extradition treaty between all civilized nations, for the delivering up of fugitives from justice, which impending treaty may or may not have a retrospective action. Therefore it is better that Mrs. Berners should be supposed to have perished in the flood, and that the secret of her rescue and continued life should be carefully kept from all, except those already mentioned.

"A last word. The only way in which my wife can keep her quiet, is by promising that you will follow her immediately. Come as soon as you can. I am weary of my charge. Why I ever undertook it, is my secret. We will await you in Liverpool. A letter addressed to 'Raphael,' through the general post-office in that city, will find us.

"And now I must seal up, wishing you a merry Christmas. From your

UNKNOWN FRIEND."

"Thank Heaven!" fervently exclaimed Beatrix Pendleton.

"Amen," earnestly responded her brother.

"You will go soon, Lyon?" eagerly inquired Beatrix.

"Soon? I would start instantly if I could. But there is no coach that leaves for Baltimore or Norfolk until the day after to-morrow. To-day I will give orders to my servants to pack up. To-morrow I will ride over to Fugitt's to inquire after my child, which for its own sake must still be left in their care, I suppose. And the day after I will leave in the early coach for Baltimore. There I shall certainly be able to meet a clipper bound for Liverpool," answered Mr. Berners, speaking very rapidly.

"And in the mean time?" anxiously inquired Captain Pendleton.

"In the meantime, that is, to-day, I must give my friend Sheridan here a power of attorney to manage this estate during my absence. For you—you hold to your purpose of visiting Europe, Pendleton?"

"Oh, yes; and if you could wait a week, while I make the necessary arrangements, Beatrix and myself might accompany you; but that is too much to ask of you under the circumstances," smiled Clement Pendleton.

"I should be so rejoiced to have you both go with me, especially as the voyage is going to be a tedious one at this season of the year; but how can I delay a day while my poor Sybil, an exile among strangers, waits for me?"

"Oh, of course you could not possibly do it. But we will follow you soon, Berners, rely upon that."

Lyon Berners pressed his friend's hand in silence, and then went to meet Minnie Sheridan, who had glided shyly and silently into the room.

She must have heard the latter part of the conversation, but without apparently understanding it; for she came forward blushing and smiling, as usual, and took her seat beside Beatrix Pendleton.

The conversation concerning Sybil ceased then. Some one started the subject of the Christmas sermon, and they talked of that until dinner was announced.

It was a much happier feast than Lyon Berners had ventured to hope for. They sat long at table. After they withdrew to the drawing-room, Mr. Berners sat the two Pendletons and the two Sheridans down to a rubber of whist, and then excused himself to them, and went out in search of Miss Tabitha Winterose.

He found that faithful creature in the housekeeper's room, sitting at a little table, drinking tea and dropping tears.

"What is the matter, Miss Tabby?" he inquired cheerfully.

"What is the matter!" she repeated, reproachfully. "Is it what is the matter you ask me, Mr. Berners; *you*? An't this Christmas-day the first Christmas-day since ever she was born, as she hasn't passed here? And to see how you all went on at dinner, eating and drinking and laughing and talking as if *she* wasn't lost and gone!"

"Now, Miss Tabby, you know well enough that Mrs. Berners is quite safe."

Miss Tabby started, spilt her tea, nearly dropped her cup, and—gazed at him in consternation.

"I know that you know she is safe," repeated Mr. Berners.

"I don't know nothink of the sort! How should I? And neither do you. How should you indeed, when even I don't?" said Miss Tabby, defiantly.

"Now, my good soul, you were present when Mrs. Berners was taken through the window of the flooded prison on to the boat," said Mr. Berners.

Miss Tabby stared at him aghast.

"How—how—how do you know that?" she gasped and faltered.

"My good creature, because the man who rescued her and her child and you, has written and told me how he did it, and all about it."

Miss Tabby's mouth and eyes opened wider than ever.

"And is she—is she safe?" she inquired.

"Yes, she is safe, on her way to a foreign country, where I shall follow her."

"Well, my good gracious me alive; how uncommon strange things do turn out! Well, I never did hear the like to that! Well, thanks be to goodness!" ejaculated the poor woman fervently, clasping her hands.

"Now, Miss Tabby, this letter-writer tells me that he bound you by an oath never to divulge the secret of Sybil's rescue; but, mark you, that he gives me the authority to release you from that oath, so that you may give me all the particulars of that event," said Mr. Berners, and then he waited for her to speak. But she kept a resolute silence.

"Come, Miss Tabby, tell me all about it," continued Mr. Berners, seating himself to listen to the story.

"I an't got nothing to tell you any more than I have told you already," answered the woman doggedly.

"Why, you never told me anything!" exclaimed Lyon Berners, impatiently.

"Yes, I did too! I told you as how the last time I seen Miss Sybil's face, or the baby's face, was when they was both a layin' side by side on the bed just before the water rushed into the broken winder; and how I myself was picked up not far from where the prison was," said Miss Tabby, stubbornly.

"Which was all a prevarication, Tabby, though to the letter true. Come. You can tell me more than that."

"No, sir; I told you that *then*, and I can't tell you no more *now*."

"But I know you can. See! this letter releases you from your oath of silence."

"No letter can't release me from no oath, sir, which I took upon the Bible," persisted Miss Tabby.

"Was there ever such fanaticism!" exclaimed Lyon Berners, impatiently.

"I don't know what sort of a schism fanaticism is, sir, but I know I an't left so far to my own devices as to be let to fall into *any* schisms, so long as I prays faithfully into the litany every Sunday to be delivered from *all* schisms."

"Heaven and earth, woman! That has nothing to do with it. Here is a man writing to release you from an oath you took to *him* to keep secrecy on a certain event, of which it is expedient now for you to speak. He frees you from your oath, I tell you."

"Which he can't do, sir, begging of his parding and yours. If so be I *took* an oath, which I don't acknowledge as I *did* take," said Miss Tabby, cautiously, "*he* can't free me from it no more 'n no one else. And if so be you could put me on the rack like a heathen and torter me to death, I would die a marture to the faith rayther than break my oath," snivelled Miss Tabby.

"Who the demon wants to put you on the rack, you intolerable old idiot?" exclaimed Lyon Berners, driven past his patience by her obstinacy. "Will you, or will you not, tell me all the particulars of Sybil's rescue?"

"No, sir, I will not, because I cannot without breaking of my oath," persisted Miss Tabby, with a constancy which compelled respect for her honesty, if it inspired contempt for her judgment.

"Well, I hope also that you will never mention the matter to any one else," said Mr. Berners, one little comfort mingling with his disappointment.

"That I never will, sir; but will suffer my tongue to be tored out by the roots first. If I have strength to withstand *you*, sir, don't you think as I shall have strength to withstand others?"

"I think it quite likely. Well, Miss Tabby, *I* know you understand me, whether you will divulge anything to me or not, and so I shall soon give you certain instructions as freely as if there were an outspoken confidence between us," said Mr. Berners, rising to leave the room.

"That you may do, sir, with full faith in me," answered Miss Tabby.

And then Mr. Berners left her, and returned to his guests.

Mr. Berners and his guests passed that Christmas evening, not in playing Christmas games, but in transacting important business.

The three gentlemen excused themselves to the two ladies, and leaving them to practice a new duet together on the piano, withdrew to the library, where documents were drawn up giving lawyer Sheridan full powers to manage the estate in the absence of its proprietors.

When these were duly signed, sealed, and delivered, and all the details of the agency and of the voyage had been thoroughly discussed, they returned to the drawing-room.

It was now late, and the guests arose to take leave, but at Mr. Berners' earnest invitation, they consented to remain, not only for the night, but for the two days that their host would be at home.

The next morning, after an early breakfast, Mr. Berners mounted his horse and rode over to the plantation where his child had been placed to nurse. He was determined, as a matter of prudence, not to divulge to the nurse the parentage of the child. He knew that to do so would start a furor of gossip and speculation that would be both unpleasant and inconvenient.

On reaching the plantation, he rode up to the gate of the substantial stone cottage belonging to the overseer, alighted, tied his horse to a post, and went up to the house door and knocked.

A rosy-cheeked girl of about twelve years of age opened the door.

"Is Mrs. Fugitt in?" he inquired.

"Yes, sir," replied the girl, stretching wide the door to admit the visitor.

Mr. Berners stepped into a very clean and comfortable room, where a woman sat with one young babe at her breast and another in the cradle beside her.

She took her foot from the rocker of the cradle and arose with the babe still in her arms to meet the stranger.

"Mrs. Fugitt?" inquired Mr. Berners.

"Yes, sir, that's my name. Will you sit down? Betsy Ann, hand the gentleman a chair."

The little girl brought forward a country made chip-bottom chair, and with a bow, the visitor seated himself.

The woman also sat down, and waited in some little curiosity to find out the object of the stranger's visit.

"You have a young child at nurse?" he said.

"Yes, sir; this one that I have upon my lap. That one in the cradle is my own."

"Are you strong enough to nurse two children?" inquired Mr. Berners.

"Betsy Ann," said the woman, turning to the little girl, "call your sister Nancy 'Lizabeth in here."

The child went into a back kitchen, and returned with another child the counterpart of herself.

"There, now! You two stand right up there before the gentleman."

The children joined hands, and stood before Mr. Berners for inspection.

"There, now, sir! You look at them."

"They are very well worth looking at; a pair of stout, rosy, healthy, happy lasses, I'm sure," said Mr. Berners, smiling at them, and feeling in his pocket for some loose coins.

"Well, sir, them's my twins. I nussed 'em both myself without any help from a bottle—either a bottle for *them*, sir, or a bottle for *myself*," said the mother, proudly.

"They do you much credit, certainly," said Mr. Berners, who had now found two half-eagles.

"Well, sir, they never had a day's sickness in their lives. I showed 'em to you, sir, to prove as I could nuss two children successful."

"I'm convinced of it."

"One of 'em is named Elizabeth Ann, and the other Ann Elizabeth. The same name because they're twins, sir, only put backwards and forwards like, so as to tell one gal's name from t'other's. And I call 'em Betsy Ann and Nancy 'Lizabeth on week-days and work days; and I call 'em Elizabeth Ann and Ann Elizabeth on Sundays and company days."

"Quite right," said Mr. Berners, smiling.

"And now, gals, you may go," said the mother.

"Here, my dears! Here is somethings to buy you a Christmas gift each," said Mr. Berners, slipping the gold coins into the hands of the children.

"There! thank the gentleman, and then run out and peel the potatoes and turnips. And be sure you don't lose your pennies," said the woman, who had no idea that the children's gifts had been half-eagles.

The well-trained little girls obeyed their mother in every particular. And as soon as they had left the room, Mr. Berners turned to the woman and inquired:

"Are those fine children your only ones?"

"I never had any but them until about three months ago, when that boy in the cradle came to put a surprise on me. Look at him, sir! An't he a hearty little chap for a three monther?"

"Indeed he is!" acknowledged Mr. Berners, as he turned down the coverlet and gazed at the fat, rosy babe. "And now," he continued, as he replaced the cover, "will you let me look at your nurse-child? I—I am its guardian, and responsible for the expense of its rearing."

"So I judged, sir, when I first saw you. The gentleman that brought the child to me, and gave me a hundred dollars with it, told me how, in about a couple of months, the guardian of the child would come to make further arrangements. And you're him, sir?"

"I am he," gravely replied Lyon Berners, as he gazed fondly down on the face of his sleeping babe, and traced in the delicate features and silky black hair and faintly drawn black eye-brows the lineaments of its mother.

"Well, sir, I can tell you, for your satisfaction, that the child is in good hands."

"I have no doubt of it. And," he continued, after some hesitation, "I can tell you, for *your* satisfaction, that the child is all right. She was born in lawful wedlock."

"I'm glad to hear that, for the child's sake, sir; though if what you tell me is true, as I suppose it is, I don't see why the parents can't own their child."

"There are good and sufficient reasons which may be made known to you at some future time," replied Mr. Berners.

"Humph! then I s'pose it's a case of a *secret* marriage, that can't be acknowledged yet a while, upon account of offending rich parents, and being cut off from their property or something. I have heard of such things before now. Well, sir, I don't want to intrude on your secrets, and I know how to keep a still tongue in my head. And as for the baby, sir, *she* has made her own way into my heart, and whatever her parents have been and done, I shall love and nuss her as if she was my own."

"You are a good woman, Mrs. Fugitt; and now to business. I, as guardian to that child, wish to make some definite arrangement for her support for the next two years at least."

"Yes, sir."

"Do you know lawyer Sheridan?"

"Of course I do, sir; he drawed up the papers between the Colonel and my old man when my old man made an engagement with the Colonel to oversee the plantation for five years."

"Very well. This Mr. Sheridan will pay you quarterly installments of money amounting to six hundred dollars a year for the support of the child."

The overseer's wife was a very simple-hearted woman, so she burst out, with her surprise:

"But that is a great deal of money, sir. More than twice too much."

"I do not think so. The child is entitled to much more, if she could use it. At any rate, that is her allowance. And here is the first quarterly payment in advance," said Mr. Berners, placing a roll of bank-notes on the woman's lap.

"But, sir, I haven't used a quarter part of what the other gentleman paid me. In truth, I only spent what I did to buy the baby's clothes, of which she hadn't a rag but what was on her when the other gentleman put her in my arms."

"So much the more reason I should advance you this money."

"Why? because I have got so much already, sir?"

"—Because you are so simple and honest. Few people would believe in such simplicity and honesty, Mrs. Fugitt."

"Then Lord forgive 'em, sir."

"Amen. And now, Mrs. Fugitt, a last word, and then good-bye. If you should ever wish to communicate with me, you may do it by inclosing a letter to Mr. Sheridan, or sending a message by him."

"Yes, sir."

"And now let me take another look at this little one."

"But there is another thing, sir: What is her name? I asked the gentleman, and he said he did not know, but you would tell me."

"'Her name?'" repeated Lyon Berners, as he gazed down upon the face of the sleeping child—the prison-born child—"Her name? It is Ingemisca; call her Ingemisca."

"Yes, sir," said the woman in a very low tone, for she was awed by the looks and words of the speaker—"Yes, sir; but would you please to write it on a slip of paper? It is a strange, solemn sort of a sound, and I'm sure I never could remember it."

Lyon Berners tore a page from his tablets, wrote the name in pencil, and handed it to her.

Then he kissed his infant daughter, breathed a silent blessing over her, and took his leave.

He returned to Black Hall, well satisfied with the woman in whose care he had left his child.

That afternoon he dined with his friends for the last time for many years. That evening, with their assistance, he concluded the very last business he had to transact, before leaving his home and country.

Beatrix Pendleton had been busy all day, looking up and packing up Sybil's costly jewels, laces, and shawls. Valuable as they all were, they filled but a small trunk, which Miss Pendleton assured Mr. Berners he could easily put inside his great sea-chest without crowding out other things.

Beatrix Pendleton and Minnie Sheridan volunteered to remain at Black Hall for a few days after the departure of the proprietor, to see that all things were properly set in order.

Among the last arrangements made was that by which honest Robert Munson, the young soldier who had befriended Sybil Berners, was appointed assistant overseer of the plantation, with the use of a cottage and garden, and with a considerable salary.

All the arrangements for the voyage of Mr. Berners, and the management of the manor during his absence, were completed that evening.

The next morning Mr. Berners accompanied by his friends, Captain Pendleton and lawyer Sheridan, set out for Blackville, to meet the stage-coach for Baltimore.

There, at the stage-office, Mr. Berners took leave of lawyer Sheridan, but not of Captain Pendleton, who made up his mind, at the last moment, to accompany him as far as the sea-port, and to see him off on his voyage.

After two days' journey, the friends arrived safely in Baltimore.

On consulting the shipping list, they found the fast sailing clipper Dispatch, Captain Fleet, advertised to sail for Liverpool the same afternoon.

Lyon Berners, with his friend, hastened to the agent to secure his passage, which he was so fortunate as to get.

He had barely time to hurry his luggage on board before the clipper set sail.

The very last words addressed to Mr. Berners by his friend Captain Pendleton were these:

"Give our love to Mrs. Berners, and tell her that Beatrix and myself will follow you soon. Heaven bless you with good luck!"

CHAPTER XXIX.

AFTER THE EXPATRIATION.

And year went by; and the tale at last

Was told as a sorrowful one long past.—MISTLETOE BOUGH.

A week after Lyon Berners went away Captain Pendleton resigned his commission in the army, placed the management of his estate in the hands of lawyer Sheridan, and, accompanied by Miss Pendleton, left the neighborhood for Baltimore, whence he sailed for Liverpool.

After this departure the secret of Sybil's escape was known but to two persons in the valley—to Mr. Sheridan, whose very profession made him reticent, and to Miss Tabby, who would have died rather than have divulged it.

Mr. Sheridan managed the manor, Miss Tabby kept the house, and both guarded the secret.

But great was the wonder and wild were the conjectures among the people of the valley on the subjects of Sybil's mysterious disappearance, Lyon's sudden voyage, and Clement and Beatrix Pendleton's eccentric conduct in following him.

Opinions were as various as characters.

Some came near the truth in expressing their belief that Sybil had been rescued on the night of the flood, secreted for awhile in the neighborhood, and then "spirited" away by her friends; that she was safe in some foreign country, and that her husband and her two friends had gone to join her.

Others whispered that Sybil had been drowned in the flood; that Lyon Berners, finding himself a widower, had proposed for Beatrix Pendleton, with whom he had always been in love, and that he had been accepted by her; that they had been anxious to marry immediately; but ashamed to do so, so soon after the tragic death of Sybil, and in her own neighborhood; and so they had gone abroad to be united, and to spend the first year of their wedded lives.

These and many other speculations were rife among the neighbors, and the "Hallow Eve Mystery," deepened by recent events, formed the subject of conversation of never-flagging interest, at every country fireside that winter.

In the midst of all this, Miss Tabby Winterose lived her quiet, dull, whimpering life at Black Hall, carefully keeping the house, waited on by Aunt

Mopsa, guarded by Joe, and solaced by little Cromartie, who had been left in her care.

Dilly, Sybil's own maid, had been taken abroad by Miss Pendleton, which fact gave additional scandal to the gossips.

"The impudence of her!" they said, "to take the late Mrs. Berners' very maid, before even she had fairly married the widower."

All this, when it came to Miss Tabby's ears, made that faithful but desponding soul whimper all the more.

Miss Tabby had but few recreations at Black Hall. Going to church every Sunday in the old carryall, with little Cro' by her side and Joe on the box, was her "most chiefest."

Then once a month or so, she went to take tea with her parents and sister; or she walked over to spend an afternoon at the cottage occupied by Robert Munson, who had married Rachel, the pretty daughter of that Norfolk inn-*keeper, who had been Lyon's and Sybil's host at the time of their first flight.

And sometimes Miss Tabby had both these families up at Black Hall, to pass a day with her.

But wherever Miss Tabby went, she always took little Cro'; and whoever came to the house had to make much of the child, or get little favor from his "aunty."

As for Joe, Robert Munson, and other of Sybil's devoted friends, they felt, in their secret hearts, that Sybil was safe in foreign parts, and that her husband and friends had gone to join her; but as no one had actually imparted this intelligence to them, they never talked over the subject except among themselves.

Thus passed the winter; but with the opening of the spring, an event occurred that for a while even superseded the "Hallow Eve Mystery," in the fever of curiosity and interest it excited in the valley.

The great Dubarry manor, so long held in abeyance, was claimed!—claimed by a gentleman in right of his wife—claimed by no less a person than Mr. Horace Blondelle, once the husband and afterwards the widower of that beautiful Rosa Blondelle who had been so mysteriously murdered at Black Hall, and now the bridegroom of Gentiliska, the great-granddaughter and only lineal descendant and heiress of Philip Dubarry and Gentiliska his wife.

During the investigation of this claim, Mr. and Mrs. Horace Blondelle occupied a handsome suite of apartments at the Blackville Hotel, and made themselves very popular by the elegant little dinners and suppers they gave, and the like of which had never before been seen in that plain village.

When their case came on for a hearing, there was but little opposition to the claimants, whose legal right to the manor was soon proved by the documents they held in their possession, and firmly established.

When the case was decided in their favor, Mr. Horace Blondelle rented Pendleton Park, which had been to let ever since the departure of its owner.

And in that well-furnished mansion on that well-cultivated plantation he settled down with his pretty young bride to the respectable life of a country gentleman.

His residence in the neighborhood gave quite an impetus to the local business.

The very first thing that he did, after his settlement at Pendleton Park, was to advertise, through the columns of the "Blackville Banner," that he intended to rebuild the Dubarry mansion, and was ready to employ the necessary artisans at liberal wages.

This gave great satisfaction to the laboring classes, who were half their time pining in idleness, and the other half working at famine prices.

But such a "reconstruction" was a gigantic undertaking. There was a wilderness to be cleared, a desert to be reclaimed, a mansion to be rebuilt, and a chapel to be restored.

All the carpenters, stone-cutters, bricklayers, plasterers, painters and glaziers, upholsterers and decorators, as well as ornamental gardeners and agricultural laborers that could be found, were at once employed at generous wages.

And the work went on merrily, and the people blessed Horace Blondelle.

But during the progress of the work, a discovery was made that changed the whole plan of the proprietor's life.

In the course of clearing the grounds, the workmen found a spring, whose water was so particularly nasty that they at once suspected it to possess curative qualities of the greatest value, and so reported it to the proprietor.

Horace Blondelle invited the local medical faculty to taste the waters of the spring, and their report was so favorable that he bottled up a gallon of it, and sent it to an eminent chemist of New York, to be analyzed.

In due time the analysis was returned. The water of the spring, it showed, was strongly impregnated with a half dozen, more or less, of the most nauseous minerals known to the pharmaceutists, and therefore were of the highest medicinal virtues.

The recent discovery of this invaluable spring on the home grounds, together with the long known existence of the magnificent cavern, or chain of caverns, in the adjacent mountains, determined Mr. Horace Blondelle to alter his whole scheme—to abandon the role of country gentleman, which a very short experience proved to be too "slow" for his "fast" tastes, and to adopt that of the proprietor of a great watering-place, and summer resort.

And so, instead of rebuilding the family mansion, he built a large hotel on the Dubarry manor, and instead of restoring the chapel, he erected a pavilion over the spring.

This was not only at the time a very popular measure, but it proved in the event a very great success.

That summer and autumn saw other changes in the valley.

First old Mr. Winterose, the overseer of the Black Valley manor, died a calm and Christian death.

Young Robert Munson succeeded him in office.

Next lawyer Sheridan received an appointment from the President as consul at a certain English seaport; and, no doubt with the consent of the proprietors, he transferred the management of the Black Valley manor to old lawyer Closeby of Blackville. And then, with his sister, he went abroad.

Then, on the thirty-first of October of that year, old Mrs. Winterose and her eldest daughter Libby received an order to remove from their cottage and take up their residence with Miss Tabby at Black Hall.

The next spring, Mr. and Mrs. Horace Blondelle removed to the "Dubarry Hotel," at the "Dubarry White Sulphur Springs," as the place was now christened, and there they commenced preparations for the summer campaign.

Mr. Horace Blondelle, was much too "sharp" not to understand the importance of advertising. He advertised very largely in the newspapers, and he also employed agents to distribute beautiful little illustrated books, descriptive of the various attractions of the "Dubarry White Sulphur Springs," the salubrious and delightful climate, the sublime and beautiful scenery, the home comforts of the hotel, and the healing powers of the water.

All these were so successfully set forth that even in this first season the house was so well filled with guests that the proprietor determined that, before another season should roll around, he would build a hundred or so of cottages to accommodate the great accession of visitors he had every reason to expect.

Another brisk season of work blessed the poor people of the place. And by the next summer a hundred and fifty white cottages were here and there on the rocks, in the woods, by the streams, or in the glens around the great hotel;

and the "Dubarry White Sulphur Springs" grew to look like a thriving village on the mountains.

The profits justified the expenditures; that second summer the place was crowded with visitors; and the lonely and quiet neighborhood of the Black Valley became, for the time, as populous and as noisy as is now Niagara or Newport.

In fact, from the advent of Mr. Horace Blondelle, and the inauguration of the "Dubarry White Sulphur Springs," the whole character of the place was changed.

All summer, from the first of June to the first of September, it would be a scene of fashion, gayety, confusion, and excitement.

But all the winter, from the first of October until the first of June, it is happily true that it would return to its aboriginal solitude and stillness.

Mr. Horace Blondelle was making money very fast indeed.

The life suited him. Many people called him a gambler and a blackleg, and said that he fleeced his guests in more ways than one.

The haughtiest among the old aristocratic families cut him, not because he was a gambler—for, oh dear! it too often happened that their own fathers, brothers, husbands, or sons were gamblers!—but because he kept a hotel and took in money!

Notwithstanding this exclusion from companionship with certain families, Mr. Horace Blondelle led a very gay, happy, and prosperous life.

We see and grieve over this sort of thing very frequently in the course of our lives. We fret that the wicked man should "flourish like a green bay tree," and we forget that the time must come when he will be cut down and cast into the fire.

That time was surely coming for Mr. Horace Blondelle.

Meanwhile he "flourished."

The third season of the "Dubarry White Sulphur Springs," was even more successful than its forerunners had been.

People were possessed with a furor for the nasty waters and flocked by thousands to the neighborhood.

But the autumn of that year was marked by other events of more importance to this story.

First, in the opening of the fall term of the Blackville Academy for young gentlemen, lawyer Closeby came to Black Hall, armed with the authority of

Mr. Lyon Berners, and straightway took little Cromartie, now a lad of seven years of age, out of the hands of Miss Tabby, and placed him in those of Dr. and Mrs. Smith, dominie and matron of the academy, for education.

Miss Tabby mourned over the partial loss of her favorite, but was consoled on the very next Hallow Eve, when a beautiful babe was left at her door.

And now that years have passed, we approach the time when the great Hallow Eve Mystery was destined to be a mystery no longer.

CHAPTER XXX.

THE GUARDIANS OF THE OLD HOUSE.

On every lip a speechless horror hung,

On every brow the burden of affliction;

The old ancestral spirits knew and felt

The house's malediction.—THOMAS HOOD.

Time does but deepen the gloom that hangs over an old mansion where a heinous crime has been committed, an awful tragedy enacted.

As the years darkened over the old Black Hall, the house fell to be regarded as a place haunted and accursed.

But as there is a certain weird attraction in the horrible, the old Black Hall came to be the greatest object of morbid interest in the neighborhood, greater even than the magnificent caverns, or the miraculous springs.

The crowds of visitors who came down to the "Dubarry White Sulphur" every summer, after tasting the waters of the spring and exploring the beauties of the caverns, invariably drove down the banks of the Black River to where it broadened into the Black Lake, from whose dark borders arose the sombre wood that shadowed the mountain's side, and from whose obscure depths loomed up the gloomy structure now known as Black Hall, the deserted home of the haughty Berners, the haunted and accursed mansion.

Here, on the murky borders of the lake, the visitors would draw up their carriages, to sit and gaze upon the fatal edifice, and listen to the story of that awful Hallow Eve, when the fiery-hearted young wife was driven by jealousy to desperation, and her fair young rival was murdered in her chamber.

"And on every Hallow Eve," their informant would continue—"on every Hallow Eve, at midnight deep, the spirit of the murdered guest might be seen flying through the house pursued by the spirit of the vengeful wife."

Visitors never penetrated into the wood that surrounded and nearly concealed the mansion, much less ventured near that mansion itself.

The place was guarded by three old women, they were told, weird as Macbeth's witches, and who discouraged all approach to their abode.

So solitary and deserted were the house and its inmates, that every path leading through the forest towards its doors was overgrown and obliterated, except one—a little narrow bridle-path leading from the house through the woods, and out upon the Blackville road. This was kept open by the weekly rides of old Joe, who went every Saturday to the village to lay in the groceries for the use of the family; by the three old women, who, seated on their safe old horses, went in solemn procession every Sunday to church; by the young Cromartie, who came trotting on his fiery steed once a month to visit his old friends; and by old lawyer Closeby, who came ambling on his sedate cob every quarter-day to inspect the premises and pay the people.

No other passengers but these ever disturbed the stillness of the forest path; no other forms than these ever darkened the doors of Black Hall. A gloomy place to live in! gloomy enough for the three quiet old women—too gloomy for the bright young girl who was growing up to womanhood under its shadows.

And never was the place darker, drearier, or more depressing in its aspect than on a certain Hallow Eve, some fifteen years or more after the disappearance of Sybil Berners and the self-expatriation of her devoted friends.

All day long the sky had been overcast by low, dark leaden-hued clouds; the rain had fallen in dull drizzle; and when the vailed sun sunk beneath the horizon, the darkness of night was added to the darkness of clouds.

A dismal night! dismal without, and even more dismal within!

The three old guardians of the premises lived in the left wing of the house, which corresponded exactly with the right wing once occupied on the first floor by the unfortunate Rosa Blondelle with her child and nurse, and on the second floor by Sybil Berners and her maid.

The old women had chosen the left wing partly because it had always been occupied by Miss Tabby, who used the lower floor for housekeeper's room and store-room, and the second floor as a bedchamber and linen closet, but *chiefly* because it was the furthest removed from the right wing, the scene of the murder, and now the rumored resort of ghosts.

On this dismal but eventful Hallow Eve of which I now write, the three old women, their early tea over, were gathered around the fire in the lower room of this left wing.

It was a long, low room, with a broad fireplace in the lower end. It was furnished in very plain country style. The walls were colored with a red ochre wash somewhat duller than paint. The windows had blinds made of cheap flowered wall paper. The floor was covered with a plaid woolen carpet, the work of old Mrs. Winterose's wheel and loom. A corner cupboard with glass doors, through which could be seen rows of blue delf dishes and piles of white tea-cups and saucers, occupied the corner on the right of the fireplace;

the old-fashioned, coffin-like, tall eight-day clock stood in the corner on the left-hand side. Flag-bottomed wooden chairs flanked the walls. At the upper end of the room stood an old-time chest of drawers. On the right-hand corner of this end, a door opened upon a flight of stairs leading to the floor above. On the left-hand corner a door opened into a back room, with a little back porch, vine covered.

There was a large spinning-wheel near the stair door, and at it the young ward of Mrs. Winterose stood spinning.

Before the fire stood a plain deal table, and on it a brass candlestick supporting one tallow candle, that gave but a dim light to the three old ladies who sat before the dull, smouldering green wood fire and worked. Old Mrs. Winterose occupied her arm-chair, between the end of the table and the fireside near the corner cupboard. She was carding rolls of white wool for the spinner.

Miss Libby sat at the other end of the table, reeling off blue yarn from broaches that had just been drawn off the spindle.

Miss Tabby was squeezed into the chimney corner next her sister, knitting a gray stocking.

There was a deep silence, broken only by the sighing of the wind through the leafless trees without, the pattering of the rain against the windows, the whirr of the spinning-wheel at the foot of the stairs, the simmering of the green logs that refused to blaze, and the audible snivelling of Miss Tabby.

The silence grew so oppressive that Miss Tabby, like the child in the Quaker meeting, felt that she must speak, or sob, or suffocate.

"Hallow Eve again," she sighed, "it have come round once more since that awful night, which I shall never be rid on seeing it before me—no, not if I live to be as old as Methusalah! And oh, what gloomy weather! How the wind do moan and the rain do pour 'round the old house! Just like heaving sighs and steaming tears! And as for me, I never feel like nothing but sighs and tears myself whenever this most doleful night comes round again."

And suiting the action to the word, the speaker drew a deep breath and wiped her eyes.

"Tabby, you're always a whimpering. When 'tan't about one thing 'tis about another. Seems to me a woman of your age, turned fifty, ought to have more sense!" sharply commented old Mrs. Winterose, as she took a roll of wool from her card and placed it softly on a pile of others that lay upon the table.

"I can't help of it, mother. I can't, indeed. Whenever this most doleful night do come round again, I feel that low sperreted I don't know what to do. And it is just such a night as that night was. Everything so miserable, outside and in. The wind moaning and the rain drizzling out there, and in here the fire not burning, but just smouldering and smoking as if it was low-sperreted too!" sighed Miss Tabby.

"I'll soon raise the fire's sperrits," said the old lady, briskly rising and seizing the poker, and giving the logs a good lunge and lift, that sent up a shower of sparks and a sheet of flame, lighting the whole room with the brightness of day.

The effect was as transient as it was brilliant, however. The sparks expired in their upward flight, and the flame died down again, leaving the logs simmering as before.

"There, now, you see how it is, mother. The very fire feels the time," sighed Miss Tabby.

"Fiddle! it is only because the wood is green. I'll cure that too. I'll make lame-legged Joe gather a heap of pine cones, that will burn the greenest wood as ever sulked on a hearth," chirped the blithe old lady, as she set the poker in its place.

And then she went to the back door of the back room, and standing on the covered porch, called out:

"Joe, Joe, fetch in a basket of pine cones to make the fire burn!"

A rumbling noise a little resembling a human voice was heard in the distance, and the old lady shut the door, returned to her seat, and resumed her reeling.

"I—don't feel to think it is the firewood, mother; I—I think it is the souls," slowly and solemnly announced Miss Libby, who had not spoken before.

"The *what?* What in patience are *you* talking about, Libby?" severely demanded the old lady, as she briskly wound off her yarn.

"The *souls*, mother, the souls—the souls that do wander about without rest on this awful night."

"Well, I do think," gravely began the aged woman, laying down the ball she was winding, and taking off her spectacles, that she might speak with the more impressiveness, "I do really think, of all the foolish women in this foolish world, my two daughters is the foolishest! Here's Tabby always whimpering about the sorrowful things in *this* world, and Libby always whispering about the supernatural things in t'other! If you had both on you married twenty or thirty years ago, you wouldn't be so full of whimsies now! But, Libby, as the oldest of the two, and a woman nigh sixty years of age, you really ought to set a better example to your sister."

And having delivered this little lecture, old Mrs. Winterose replaced her spectacles on her nose, and resumed her reeling.

"It's all very well for you to talk that a way, mother, and it's all very right; but for all that, you *know* as how the old folks *do* say, as on this awful night, of all the nights in the year, the 'churchyards yawn and the graves give up their dead,' and the unsheltered souls do wander restlessly over the earth; and though we may not see them, they come in at our doors and stand beside us or hover over us all the night. Ugh! It do make me feel as if ice water was a trickling down my backbone only to think of it! For what if as how *her* soul was a wandering about here now!" continued Miss Libby, solemnly clasping her hands and rolling up her pale-blue eyes. "Yes! what if as how *her* soul was a wandering about here now—*here*, where, all unprepared to go, on just such a dismal Hallow Eve as this, it was wiolently druv out'n her body! Ah! good land! what was that?" suddenly exclaimed Miss Libby, breaking off with a half-suppressed scream.

"It was nothing but Gem's wheel stopping suddenly, as her thread snapped, you goose," said the old lady.

"Ah! but it sounded just like an awful groan, as it might be an echo of *her* dying groan as her soul fled from the body, and rewived by memory, if so be she should be walking now," shuddered Miss Libby.

"And surely, if any soul ever *did* wander over the earth anywhere, at any time, her soul, of all souls, would wander in this place of all places, on this night of all nights, when she—"

"Hush, for Heaven's dear sake, both of you!" exclaimed the old lady. "Tabby is so sentimental and Libby is so superstitious, that what with the snivelling of one of you and the shuddering of the other, and the talking of both, I should get the horrors myself if it weren't for Gem, my bright Gem there, humming a tune to her humming wheel!" said the old lady, with an affectionate glance towards the young girl. "And I wonder," she added, "what has become of Joe? I shouldn't wonder if the poor fellow had gone out to the pine woods to collect the cones. But now, Tabby and Libby, let me hear no more of your snivelling and shivering."

"But I can't help of it, mother. I should die if I didn't cry. Hallow Eve, especially a dark, drizzly, windy, dreary Hallow Eve like this, always brings back that awful night so vividly again. I seem to see it all again. I seem to see my child, raging and burning like the Spirit of Fire she called herself. I seem to hear that piercing shriek that woke up all the house. I seem to meet that flying form in the flowing white dress, and with the scared and pallid face. I seem to feel the hot blood flowing down upon my hands and face, as I caught her in my arms and tried to stop her, when she broke from me and fled screaming into the library, and threw herself upon Lyon Berners' breast, dying. How can I help it? How can I help it?" cried Miss Tabby with a burst of tears.

"It is her spirit a hovering over you, and impressing on you, Tabitha," solemnly whispered Miss Libby.

"I shouldn't wonder! no, I shouldn't wonder the least in the world," assented Miss Tabby, with a serious nod of her head.

"And remember, Tabby, that her murderer is still at large, and her spirit cannot rest until that murderer is brought to justice," whispered Miss Libby.

"Ah, but who was her murderer? Surely Elizabeth Winterose, *you* do not dare to hint as it was my darling, that beautiful and noble lady who was so nearly executed for the crime she never could have committed?" demanded Miss Tabby, with awful gravity.

"Tabitha Winterose, you know I don't," answered Miss Libby, in solemn indignation.

"I'm glad to hear you say so, for she never did it, nor yet could have done it, though she had cause enough, poor dear! cause enough to go raving mad with jealousy, and to hate her rival unto death, if ever a lady had. But she never was that poor woman's death, though well the woman might have deserved it at her hands. But she never did it! No, she never did it!" reiterated Miss Tabby, with many vain repetitions, as she wiped her faded blue eyes.

"And if Rosa Blondelle's spirit cannot rest in her grave, it an't so much because her rale murderer is at large, as it is because Sybil Berners, her benefactress, as she wronged so ungratefully when she was alive, is now falsely accused of her death," whispered Miss Libby.

"Yes, and, would a been just as falsely executed for it too, if she hadn't a been reskeed on that dreadful night of the flood. And where is she now? Where is the last of the Berners now? An exile and a wanderer over the face of the earth! A fugitive from justice, they call her! 'A fugitive from justice!' when all she needs to make her happy in this world, if she still lives in it, is jest simple justice. Oh! I shall never, never, forget that awful night of the storm and flood, when with her infant of a few hours old, which they had waited for it to be born before they meant to murder her, she was suddenly snatched out of the flooded prison and carried away from sight, as if the waters had swallowed her! And that was the second horrible Hallow Eve of my life!" sobbed Miss Tabby.

"Hush! hush! why harp upon the horrors that happened so many years ago? 'What's done is done,' and can't be undone," urged the old lady.

"I know it, mother; but it is some sort o' relief to talk—it keeps me from thinking too deep about—"

"About what, Tabby? Don't be a fool!"

"About this, then; as there never was no dreadful thing ever happened to us as didn't happen to happen on a dark, drizzly, dreary Hallow Eve!" whimpered Miss Tabby.

"It is a fatality!" whispered Miss Libby.

"It is a fiddlestick!" snapped the old lady.

"Oh, mother, mother, you can't dispute it! Wasn't it on a Hallow Eve at night that Rosa Blondelle, sleeping calmly in her bed, was mysteriously murdered?" inquired Miss Tabby.

"Yes, yes," impatiently admitted the old lady.

"And wasn't it that same night in the storm that Sybil Berners fled away from her home, some said driven mad by horror, and some said by remorse?"

"Oh yes!" sighed the old lady; "and that was the worst thing as ever she did in her life, for her flight was taken as a proof of conscious guilt. I was very sorry she fled."

"Yes, but she was persuaded by those as was wiser than we. And besides, what could she do but fly, when the evidence was so strong against her? so strong that everybody believed her guilty? so strong that even when she came forrard and give herself up, it convicted her, and she was doomed to death! that beautiful, noble lady! and only spared until she could bring her babe into the world—her babe born in the condemned cell."

"I know it, I know it; but for all that, it was her first flight that prejudiced people's minds against her."

"And do you remember, mother, that awful night when the child was born in the prison? You and I and the prison doctor was with her in that stone cell! And oh, how we prayed that she might die! But she was strong, and could not die, nor could the babe. Both lived."

"Yes, thank Heaven! despite our short-sighted, sinful prayers, both lived," fervently exclaimed Mrs. Winterose.

"But that awful night of storm and flood, when the condemned mother gave birth to the child in the condemned cell, that awful night was also Hallow Eve, and do you mind how, when all was over, and, the baby was dressed and the mother was lying in stupor, how you had to leave us, and go away in the storm to tend my father's sick-bed?"

"Ah, child, don't I remember it all!" "And now I'm going to tell you what happened after you left!"

"Why, Tabby, you never would tell us before," said Mrs. Winterose, taking off her spectacles and becoming very attentive.

"No, mother, because I was bound by an oath. It is true, the man I made the oath to released me from keeping of it! But still I never did feel free to tell all I knew until to-night."

"And why to-night, Tabby?"

"Because it is borne in upon my mind that something will happen on this very Hallow Eve to clear up the whole mystery, that I feel free to reveal my part of it!"

"But what makes you feel as if something was going to happen to reveal the secret, Tabby?" inquired her mother.

"Because I had a dream last night as foretold it! I dreamed as I was a walking in the haunted wing, in the wery room where Rosa Blondelle was murdered, and suddenly the sun shone full into the room, lighting it up like noon-day."

"And to dream of the sun shining into a room, is a sure sign of the revelation of secrets and the discovery of hidden things," said Miss Libby, mysteriously.

"Stuff and nonsense about dreams and visions!" sharply exclaimed Mrs. Winterose; "but whatever has caused you to change your mind about Mrs. Berners' reskee, I shall be very glad to hear the particulars, Tabby; so go on."

"Well, goodness knows there an't much after all, as I *have* to tell, but you shall hear it! Well, soon after you left, mother, the prison doctor *he* got up to go home; and he asked Mr. Berners, who had been waiting out in the lobby to hear from his wife, if *he* would go along with him to bring back some medicine; and Mr. Berners and him they both went out in the storm, and oh, how it was a storming to be sure!"

"Yes, that it was!" assented Mrs. Winterose. "I thought as I should never a got through it myself!"

"Well, I sat there hour after hour, holding the new-born baby in my lap, watching the unconscious mother and waiting for Mr. Berners to come back with the medicine. Well, I might a waited!"

"Yes, for there was no getting back that night!" put in the old lady.

"No, for the storm got worse and worse! The rain poured, the wind howled, the waters rose! Oh, what a horrible night! It was as if the end of all things was come, and the world was about to be destroyed by water, instead of by fire!"

"I know what sort of a night it was, Tabby. I can never forget it! Tell me how Sybil Berners was reskeed?" said Mrs. Winterose, impatiently.

"I am a telling of you as fast as ever I can; which she never would a been reskeed neither, if it hadn't a been for that there blessed flood, which you don't even want me to tell about," complained Miss Tabby.

"Tell me about the reskee!" commanded Mrs. Winterose, peremptorily.

"Well, then, just as I had discovered as the waters had ris' almost up to the level of the windows, and was even oozing through the walls like dew, and rising higher every minute, and I was in deadly fear of our lives, and screeching as loud as I could screech, for some one to come and let us out, which nobody could hear us because of the hollering, and bawling, and running, and racing, and banging, and slamming of doors and windows, and all the rout and rumpus made by the people as were trying to save their own lives, suddenly the window was busted in. And before I had time to say my prayers, in jumped a big man followed by a little man."

"Lor!" exclaimed Mrs. Winterose and Miss Libby, in a breath.

"And the big man, in all his haste and hurry, he took *her* up, Sybil, as tenderly, and wrapped her up as carefully as if he had a been her mother. He cussed some about the baby, which was a sort of surprise to him; but Raphael——"

"Raphael!" exclaimed Mrs. Winterose and Miss Libby, in a breath.

"Yes, Raphael! He was the little man I soon discovered. Raphael pleaded for the baby, and so the big man he let him save her; but he said how he must leave the 'ole 'oman' meaning me, to be drownded, though goodness, knows, for that matter, I wasn't so old as to be tired of life, being only just turned of thirty-three——"

"Oh, bother about your age, Tabby! tell us about the reskee!" snapped her mother.

"An't I a telling of you as fast as I can? But he did call me an ole 'oman, and me not thirty-four then, which I would say it if I was to die for it, and he would a left me to be drownded, but Raphael he pled for me like he did for the baby, and the waters was rising higher and higher, and the uproar in the prison was getting louder and louder, and the big man he swore at Raphael, and told him to fetch me on; but first he made me swear on the Bible never to tell how we was reskeed. Then he took us off on the boat which I tell you, mother, it was just awful to be a riding on the high floods over the tops of the houses. It had done raining, which was a good thing for my poor child, who was well wrapped up also. They rowed me up to the Quarries, and put me out high, and on a ledge of the mountain, and rowed away with my child, and that's the last I ever saw or heard of her or her baby until that letter come to Mr. Berners, a telling of him how she was took off to foreign parts, and a releasing of me from my oath of silence."

"But you never told us, for all that."

"Because, as I said afore, I never felt free to do it until to-night, and to-night it is borne in upon my mind as some thing will happen to clear up that Hallow Eve mystery."

"It is a presentiment," said Miss Libby, solemnly.

"It is a fiddle!" snapped the old lady.

"You may call it a fiddle, mother, but I believe you know more about the fate of Mrs. Berners and her baby too, than you are willing to tell," said Miss Libby.

"May be I do, and maybe I don't," answered the old lady. Then suddenly breaking out angrily, she exclaimed, "I told you both before as I didn't want to talk of these here horrid ewents! And I don't! And here you draw me on to talk of them, whether or no! *And look at Gem there*," she added, lowering her voice, and directing her glance towards the girl at the spinning-wheel; "she knows nothing about these dreadful doings, and ought to know nothing about them. Yet there she stands, with her wheel still, and she a drinking down every word."

CHAPTER XXXI.

GEM.

A maiden meek, with solemn, steadfast eyes,

Full of eternal constancy and faith,

And smiling lips, through whose soft portal sighs

Truth's holy voice, with every balmy breath.—MRS. KEMBLE.

Three pair of eyes were turned towards Gem. She was well worth looking at, as she stood there beside the pausing wheel, with the thread of yarn suspended in her hand between the delicate forefinger and thumb, and with her large, luminous dark eyes, fixed upon the face of the speaker. Yes, look at Gem—a slight, elegant creature, whose form was perfect symmetry, whose every motion was perfect grace, whose small stately head was covered with shining jet-black ringlets that hung down each side and half shaded a bright young face of exceeding beauty—an oval face, with regular features, large, soft, dark-blue eyes, vailed with thick, long lashes, and arched over by slender, jet-black brows, and with roseate cheeks and crimson lips. This will do for a pen and ink sketch; but how can I picture the light, the life, the gleam and glow of that brilliant and beautiful countenance?

She wore a plain brown linsey dress, that perfectly fitted her symmetrical form; and this rustic suit was relieved by a little linen collar that clasped her throat, and a pair of little white linen cuffs that bound her wrists.

The setting was plain enough, but the gem was a very rich and rare jewel, whoever might be destined to wear it.

Only for an instant she stood thus, like a bright and beautiful image, and then she suddenly darted across the room, sunk down beside the old lady's chair, and looking up into her face, said:

"Grandma! I know more of that awful tragedy than you think I do. Of course, in all these years, I have chanced to hear much from the talk of women and children seen in church or in school. And to-night I have heard too much from you, not now to be told more! What is all this mystery and horror connected with this anniversary of Hallow Eve? And—who am I?"

"You are my own darling child, Gem!" answered the old lady, in a trembling voice.

"I know that I am your foster-child, but that is all I, or any one else except you, seems to knew about me! But you know who I am, grandma! Now tell me—who am I?" she pleaded, taking the withered old hands within her own, and gazing imploringly up into the kind old eyes that looked compassionately down on hers.

"You are my pet, and my darling, and my blessing, Gem! That is enough for you to know!" answered the old lady, still in a tremulous tone.

"Am I that prison-born child? Am I the daughter of that poor lady who was crucified and cast out among human creatures? Am I? Am I?" persisted the young girl beseechingly, while Miss Tabby wept and Miss Libby moaned.

"Gem," said the aged woman gravely, and sorrowfully pressing the maiden's hands, "Gem, have I been a good grandma to you?"

"Oh, you have! you have!" answered the young girl, earnestly.

"And can you still trust me to be good to you, and true to your best interests?"

"Oh, yes, yes, yes! dear grandma!"

"Then, my own little one, trust me, by obeying me, when I tell you to ask me no questions about yourself; because I cannot answer them yet a while. Will you do so, my little Gem?"

"Yes, yes, I will! I will! But, dear granny, I know! I know! although you are too tender to tell me, I know!"

"Know—what, Gem?" questioned Mrs. Winterose, in alarm.

"I know that some mystery and horror hung over my birth—hangs over my life! I have known this a long time. They call me 'Ingemisca;' that means, 'Bewail! Bewail!' Some one bewailed my birth, and bade *me* bewail it! Some one sung the refrain of a requiem at my baptism, as they do at the burial of others! And oh, grandma! to-night! to-night! in what has reached my ears, I have found a clue to the solving of my mystery!"

"Gem! Gem! if ever I have been kind to you, mind me now! Never think, never speak of these things again. Look on yourself as my child, and nothing more," urged the old lady with so much earnestness, and even pain, that her pet hastened to caress her, and to say:

"I will mind you as much as I can, best, dearest granny! I will never speak of this again until you give me leave."

"That is my darling girl! And now put away your wheel and come and sit down here, and let us have a pleasant talk after all this solemn nonsense. And when Joe comes in—Where the mischief is that fellow, and why don't he come with the cones, I wonder? Anyhow, when he does come I will send him down in the cellar for some nuts and apples, and we will have a little feast."

Gem sat back her wheel, and came and took her seat on a stool at the old lady's feet.

"Gem," said Mrs. Winterose, passing her hand through the girl's dark curls, "my two daughters have been horrifying us by telling of some awful events that happened on certain long past Hallow Eves. But they have said nothing of the pleasant things that have happened on later Hallow Eves! They haven't said a word of that Hallow Eve when me and my Libby was a sitting in our cabin without provisions, and a wondering where the money to buy them was to come from, and how long the agent would let us live there, seeing as we had no right, after my old man, who was the overseer, died, when in walks the agent himself, and offers of us a home rent free here, with the use of the garden, the orchard, and the wood, with a small salary besides, if so be we would come here and live with Tabby, and help keep rats and thieves and rust and mould out of the old house. You may depend, Gem, as we jumped at the offer, and came here the very next day."

"That was all the kindness of my child! It didn't need nobody but me to do all that. But, my sweet angel, she wanted to provide for you and Libby, and to make us all comfortable and happy together," said Miss Tabby.

"Yes, I know. Heaven bless her, wherever she is! And that was a happy Hallow Eve. But the next one was even happier, Gem."

"Yes, dear grandma, I know," smiled the girl.

"Yes, for just one year from that time, when Hallow Eve came around again, I got up early in the morning, as I used to do *then* as well as now, and I came down into this very room, and went through to that back door and into the back room, and opened the back porch door to let in the morning air, and there on the porch with the sun shining bright on the scarlet seed-pods of the rose vines all over the shed, there, like a cradle, stood a large wicker basket, with a two year old baby comfortably tucked up into it, and fast asleep."

"That was I," said the maiden.

"Yes, Gem, it was you. But just think of my astonishment when I found you there! I stared at you, and was as 'fraid to touch you at fust as if you'd been a bombshell to blow me up! I rubbed my eyes to see if I was awake. I crept up to you and shrank back from you ever so many times, before I could venture to touch you. Then I saw a card tied to the handle of the basket. I took it off, put on my specks, and read this:

"'A GEM FOR MRS. WINTEROSE.'

"Then, my dear, I saw that somebody who wanted to get shet of a baby, had put it off on to me. And, Lord forgive me, I struck mad as hop, and said I wouldn't have the brat, and would send it to the alms-house. But, lor! there is a power in helplessness compared to which the power of a monarch is all moonshine! And however angry I might a felt at that minute with the unnatural monsters who I thought had dropped the baby there, why, I could no more a sent it to the alms-house than I could a smothered it in its basket," said the soft-hearted old dame, wiping away the tears that rose to her eyes at the very idea of such a piece of cruelty.

"So you took the little creature in?" smiled Gem.

"What else could I do? I was shivering with cold myself. Could I leave it out there? No. I took hold of the handle of the basket—which it was a large open clothes basket with a handle at each end, and very useful I have found it ever since to put the siled clothes in—and I began to drag it through the door and through the back room into this very room. But the motion waked the baby up, and it opened the darkest blue eyes I ever had seen in my life, and looked at me as calm and quiet as if it had known me all my life, and then it opened its little rosy lips, and said:

"'GAMMA!'

"Yes, my dear Gem, that was what you called me from the first, 'Gamma.' It went straight to my heart, Gem! And why? Because I was sixty years old then, and my hair was as white as it is now, and I never had a baby in the world to call me grandma: all because Tabby and Libby didn't marry as they ought to have done twenty years before that."

"You're always hitting of us in the teeth about that, mother, as if it was our fault. As for me I would have married fast enough if William Simpson hadn't a proved false," snivelled Miss Tabby.

"Bosh! there's as good fish in the sea as ever was got out of it," snapped the old lady.

"It was our fate," said the superstitious Miss Libby.

"You made your own fate," answered the inexorable old lady.

"So you adopted the poor little forsaken child," put in Gem, to stop the altercation between the mother and daughters.

"Yes, Gem, of course. But oh! the day you were given to us was a day of jubilee! While I was lifting you out of that basket, lame leg Joe came in to make the fire. When he saw me with a babe in my arms he let his wood fall, and lifted up his arms and opened his eyes in dumb amazement. And when I told him where I found it, he recovered his speech, and advised me to send it to the alms-house.

"'Joe,' I said, '*if ever* you mention alms-houses and babies in the same breath to me again, you and I will have to part."

"Yet poor old Joe spoke in your interests, grandma," said Gem.

"I know he did, dear, or he thought he did; but my real interest was to keep my Gem, for she has been the brightness of my life, and not only of mine, but of Tabby's and Libby's, poor childish old maids, and of Mopsy's and lame leg Joe's."

"It is because we all love each other so much, and it is such a happiness to love," said Gem.

"We all loved you, my darling, from the very first. We could not help it. Ah! you should have seen what a sunbeam you were in our dull house that day and all days after that. When I took you out of the basket and set you upon your feet, you tottered all about the room, eagerly examining all that was new to you; the chip-bottom chairs, the turkey-wing fans, the peacock's feathers, even poor Joe's crooked leg. And me and Joe watched you in your little crimson dress, as one watches some bright-plumed bird, hopping from twig to twig."

"How I wish I could remember that day, grandma."

"You were too young; not more than two years old. But oh! you should have seen the surprise and delight of Tabby and Libby, when, after they had made the beds up stairs, they came down to help me to get breakfast. They were as silly over you as ever you saw children over a new pet kitten. I thought you would have been pulled to pieces between them, which was another sign that they ought to have been married twenty years before."

"Oh, mother!" began Miss Tabby.

"Well, there! I won't say anything more about that But the way they talked to you, Gem!"

"'What's your name, little one?' they asked.

"'Gem,' you answered.

"'Who's your mother, baby?'

"'Gamma,' you replied. You had only them two words, my darling—'Gem' and 'Gamma.'"

"Did you ever afterwards find out who I was, grandma?" inquired the girl.

"Maybe I did, and maybe I didn't, Gem. Anyway there was no clue to your history there in that basket, Gem. There was heaps of baby clothes, nicely got up and marked 'In-gem-is-ca,' and there was a small bag of gold coins, amounting to just one hundred dollars. That was all. And now, didn't you give me your word never to ask me any questions about yourself?"

"I know I did, grandma, and I will keep my word; but oh, grandma, I can't help thinking about it and suspecting who I am."

"Hush! hush, Gem! Put away such troublesome thoughts. I had rather see a little natural silliness than so much gravity in one so young as you are. Be a girl while girlhood lasts. The season is short enough. This is Hallow Eve. When I was young, it used to be a gay festival, and not the funeral feast my mournful daughters would make it. When I was young, the lads and lasses, on a Hallow Eve night, used to try spells to find out their sweethearts and lovers. And if ghosts walked then, they were merry sprites who only came to tell the youths and maidens whom they were to love and marry. Come, now, I'll teach you a sure spell. Here are some chestnuts," she said, rising and taking a little basket from the chimney shelf, and emptying it into Gem's lap.

"What am I to do with these, grandma?" smiled the girl.

"You are to take half a dozen large ones, scratch on each the first letter in the name of some young man you know. Then on another, 'Str.' for stranger; on another 'Wid.' for widower; on the last one, a cross for old maidenhood."

Smilingly Gem complied with the directions, and marked the chestnuts, while the old lady, with spectacles on nose, watched her carefully.

When they were all ready, Gem looked up, saying:

"Well, they are marked! Nine of them altogether."

"Now lay them in a row on the hot hearth, close to the coals, to roast."

"It is done," said Gem, after she had arranged them according to rule.

"Now, then, my dear, you must sit and watch them in perfect silence, until they are roasted, when they will begin to pop; and the first one that pops will be your fate, whether it be one of the young men, or the widower, or the stranger, or whether it be the cross that stands for old maidenhood."

Smilingly Gem folded her hands, and composed herself to perfect silence and stillness.

While she watched her roasting chestnuts, the old lady watched her.

Each of these women, the ancient dame and the youthful maiden, was making herself silly to please the other. Mrs. Winterose, wishing to divert Gem from her troublesome thoughts, and Gem willing to gratify her "grandma."

But the law of silence was not laid upon any one else but the trier of the spell. And Miss Tabby and Miss Libby chattered together like a pair of sister magpies for some minutes, when suddenly Miss Tabby exclaimed:

"Look out, Gem! Your chestnuts are beginning to crack; they will shoot you presently, if you don't mind."

The warning came too late. A blazing chestnut was suddenly shot from the hearth like a small bombshell, and struck Gem upon the right hand, inflicting a slight burn.

With a faint cry she sprang up and shook it off; and she sat down startled and trembling, for she was very delicate and very sensitive to pain.

"Never mind, never mind a little smarting! When I was young I would have been willing to have been scorched worse than that, to have had such a powerful sign that some one loved me so fiercely as all that! Goodness! how he loves you, to be sure! and how quickly he is coming to see you! Come, pick up your chestnut, child, and see what mark it bears. Come, now! Is it Cromartie?" inquired the old lady with an arch smile.

But the girl made no reply. She had picked up and blown out the blazing emblem that she had playfully made a messenger of fate, and she was gazing upon it. She remained pale and mute.

"Come, come; did you name it for that auburn-haired youth?" persisted the old lady.

"I named it for—*the exile*—the lady who was borne from the flooded prison that stormy night; I named it for—*my mother*," answered the maiden in a low tone.

Silence like a panic fell upon the little party.

Mrs. Winterose was the first to break it.

"Gem! how dare you do such dreadful things?" she demanded, speaking more harshly than she had ever before spoken to her spoiled child.

"It's enough to break anybody's heart to hear her say that," whimpered Miss Tabby, wiping her eyes.

"And, oh! what a sign and an omen! If there's any truth in the spell, her mother—if so be *she* is her mother and is a living—her mother loves her better than any one in the world, and is a hurrying to see her now! For I never knew that to fail," said Miss Libby, clasping her hands and rolling up her eyes.

Gem turned and gazed at the last speaker, while a superstitious faith in the omen crept into her heart.

"There is nothing at all in it! I was only trying to amuse the poor child by the old love spell. I had no thought it would turn out this way," said Mrs. Winterose, glancing uneasily at Gem.

But Miss Tabby sighed, and Miss Libby shook her head, and Gem continued to look very grave.

"Well, I declare! I am out of all patience with Joe!" exclaimed the old lady, by way of changing the whole conversation. "It has been full forty minutes or more since I sent him after them cones! And now I am going to call him."

And so saying she went and opened the back door.

But she had no sooner done so, than she started with a cry of horror and fled back into the room.

And well she might!

Behind her came three men, bearing in their arms the mutilated and bleeding body of a third man!

Following them limped lame-legged Joe.

The affrighted women shrank back to the chimney corner, where they clung together in that dumb terror which is the deeper for its very silence.

"Now don't you be scared, ladies," said Joe, soothingly. "Nobody an't a going to do you no harm. It is only some man as has been murdered out there."

"*Murdered!*" echoed Mrs. Winterose, in an awe-deepened tone.

"Another Hallow Eve murder!" groaned Miss Tabby, wringing her hands.

"It is doom!" muttered Miss Libby solemnly.

Gem vailed her eyes and said nothing.

"Lay him down here on the floor, men, and let us take a look of him to see if we know him," said Joe, as he took a candle from the table.

The bearers laid their burden gently down.

Joe held the candle to the face of the murdered man.

Old Mrs. Winterose cautiously approached to view it.

"Good angels in Heaven!" she exclaimed.

"Who is it, mother??" inquired her daughters, in terrified tones.

"MR. HORACE BLONDELLE!" she whispered.

- 255 -

CHAPTER XXXII.

THE LAST FATAL HALLOW EVE.

So do the dark in soul expire,

Or live like scorpion girt with fire;

So writhes the mind remorse hath riven—

Unfit for earth, undoomed for heaven,

Darkness above, despair beneath,

Around it flame, within it death.—BYRON.

The awe-stricken women drew nearer to gaze upon the murdered man.

"Grandma, he is not dead! He breathes," exclaimed Gem, whose young eyes had detected the slight, very slight motion of the man's chest.

The old woman knelt down beside the body, and began to examine it more closely. The shirt-bosom, vest, and coat front were soaked with blood, that still seemed to ooze from some hidden wound.

She hastily unbuttoned his clothing, and found a small round blackened bullet hole over the region of the left lung.

"Turn him over on his left side, men," she said, half rising from her knee.

As they followed her directions, the blood flowed freely both from the wound and from the mouth of the man.

"Joe, mount Fleetfoot and gallop to Blackville as fast as you can go, and bring Dr. Hart, though I don't believe it will be a bit of use; but still it is our duty. And, Tabby, and Libby, stop wringing of your hands and rolling of your eyes, and go up stairs and fetch down the cot bedstead to lay him on, for it stands to reason we can't carry him up-stairs without hastening of his end," said the old woman, as she busied herself with stanching the wound in the chest.

All her orders were immediately obeyed.

The cot bed was made up in the corner of the room, and the wounded man was tenderly raised by the two laborers, and laid upon it.

"Now stand out of my way, all of you, and don't ask any questions, but be ready to fly, the minute I tell you to do anything," said the dame, as she stood over the injured man and still pressed a little wad of lint over the bullet hole to stanch the blood.

The other women and the men withdrew to the fireplace and waited.

"He is very nasty and uncomfortable-looking, lying here in all these stained clothes, but I am afraid to undress him for fear of starting the wound to bleeding again, and that's the sacred truth," said Mrs. Winterose.

"No; don't move me," spoke a very faint voice, which, as she afterwards said, sounded so much as if it might have come from the dead, that the old lady withdrew her hand and recoiled from it.

"Brandy! brandy!" breathed the same voice.

"Tabby, get the brandy bottle and pour some into a glass and bring it here. Quick!" she exclaimed.

Miss Tabby, too much awed to whimper, brought the required stimulant, which Mrs. Winterose immediately administered to the patient.

The effect was good. He breathed more freely and looked around him.

"Now, be of good cheer! I have sent a man on a fast horse for the doctor. He will be here in an hour," said Mrs. Winterose encouragingly.

The wounded man laughed faintly, as he replied:

"Why, what can the doctor do for me? I'm shot to death. I'd like to see a magistrate, or a lawyer, though."

"Would you? Then you shall. Hey! one of you men, run out to the stable as fast as you can, and see if Joe's gone. If he isn't, tell him to fetch lawyer Closeby, as well as the doctor," said Mrs. Winterose.

Both of the laborers started on the errand.

Mrs. Winterose turned to her patient.

"What place is this; and who are you?" he inquired.

"Why, don't you know? This is Black Hall, and I am the caretaker."

"Black Hall!" echoed the man, starting up and gazing around him with an excitement that caused his wound to break out bleeding again. "Black Hall! Is it here that I must die? Here, and—great Heaven!—in the very room where the crime was committed! In the very room haunted by her memory!"

And covering his face with his hands, he fell back upon the pillow.

"Tabby, more brandy!" hastily exclaimed the old lady, as she nervously pressed a fresh piece of lint into the gushing wound.

"Yes, more brandy," he faintly whispered; "keep me alive, if possible, till the lawyer comes."

Miss Tabby brought the stimulant, and Mrs. Winterose put it to his lips.

"But, oh, this room! this fatal room! this haunted room!" he murmured, with a shudder.

"Be quiet, good man; this an't the room where the lady was murdered," said Miss Tabby.

"And which is haunted by her ghost to this day," put in Miss Libby, who had come up to the side of the bed.

"Not—not the room where Rosa was murdered this day fifteen years ago?" murmured the man, gazing around him. "Am I delirious, then? It seems the very same room, only with different furniture."

"It is the correspondial room in this wing. T'other room is in t'other wing," explained Miss Tabby.

"And yet, what difference? what difference?" he murmured, restlessly.

"Mother," whispered Miss Tabby, "it seems to me as I've see a this man before."

"Shouldn't wonder," replied the old lady in a low tone. "Mr. Horace Blondelle has been living at the Dubarry Springs, within ten miles of us, for the last thirteen or fourteen years, and it would be queer if you hadn't seen him before."

"Queer or not, I never *did* see Mr. Horace Blondelle, to know him as sich, in all my life before. And that an't what I mean neither, mother. I have seen this man in a fright somewhere or other."

"The man in a fright?"

"No; *me* in a fright when I saw him."

"Hush! don't whisper! See, it disturbs him," said the old lady.

And in truth the wounded man had turned to listen to them, and was gazing uneasily from one to the other.

When they became silent, he beckoned Miss Tabby to approach.

She bent over him.

"Now, look at me well, old girl," he whispered faintly, "and see if you can't recollect when you met me last."

"Ah!" screamed Miss Tabby, as if she had seen a ghost. "It was on the night of the flood! And you reskeed of us!"

"That's so."

"Well, then, my good gentleman, it ought to be a comfort and a conserlation to you, a laying wounded there, to reflect as how you *did* reskee us from drownding that night," said Miss Tabby, soothingly.

"I don't know as far as the rescuing of you is concerned, old girl, whether the act will be found set down on the debit or credit side of my account at the last day," he said, with a gleam of his old humor sparkling up from beneath all his pain of mind and body.

"So this was the man," said the old lady to herself, while Miss Libby and even Gem, looked at him with a new interest.

"Mr. Blondelle, can you tell me how you came to be wounded?" inquired the old lady.

"No, not now. I must save all my strength for what I have to say to the lawyer. Give me more brandy. And then let me alone," he said, speaking faintly and with difficulty.

His request was complied with, and then the three old women, with Gem, withdrew to the fire.

The two laboring men came in from their errand and joined them at the fire.

"Did you catch Joe?" inquired the dame.

"Yes, mum, just as he was riding off. We had to run after him and shout; but we stopped him, and gave him your message."

"All right; and now tell me—for I hadn't a chance to ask before—how came this gentleman to be wounded?"

"Don't know, mum. We was on our way to a little Hallow Eve merry-making at a neighbor's house in the Quarries, when we fell in long o' Joe, who had been to the pine woods to gather cones; and we was all jogging along, Joe foremost, when he stumbled and fell over something, which proved to be this man, which, to tell the truth, we took to be dead at the time," replied one of the men.

"And have you no idea who shot him?"

"No more than you have yourself, mum. You see—"

A groan from the wounded man interrupted the conversation.

"Hush! we disturb him. I ought to have known better than to talk," whispered Mrs. Winterose, and then she walked to the bedside and inquired:

"What is the matter? Can I do anything for you?"

"No; let me alone, and be quiet," was the feeble reply.

The old woman went back to the fireplace, and sat down in silence. The two laboring men, uninvited, seated themselves at a short distance. All thoughts of going to a merry-making were given up for that night.

And a weary death-watch commenced, and continued in awful silence and stillness until it was interrupted by the sound of horses' feet in front of the house, and soon after by a loud knocking.

Miss Tabby sprang up to open the door and admit the doctor and the lawyer.

"This is a terrible thing, Mrs. Winterose," said Dr. Hart, as he shook hands with the old lady, and bowed to the other members of the family.

"Terrible indeed, sir," replied Mrs. Winterose, as she led the way to the bedside.

"I am sorry to see you wounded, Mr. Blondelle; but we shall bring you round all right," said Dr. Hart, as he took the hand of the dying man.

"Doctor, you know, or you will soon know, that you cannot do any such thing. So let us have no flattery. But if you can give me anything to keep me alive until I shall have finished a statement, that it may take me an hour to make, you will do the only thing you possibly can do for me," said Mr. Blondelle, speaking faintly, with difficulty, and with frequent pauses.

"Let me examine your injuries," said the doctor, gently.

"Do so, if you must and will. But pray occupy as little of my precious time as possible," pleaded the dying man.

The doctor proceeded to make his examination.

When he had finished it, he made not a single comment.

"I told you so," said Mr. Blondelle, interpreting his silence. "And now give me something to keep me going until I finish my work, and then send all these women out of the room, so as to leave us alone with the lawyer; but let them supply him with writing materials first."

"I will do as you direct; but meanwhile, shall I not send for your wife?" gently inquired the doctor.

"No; what would be the use? It will be all over with me before she can possibly get here," answered Mr. Blondelle.

The doctor did not urge the point; he probably agreed with his patient.

When he had administered a stimulant, he whispered to Mrs. Winterose to place writing materials on the little stand beside the cot, and then to take her daughters and Gem up stairs.

When the women had left the room, the doctor bade the two laboring men retire with Joe to the kitchen, where he himself would have followed them, seeing that the rest of the house was closed up and fireless; but at a sign from the dying man, he stayed, and took a seat by the bedside.

The lawyer sat between the bed's head and the little stand upon which pens, ink, and paper had been placed.

"It is a will," said Mr. Closeby, as he rolled out a sheet of parchment he had taken the precaution to bring.

The dying man laughed low as he replied:

"No, it is a confession. I can make it now, when it will redeem *her* life without ruining mine."

The lawyer and the doctor exchanged glances, but made no comment.

What Mr. Horace Blondelle's confession would be they had already surmised. What it really was will be seen presently.

The work occupied something more than an hour, for the narrator was very weak from loss of blood, and spoke slowly, faintly, and with frequent pauses, while the lawyer, at leisure, took down his words, and the doctor from time to time consulted his pulse and administered stimulants.

Meanwhile the three old women, with Gem, remained up stairs, gathered around the small fire in their bed-room. Awe hushed their usually garrulous tones, or moved them to speak only in whispers. Never seemed an hour so long. At length it was past, and more than past, when the door at the foot of the stairs was opened, and the doctor's voice was heard calling upon them to come down.

"Is it all over?" whisperingly inquired Mrs. Winterose.

"The work is over."

"But the man, I mean."

"It is not all over with him yet. He still lives, though sinking fast."

"Don't you think he ought to have a clergyman?"

"He would be dead before a clergyman could be brought here."

This rapid, low-toned conversation took place at the foot of the stairs, out of hearing of the dying man, whose senses were fast failing.

Mrs. Winterose then came down into the room and took her seat by the bed, and from time to time bathed the sufferer's brow with her own preparation of aromatic vinegar, or moistened his lips with brandy and water.

Tabby, Libby, and Gem sat around the fire. The doctor and the lawyer stood conferring in a low tone at a distant window.

Thus the death-watch was kept in the silence of awe, until Miss Tabby, unable to resist her desire to do something for the sufferer, crept up to the side of the cot opposite to which her mother sat, and "shook his sands," by asking him in a low tone:

"Is there *no* one in the world you would like to see, or to send a message to?"

"No—no one—but Sybil Berners—and I have written a message to—her; but—to see her—is impossible," gasped the man at intervals.

"Tabby, go sit down and keep quiet. You only worry the poor soul!" said Mrs. Winterose.

Miss Tabby complied, and the silent death-watch was resumed, and continued unbroken except by the howling of the wind, the beating of the rain, and the rattling of the leafless trees, until at length—inexplicable sound!—wheels were heard, grating over the rough, neglected avenue, and approaching the house.

Who could it be, coming at that late hour of a stormy night, to a house to which, even in daylight and good weather, scarcely a visitor ever came?

The sound of the wheels ceased before the door, and was immediately followed by a knock.

"Burglars never come in wheeled carriages," said Miss Tabby to herself, as she recovered her courage, and went and opened the door.

She recoiled with a loud cry.

Every one started up, and hurried forward to see what could now be the matter.

CHAPTER XXXIII.

RETURN OF THE EXILE.

Long years had seen her roaming

A sad and weary way,

Like traveller tired at gloaming,

Of a sultry summer-day.

But now a home doth greet her,

Though worn its portals be,

And ready kindness meet her,

And peace that will not flee.—PERCIVAL.

Sybil Berners stood before them! Sybil Berners, in magnificent beauty! Sybil Berners, developed into a woman of majestic dignity and angelic grace!

Yet they all knew her in an instant.

The scene that followed is indescribable, unimaginable.

Forgotten was the dying man! Unseen was Lyon Berners, whose fine form filled up the door-way.

They crowded around *her*, they caressed her, they cried over her, they exclaimed about her, they asked her a score of questions, and without waiting for a single answer asked her a hundred others.

"God bless my dear old home, and all the people in it!" were the first words that Sybil spoke after she was permitted to catch her breath.

"And you, my darling, you! God bless you in coming home!" fervently exclaimed the old woman.

"Now, where is my child; Mrs. Winterose? Where is my Gem?" the lady inquired, looking eagerly around the room.

"Gem, come here," said the dame.

And the beautiful young girl who had been timidly lingering in the background, yet with some suspicion of the lady's identity too, came modestly forward, and was silently folded in the arms of her mother.

A moment they clung thus; and then Sybil lifted the young head from her bosom, and holding it between her hands gazed tenderly down in the sweet face.

"My daughter! my little Gem!" she murmured. "It is but a few months since I knew that I possessed you."

"But I always knew that you were my mother. I always knew it, though no one ever told me!" sobbed Gem.

"And did you think that I had deserted you all this time, my daughter, my daughter?" inquired the lady, lingering on the last word, and tenderly gazing into her dark eyes.

"I thought you were compelled to do it, mother!"

"What! to leave you here alone, uncared for and unschooled, all these long years? No, my daughter; no, no, no. I did not know that I was blessed with a daughter; I did not know that you lived, until within a few months past. Mistaken love for me, inordinate care for me, induced all those who were nearest to me to conceal your existence from me, lest, if I should know it, I should compromise my safety, my liberty and life, Gem, by seeking to see you!"

"Oh, mother!"

"And they were so far right, my darling, that as soon as at last, your father informed me of your existence, and of a necessity to bring you over to us for education, I became so impatient that I could not wait for you to be brought to me. I felt that I must fetch you, at all risks, for the sake of seeing you some few weeks earlier than I could by waiting for you over there! So here I am, my daughter!"

"But oh! dearest, dearest mother, at what a hazard!" sighed Gem.

"I do not believe it, my darling. I do not believe, after all these years, that any one will seek to molest me for the few days that I shall remain here, even if my presence should be suspected, which will be very improbable, as I have taken and shall take every precaution for secrecy. I have travelled only by night, Gem, and this is the first time I have raised my thick veil."

"But oh, mother!" she said, giving an alarmed look around, for she suddenly remembered that there were the doctor and the lawyer in the house; but she did not see them. They had discreetly withdrawn into the back room.

"And now, dear Gem, here is your father, who is waiting to embrace you," said Sybil.

And Lyon Berners, who had forborne to interrupt the meeting between the mother and daughter, and who was standing apart, talking in low, eager tones with Mrs. Winterose, now came forward and folded his daughter to his heart, and laid his hand upon her head and blessed her.

"But who is that?" exclaimed Sybil, in a startled tone, as she turned her eyes upon a ghastly and blood-stained form, sitting bolt upright on the cot bedstead, and staring in a death panic at her.

At her exclamation all eyes were turned in the direction that hers had taken, and Mr. Berners looked inquiringly towards Mrs. Winterose who hastened to reply:

"Oh, I forgot. In my joy at her arrival, I forgot all about the poor dying man! Sir, he is Mr. Blondelle, who owns the great Dubarry Springs up yonder. He was set upon and murdered by—the Lord only knows whom—but he was found by Joe lying in the pine woods, and with the help of two laborers he was brought here. We sent for the doctor, but he could do nothing for him. He must die, and he knows it," she added, in a whisper.

In the mean time, Sybil, staring at the ghastly face which was staring back at her through its glazing eyes, recognised an old acquaintance.

"It is Satan!" she gasped. "It is Captain 'Inconnu!'"

And Miss Tabby moved by compassion, went up to him and whispered:

"Listen, now. You said there was only one person in the world as you wanted to see, and that it was impossible to see her. But here she is. Do you understand me? Here she is."

"Who? Who?" panted the dying man, listening to Miss Tabby, but still staring at Sybil in the same dazed manner.

"Sybil Berners! Sybil Berners is here!"

"Is—that—her?"

"Yes, yes; don't you see it is?"

"I thought—I thought—it was her phantom!" he gasped.

Sybil gravely approached the bed, and put her hand on the cold hand of the corpse-like man, and gently inquired:

"Mr. Blondelle, or Captain 'Inconnu,' did you want to see me?"

"The expiring flame of life flashed up, once more—flashed up brilliantly. His whole face brightened and beamed.

"It is you! Oh, thank Heaven! Yes, I did want to see you. But—It is growing very dark. Where have you gone?" he inquired, blindly feeling about.

"I am beside you. Here, take my hand, that you may feel that I am here," said Sybil, compassionately.

"Yes. Thanks. Lady, I did try very hard to save you from the consequences of my crime."

"Wretched man!" exclaimed Sybil impulsively snatching away her hand in abhorrence, "You murdered that unhappy woman, of whose death I was falsely accused."

"No, lady; no! Give me your hand again. Mine is not stained with her blood. Thank you," he said, as Sybil laid her hand in his.

"A wild, bad man I was and am, but no murderer; and yet it is no less true that it was through my fault that the poor woman was done to death, and you driven to insanity. That was the reason why I tried to save you by every other means but the only sure one—confession. But now, when a confession will redeem your life without ruining mine—mine—which is over—I have made it, under oath, signed it, and placed it in the hands of your solicitor, lawyer Closeby."

He ceased to speak, and he breathed very hard.

She continued to hold his hand, which grew colder and colder in her clasp.

"Lie down," she whispered gently. "You are too weak to sit up. Lie down."

"No, not yet," he panted hard. "Tell me: do you forgive me?"

"As I hope to be forgiven, I forgive you with all my heart and soul; and I pray to the Lord to pardon you, for the Saviour's sake," said Sybil, earnestly.

"Amen and amen!" faintly aspirated the expiring man. And his frozen hand slipped from Sybil's clasp, and he fell back upon his pillow—DEAD.

Sybil's sudden cry brought the three old women to the bedside.

"It is all over, my dear child. The poor man has gone to his account. Come away," said the experienced dame, when she had looked at the corpse.

"I am very glad as you happened to come in time, and as you was good to him and forgave him, whether he deserved it or not," wept the tender-hearted Miss Tabby.

"Every one who is penitent enough to ask for forgiveness deserves to have it, Miss Tabby," said Sybil, solemnly.

"But, oh! the signs and omens as ushered in this awful ewent!" whispered Miss Libby.

"Hush! hush!" said the dame. "To more vain talk. We are in the presence of death. Mr. Lyon, my dear sir, take your wife and daughter into the parlor. It is not damp, or close. It was aired yesterday. The whole house has been opened and aired faithful, once a month, ever since you have been away. And Joe went and made a fire in the parlor about a quarter of an hour ago. Take them in there, Mr. Lyon, and leave me and my daughters to do our last duties to this dead man," she added, turning to Mr. Berbers.

He followed her advice, and took his wife and daughter from the room of death.

As they entered the old familiar parlor, now well aired and warmed and lighted, Joe, who was still busy improving the fire, and Mopsy, who was dusting the furniture, came forward in a hurry to greet their beloved mistress. They loudly welcomed her, wept over her, blessed her, kissed her hands, and would not let her go until the door opened, and Dr. Hart and lawyer Closeby entered the room.

"Go now," said Sybil gently to her faithful servants. "Mopsy, see to having my bed-room got ready; and, Joe, carry up a plenty of wood."

And of course she gave them these directions for the sake of giving them something to do for herself, which she knew would please them.

Delighted to obey their beloved mistress, they left the room.

Dr. Hart and lawyer Closeby came up to Sybil.

"Let us welcome you home, Mrs. Berners! And you, sir! Words would fail to express our happiness in seeing you. You arrive in an auspicious hour too. If you had not come I should have dispatched a special messenger to Europe after you by the next steamer," said lawyer Closeby, grasping a hand each of Sybil and Lyon.

"Welcome, my child! Welcome, Sybil! Welcome home! I thank Heaven that I have lived to see this day. Well may I exclaim with one of old, 'Now, Lord, let thy servant depart in peace, for I have seen the desire of my eyes!'" fervently exclaimed old Dr. Hart, as he clasped and shook Sybil's hands, while the tears of joy filled his eyes.

But Sybil threw her arms around his neck and kissed him, for she could not speak.

Then he shook hands with Mr. Berners, and warmly welcomed him home.

When the congratulations were all over, and the friends were seated around the fire, Mr. Closeby drew a parchment packet from his pocket, and said:

"I told you, Sir, and Madam, that you had arrived in time to prevent my sending for you. I hold the cause of my words in my hand."

"The confession of Horace Blondelle?" said Mr. Berners, while Sybil listened eagerly.

"Yes; the confession of Horace Blondelle, *alias* Captain Inconnu, *alias* Satan. This confession must first be read to you, then sent up to the Governor of Virginia, and finally published to the whole world; for it fully vindicates your honor, Mrs. Berners."

"At last! thank Heaven!" exclaimed Sybil, while her husband took one of her hands and pressed it, and her daughter took the other one and kissed it.

"The writing down of this confession from the lips of the dying man occupied an hour and a quarter; the reading of it will take perhaps fifteen minutes. Can you hear it now, or are you too much fatigued with your journey, and would you prefer to put off the reading until to-morrow morning?" inquired the lawyer, looking from Sybil to Lyon.

"Put off the reading of that document until to-morrow? By no means! Read it at once, if you please," replied Mr. Berners, with a glance at his wife, which she at once understood and acted upon by hastening to say:

"Oh, yes! yes! read it at once! I could not sleep now without first hearing it."

"Very well, then," said the lawyer, as he unfolded the paper and prepared to peruse it.

The confession of Horace Blondelle need not be given in full here. A synopsis of it will serve our purpose.

As the son of a wicked old nobleman and a worthless young ballet dancer, he had been brought up in the very worst school of morality.

His mother closed her career in a hospital. His father died at an advanced age, leaving him a large legacy.

His beauty, his wit, and his money enabled him to insinuate himself into the rather lax society of fashionable watering places and other public resorts.

He had married three times. First he married a certain Lady Riordon, the wealthy widow of an Irish knight, and the mother of Raphael, who became his step-son. He soon squandered this lady's fortune, and broke her heart.

After her death he joined himself to a band of smugglers trading between the French and English coast, and consorted with them until he had made money for a fashionable campaign among the watering places. He went to Scarborough, where he met and married the fair young Scotch widow Rosa Douglass.

He lived with her until he had spent all her money, and swindled her infant out of his inheritance, and then he had robbed her of her jewels and deserted her.

About the same time a smuggling craft, unsuspected as such by the authorities, had entered the port of Norfolk, sailing under the British flag.

Mr. Horace Blondelle, going to take passage in her, recognized the captain and the crew as his own old confederates.

As he was quite ready for new adventures, he joined them then and there. The ship sailed the next day. And the next week it was wrecked on the coast of Virginia.

The lives of the captain and crew, and also the money and jewels, the silks and spirits they had on board, were all saved. They reached the land in safety.

There a new scheme was formed in the busy brain of Mr. Blondelle. Accident had revealed to him the fact that the little Gentiliska, the orphan daughter of a dead comrade, was the heiress of a great Virginian manor, long unclaimed. He made up his mind to go and look up the estate, marry the heiress, and claim her rights.

Without revealing his whole plan to his companions, he persuaded them to accompany him to the neighborhood.

There is a freemasonry among thieves that enables them to recognize each other even at a first meeting.

Blondelle and his band no sooner reached the neighborhood of the Black Mountain, than they strengthened their forces by the addition of all the local outlaws who were at large.

They made their head-quarters first at the old deserted "Haunted Chapel." They penetrated into the vault beneath it, and there discovered the clue to the labyrinth of caverns under the mountain that henceforth became their stronghold.

Thence they sallied out at night upon their predatory errands.

On the night of the mask ball, two members of the band determined to attend it in disguise, for the double purpose of espionage and robbery. Mr. Blondelle had learned to his chagrin that his deserted wife was in the neighborhood, at Black Hall, where her presence of course would defeat his plan of marrying the little Dubarry heiress.

He arrived as an ordinary traveller at the Blackville Inn, where he assumed the ghastly and fantastic character of "Death," and went to the ball.

His companion, known in the band as "Belial," took the character of Satan, and met him there.

With great dexterity, they had lightened several ladies and gentlemen of valuable jewels before supper was announced. And then they went and concealed themselves in the heavy folds of the bed-curtains in Mrs. Blondelle's room, intending to rob the house that night.

An accident revealed the presence of Belial to Mrs. Blondelle, who, on catching sight of him, screamed loudly for help. The robber was at her throat in an instant; in another instant his dagger was buried in her bosom; and then, as Sybil's steps were heard hurrying to the help of her guest, he jumped out of the low window, followed instantly by Blondelle. They clapped the shutter to, and fled.

Subsequently, when Mr. Blondelle discovered that the beautiful Sybil Berners was accused of the murder, he sought to save her in every manner but the only sure one—confession. He could not confess, for two reasons. He was bound by the mutual compact of the band, never to betray a comrade; and also he was resolved now that he was free, to marry the Dubarry heiress and claim the manor, which he could never do, if once he were known as an outlaw.

The death of Belial and the disbanding of the robbers released him from his compact; but still self-preservation kept him silent until the hour of his death, when he made this confession as an act of tardy justice to Sybil Berners. His violent death had been the direct result of his lawless life. A brutal ex-confederate in crime had long successfully black-mailed him, and at length waylaid, robbed, and murdered him. The criminal subsequently fled the neighborhood, but no doubt somewhere, sooner or later, met his deserts.

The confession was ended. At the same time Miss Tabby knocked at the door and announced supper.

And after this refreshment the friends separated, and retired to rest.

There is but little more to tell.

The next day news of the tragedy was taken to the Dubarry Springs.

Raphael Riordon and his step-mother, Mrs. Blondelle, came over to view the corpse and see to its removal.

Gentiliska, now a very handsome matron, gazed at the dead body with a strangely mingled expression of pity, dislike, sorrow, and relief. She had not been happy with the outlaw, whom, in her ignorance and friendlessness, she had been induced to marry; and she was not now unhappy in his death.

Raphael, now a grave and handsome man, met Mrs. Berners with a sad composure. He worshipped her as constantly and as purely as ever. He had known no second faith.

Mr. Blondelle was buried at Dubarry.

His confession was duly laid before the Governor of Virginia, who, in granting Sybil a pardon for the crime she had never committed, also wrote her a vindicatory letter, in which he expressed his respect for her many virtues, and his sorrow that the blundering of the law should have caused her so much of suffering.

The criminal's confession and the Governor's letter were both published through the length and breadth of the land. And Sybil Berners became as much loved and lionized as ever she had been hated and persecuted.

In the spring other exiles returned to the neighborhood: Captain Pendleton and his wife, once Miss Minnie Sheridan; and Mr. Sheridan, with his wife, once Miss Beatrix Pendleton.

Both these couples had long been married, and had been blessed with large families of sons and daughters.

The widow Blondelle sold out her interest in the Dubarry White Sulphur Springs, and with her step-son Raphael Riordon, returned to England. Under another name, those springs are now among the most popular in America.

Mr. and Mrs. Berners have but one child—Gem! But she is the darling of their hearts and eyes; and she is betrothed to Cromartie Douglass, whom they love as a son.

Milton Keynes UK
Ingram Content Group UK Ltd.
UKHW040831071024
449371UK00007B/733